BEYON

DETENT

Toward an Ame

Foreign Polic

BEYOND DETENTE

Toward an American
Foreign Policy

Paul Eidelberg

Sherwood Sugden & Company
PUBLISHERS

1117 Eighth Street, La Salle, Illinois 61301

E
840
8
.E37

ISBN 0-89385-000-4

First Edition, 1977

Sherwood Sugden & Company, Publishers
1117 Eighth Street
La Salle, Illinois 61301
(815) 223-1231

To Joseph Levinson

It is my purpose . . . to show how easily the tragedy of the Second World War could have been prevented; how the malice of the wicked was reinforced by the weakness of the virtuous; how the structure and habits of democratic states, unless they are welded into larger organisms, lack those elements of persistence and conviction which can alone give security to humble masses; how, even in matters of self-preservation, no policy is pursued for even ten or fifteen years at a time. We shall see how the counsels of prudence and restraint may become the prime agents of mortal danger; how the middle course adopted from desires for safety and a quiet life may be found to lead direct to the bull's-eye of disaster.

—*Winston Churchill*
The Gathering Storm

CONTENTS

ACKNOWLEDGMENTS

Beyond Détente is the sequel to another work, *On the Silence of the Declaration of Independence*. The two volumes, comprising an inquiry into the foundations of American and Soviet foreign policy, were written under the auspices of the Henry Salvatori Center of Claremont Men's College. I am grateful to the Center and to the College for making this project possible. Research for Chapters 5, 6, and 8 was conducted at the Hoover Institution of Stanford University and assisted by a grant from the Earhart Foundation.

I wish to thank Donald Maletz, William Morrisey, and Peter Stark for their helpful comments on the manuscript. Mr. Stark, who has served as a congressional aide for national security affairs, has been especially helpful on strategic questions. I am also indebted to Professor Harold Rood of Claremont Men's College who, since 1969, has served as a consultant to the Defense Department. Professor Rood's "briefings" at the "Hub" have been an education for me in geopolitics.

I am especially grateful to Robert Reilly. His friendship and public spiritedness have contributed very much to the publication of this book.

To my wife Phyllis, who typed the manuscript, and for the encouragement of its publisher, Sherwood Sugden, profound gratitude.

Jerusalem
January 1977

PREFACE

Neither after the Crimean War, nor more recently, after the war with Japan, nor in 1916, 1931 or 1941, would even the most unbridled patriotic soothsayer have dared to set forth so arrogant a prospect that the time was approaching, indeed, was close at hand, when all the great European powers taken together would cease to exist as a serious physical force; that their rulers would resort to all manner of concessions simply to win the favor of the rulers of a future Russia . . . ; that they would grow so weak, without losing a single war; that countries proclaiming themselves "neutral" would seek every opportunity to gratify us and pander to us; that our eternal dream of controlling straits, although never realized, would in the event be made irrelevant by the giant strides Russia took into the Mediterranean and the oceans; . . . and that even the mightiest transatlantic power, having emerged all-victorious from two world wars as the leader and provider of all mankind, would suddenly lose to a tiny, distant Asiatic country, and show internal dissension and spiritual weakness.

—*Alexander Solzhenitsyn*
September 5, 1973

The subtitle of this book, "Toward an American Foreign Policy," might prompt some readers to wonder, 'Don't we have a foreign policy already?' If so, in vain do we look for a clear, candid, and consistent articulation of its moral and geopolitical principles. Whatever our foreign policy, it has manifestly failed to instruct and encourage the nation, or to sustain and advance the principles which this nation inaugurated some two hundred years ago. To the contrary, Spenglerian gloom hovered over the Bicentennial following America's defeat in Indochina. The traditional optimism of the American people has given way to an all-pervasive pessimism. Confusion as to national purpose is everywhere evident. Self-doubt and self-hatred now paralyze the nation's will. Vietnam alone did not occasion this mood of defeatism.

i

The present crisis of confidence and conviction is rooted in causes more difficult to apprehend than that of military disaster. As Churchill so well understood, defeat may be followed by defiance rather than by despair. What, then, are the causes of our despair rather than of our defeat? To pose this question is to go back in time before the debacle of Vietnam. Post-mortems on that tragedy I leave to others. What concerns me is to avoid a larger tragedy: the decline of the United States as a free and independent nation confident in the justice of its cause.

What is the cause of this nation? Has it been forgotten and forsaken? What must be done to restore it, to restore the nation's will, its pride of purpose?

What this nation lacks, and what the present book attempts to provide, are philosophically articulated principles of a foreign policy based on the statesmanship of America's founding fathers. Such a policy should permit and encourage political-military vigor and decisiveness on the one hand, and adherence to principles based on civility and magnanimity on the other. Avoiding sentimentalism and chauvinism, it should satisfy the hard demands of political reason as well as the dictates of what is right and honorable. It should provide statesmen not only with philosophic insight into this country's enduring values, its strengths and weaknesses, but also a deeper understanding of the character and objectives of our enemies. Thus informed, statesmen would be able to comprehend the defects of contemporary American foreign policy and to undertake measures designed to remedy those defects.

The first chapter contrasts the animating principles of contemporary American statesmen on the issue of Communism with those of Lincoln on the issue of slavery. There I sketch a critique of present-day moralism and pragmatism, and introduce an alternative mode of thought based on my *Discourse on Statesmanship*.[1] This alternative mode of thought will provide the foundation for the articulation, in the concluding chapter, of an American foreign policy which transcends "détente", "liberation", and "containment". To justify calling this an *American* foreign policy and, at the same time, to dispel the profound confusion concerning our nation's purpose, it will be necessary to return to our roots, to the founding of the Republic, to the teachings of our founding fathers. This I have done in *The Philosophy of the*

ii

American Constitution and *On the Silence of the Declaration of Independence* but without enlarging upon the problems of foreign policy to the extent required by the present crisis.[2] While I shall, throughout this volume, draw upon my work on the Declaration, the second and third chapters will focus on Washington's Farewell Address, perhaps the most philosophically insightful presidential paper on the American polity in general, and on American foreign policy in particular.[3] The paramount theme of the Address is national unity. Hence, Chapter 2, corresponding to the first half of the Address, will explore the theme of unity in relation to the very founding of the American polity, an extended and more or less fragmented republic troubled (and today, troubled once more) by a weak sense of national consciousness or character.[4] Reflection on this problem will reveal why, without great rhetorical skills, American statesmen will ever find it extremely difficult to pursue a comprehensive, coherent, and long-range foreign policy. Chapter 3, corresponding to the second half of the Farewell Address, will explore the theme of unity in connection with the problem of preserving the character of a republic in the midst of an international environment hostile to the republican form of government. The operational principles of American foreign policy, as prescribed by Washington, will be discussed along with the moral standards intended to govern this nation in the world at large. The key problem emerging from this discussion is: How to enlighten the public about the realities of contemporary international relations so as to prevent hostile powers from dividing the American people from their government? Both Chapters 2 and 3 will draw upon *The Federalist*, whose main authors, Hamilton and Madison, contributed to the drafting of the Farewell Address. *The Federalist* provides collateral evidence indicative of the unique character of the American polity, its strengths and weaknesses—evidence that elucidates the generic problems of American foreign policy.

Chapters 4 through 6 are addressed to the key problem emerging from Chapter 3, the problem of educating the American people about the true character and ultimate intentions of the Soviet Union without arousing unruly passions.

Accordingly, Chapter 4 portrays the philosophical principles governing Soviet foreign policy. The significance of those principles will be magnified by contrasting the *Communist Manifesto* and the

Declaration of Independence—two documents intended to foment revolution, yet fundamentally opposed in their teachings regarding the role of force in human affairs. Chapter 4 will also show how certain "early" writings of Marx attest to what is at stake in the conflict between liberal America and Communist Russia. Chapter 5 offers a new interpretation of why the United States accorded diplomatic recognition of the Soviet Union some sixteen years after the Bolshevik Revolution. That dramatic shift in American foreign policy is linked to a profound change in the political character of the American regime foreshadowed in my *Discourse on Statesmanship*. Chapter 6 explores the meaning of "peaceful coexistence" or "détente", revealing in the process certain fundamental changes in the political thought of Henry A. Kissinger. Finally, after a philosophical interlude in Chapter 7 further elaborating upon the Declaration of Independence, Chapter 8, as indicated earlier, outlines an American foreign policy that transcends moralism and pragmatism. Included is a presidential State of the World Message on geopolitics. That message derives its principles from statesmen who made great demands on their readers. This book will attempt no less.

---

*When this book goes to press, America will have a new President. But will it have a new foreign policy? Thus far, nothing in the pronouncements of Mr. Carter, certainly nothing in the writings of his National Security Adviser, Professor Brzezinski (see below, p. 218n18), is indicative of geopolitical principles which go beyond the delusions and deceptions of "détente". Candor was a major theme of the 1976 presidential campaign. Yet one looks in vain for any public acknowledgement of the treachery of the Soviet Union and its unrelenting drive toward world supremacy. With statesmen unwilling or unable to confront the public with the truth about Russia's geopolitical objectives and with the burdens which this truth entails, the United States remains without a long-range and comprehensive foreign policy—a constructive policy capable not only of halting the spread of Communism, but of advancing genuine peace and liberty.

CHAPTER 1

BEYOND MORALISM AND PRAGMATISM

Let every nation know, whether it wishes us well or ill, that we shall pay any price, bear any burden, meet any hardship, support any friend, oppose any foe to assure the survival and success of liberty.

—*President John F. Kennedy*
Inaugural Address, *1961*

America cannot—and will not—conceive all the plans, design all the programs, execute all the decisions and undertake all the defense of the free nations of the world.

—*President Richard M. Nixon*
State of the World Message, *1970*

The Soviets' inability to acquire loyalty in Eastern Europe is an unfortunate failure, because Eastern Europe is within their scope and area of natural interest. . . . So it must be our policy to strive for an evolution that makes the relationship between the Eastern Europeans and the Soviet Union an organic one.

—*State Department, 1976:*
from the official summary of the
remarks of Secretary Kissinger and
Helmut Sonnenfeldt to the London
meeting of American ambassadors in
December, 1975

Are there certain fundamental but virtually unrecognized defects in the mentality of American statesmen? Clemenceau, referring to the problem of securing peace between a democratic regime like France and a Germany long nurturing, unconcealed, an anti-democratic "doctrine of universal supremacy", in vain warned his countrymen, in 1930, that "for a lasting peace it is necessary for both sides to have the same fundamental ideas of right and the same quality of good faith"—in other words, the same basic principles of justice and honor.[1] Are American statesmen—are the architects of détente —governed consistently by this simple truth? Do they understand with any profundity the basic principles, the roots, of Soviet foreign policy? Do they understand with any profundity the roots of American foreign policy, or rather, what America once stood for as a nation? Hence, against a tyranny like the Soviet Union, do they know how to conduct the foreign policy of a *republic*: do they know how to reconcile wisdom and consent? how to employ power on behalf of liberty but in consonance with reason and civility? If not, this country's future, its security, is indeed precarious. Dr. Kissinger once said that "national security policy is not primarily a technical problem, but a challenge to political understanding and ultimately, to philosophical insight."[2] Do American statesmen possess philosophical insight?

I

The statesman's need for philosophical insight is made urgent by the inability of contemporary modes of thought to enlighten the American people, to restore that sense of national unity and confidence necessary to halt the decline of the United States and the corresponding ascendency of the Soviet Union. A naïve moralism as well as a naïve realism or pragmatism have distracted and enfeebled the actual conduct of American foreign policy.[3] Moralists and pragmatists equally misconceive the nature of morality, despite their disagreement over what ought to be the role of moral considerations in the conduct of international affairs.[4] Both commit the common error of reducing morality to moral *precepts* or principles, in contradistinction to moral *judgment* or prudence. There are many moral principles, and these cannot but come into mutual conflict. Moral judgment or prudence involves nothing less than the mutual adjustment of moral principles or the coördination of competing values so as to maximize goodness or minimize evil. Whereas moralists subordinate politics to inflexible dogmas, pragmatists subordinate politics to narrow interests. Moralists and pragmatists thus obscure not only the complexity but the architectonic character and potential grandeur of politics. Closer examination of moralistic dogmas and the interests of pragmatists reveals, however, that moralism and pragmatism are not antithetical in the most decisive respect. For the primacy of altruism in the mentality of most moralists cooperates with the primacy of safety and material well-being in the mentality of pragmatists to produce a foreign policy whose highest aim is a peace reduced in significance to the mere avoidance of conflict. In other words, animating most moralists and pragmatists is a "politics of survival", a politics which Professor Kissinger once deemed ultimately "destructive of purpose and values".[5] Moralism and pragmatism are thus less than they seem. On the surface, one appears sentimental, the other coldly calculating. Probing deeper one discovers that pragmatists, like moralists, are sentimental enough to regard war as the greatest evil, a sentiment which renders moralists, like pragmatists, calculating enough to tolerate the subjugation of other nations rather than disturb the tranquillity and material well-being of our own.[6] And yet, in the sometime opinion of Professor Kissinger:

> Whenever peace—conceived as the avoidance of war—has been the primary objective of a power or a group of powers, the international system has been at the mercy of the most ruthless member of the international community. Whenever the international order has acknowledged that certain principles could not be compromised even for the sake of peace, stability based on an equilibrium of forces was at least conceivable.[7]

This suggests that whereas moralism lacks certain dimensions of morality, pragmatism lacks certain dimensions of reason. The former fails to reach the level of the noble or the magnanimous; the latter fails to reach the level of wisdom or philosophy.[8] Neither is therefore capable of inspiring the American people or of achieving genuine peace, a peace which knows friendship and not merely the word but the substance of honor.

If American foreign policy has at times been distracted or diverted by moralism, the European Security Conference of 1975—call it the

3

"spirit of Helsinki"—suggests the actual as opposed to the verbal primacy of pragmatism.* What pragmatism fails to provide is a dynamic yet prudent policy informed by universality of principle or purpose. Needed is a policy capable of promoting the liberty and civility of Republicanism in the world while avoiding armed conflict with the Soviet Union. Putting aside that wishful thinking which only furthers the aims of the Kremlin, there is no reason to doubt that Russia, for its part, will persist in its efforts to export Communism while avoiding armed conflict with the United States, that is, so long as we are not deterred on the nuclear level.† The task, therefore, is not merely to combine sentimental moralism and calculating pragmatism which, as we have seen, are not in all respects antithetical, but rather to transcend both in a higher synthesis issuing in a tough-minded "politics of magnanimity". Such a politics would be comparable to the prudence which classical political philosophy identified with practical wisdom. Taking prudence, which is presently understood as expediency, and infusing it with principle and manliness, the statesman will be able to harness the intellectual, moral, and material resources of the American people in such a way as to advance the cause of liberty and civility without threatening the Soviet Union. At the same time, he will demonstrate to the Kremlin that we shall forcefully resist any efforts on its part to undermine the vital interests of the United States. Not "selective détente" as orchestrated by Moscow, but selective détente orchestrated by Washington—this should be one description of American foreign policy.[9] Another, necessarily, is "selective containment". The one ever seeks areas for negotiation and cooperation consistent with civility. The other never shirks competition or even confrontation in defense of liberty. But there is another way of describing the foreign policy to be developed in these pages, for the purpose of which I turn to the statesmanship of Abraham Lincoln.[10]

Lincoln was a master of synthesizing ordinary prudence and lofty principle. Unlike his contemporary moralists, Lincoln was prepared to tolerate the existence of slavery in the South as a necessary evil, but only to avoid a still greater evil, the destruction of the Union.[11] Unlike

---

*See Appendix 1.

†Of course, Russia could avoid armed conflict by achieving a *preclusive* first strike capability (or an effectual damage-limitation on U.S. strategic forces, thereby imposing on this country a no-fire policy). See below, pp. 112-113, 168-169, 174.

his contemporary pragmatists, however, Lincoln was unequivocally and uncompromisingly opposed to the extension of slavery in the territories. For to tolerate slavery in the territories, allowing the white settlers to decide the issue by majority vote, would publicly signify the repeal of the Declaration of Independence and the principle that all men are created equal. Lincoln knew, and the South knew, that if slavery were kept out of the territories, these would eventually be admitted to the Union as free states. Sooner or later free states would outnumber the slave states, in consequence of which the Constitution could be amended abolishing slavery throughout the Union. By equal reason, if the territories (as a result of the Dred Scott decision), were to become slave states, there would be no *publicly affirmed moral principle* in terms of which slavery could be prevented from encroaching upon or infiltrating the free states. Lincoln thus agreed with the moralists in publicly declaring slavery an evil. But he agreed with pragmatists that the abolition of slavery in the slave states, as proposed by moralists, would destroy the Union. What moralists did not see was that the destruction of the Union would not necessarily lead to the abolition of slavery. What pragmatists did not see was that the toleration of slavery in the territories would not necessarily preserve the Union. Both moralists and pragmatists lacked long-range or comprehensive vision, that which comes with holistic or philosophic insight.

Lincoln understood that a republic which does not *publicly* deplore slavery and oppose its extension will not, in the long run, preserve its freedom:

> Either the *opponents* of slavery, will arrest the further spread of it, and place it where the public mind shall rest in the belief that it is in the due course of ultimate extinction; or its *advocates* will push it forward, till it shall become alike lawful in *all* states, *old* as well as *new*....[12]

Clearly, in opposition to the "spirit of Helsinki", Lincoln would never have given his signature to a document which could be construed by the public to have rendered lawful the communist domination of Eastern Europe. By no means, however, would he have supported a policy of "liberation". He called not for the *immediate* but for the *ultimate* extinction of slavery, and then only in our own country. "We deal with it", he said in his sixth debate with Douglas, "as with any other wrong, in so far as we can prevent its growing any larger. . . . [W]e have a due regard to the . . . difficulties of getting rid of it in any satisfactory way. . . . [W]e have no right at all to disturb it in the states where it exists. . . . We insist on the policy that shall restrict it to its present limits."[13] Lincoln publicly emphasized the wrongness of slavery precisely because, in the repeal of the Missouri Compromise as well as in the Dred Scott decision, the government of the United States had conveyed a public teaching that slavery is not a wrong. Here is his own statement of the fundamental difference between himself and Douglas:

> I suggest that the difference . . . reduced to its lowest terms, is no other than the difference between the men who think slavery a wrong and those who do not think it a wrong. The Republican party think it wrong—we think it is a moral, a social and a political wrong. . . . Because we think it wrong, we propose a course of policy that shall . . . so deal with it that in the run of time there may be some promise of an end to it.[14]

The key issue of the Lincoln-Douglas debates thus turned on the question of what teaching was to shape public opinion: the teaching of Lincoln that slavery was a wrong, or the teaching of Douglas that looked upon slavery with indifference, not caring whether it was voted down or voted up.[15] If mere majorities, however, can determine the question of freedom or servitude, there is an end to republican government and we are back to the *fundamental* issue of the American Revolution: whether *all* men are created equal in their *unalienable* rights to life, liberty, and the pursuit of happiness. Lincoln was willing to bring this country to war rather than sacrifice that first principle of republican government, the fondest hope of mankind. Still, his statesmanship or prudence, which transcended moralism and pragmatism, remains a model for those who seek to preserve republican government in the nuclear age. Let us apply his statesmanship to the outstanding conflict of this age, the conflict between Communism and liberal democracy.

As a form of servitude (and let us not forget those Soviet slave-labor camps in comparison with which Southern slavery was a beneficent institution!) Communism, in areas contiguous with the Soviet Union, must be tolerated as a necessary evil in order to avoid a still

6

greater evil, the destruction of mankind. A policy of "liberation" could lead to nuclear holocaust. Nevertheless, the United States and its allies must be unambiguously and unalterably opposed to the expansion of Communism in the territories of the Third World. The nations of that world, only recently released from colonial status, have yet to develop, in many cases, the resources essential for republican government. For this reason they are the more susceptible to authoritarianism, hence to communist imperialism. If they are to avoid or overcome servitude and be admitted, as it were, into the union of free states, they will require the support of the Free World: its political and administrative skills, its food technology and surpluses, but above all, *conviction*—conviction in the moral superiority of Republicanism over Communism. This last will require from the West infinitely more than the platitudes of Helsinki or Western professions of faith. Ultimately, the peoples of Asia, Africa, and Latin America will (or at least ought to) judge us by the sacrifices we are willing to make on behalf of our faith. Still, a prudent policy of selective containment calls for distinctions, say on a scale of one to five, between strategic and non-strategic areas. The allocation of resources, not simply for defending, but for liberalizing any particular area will of course depend on its strategic significance. And so another description of American foreign policy is that of "selective liberalism". This is part of a sober policy of magnanimity intended not only to spread the blessings of liberty and republicanism to the peoples of the Third World, but to preserve those blessings in the Free World as well.

Failure to oppose the spread of communism or of communist influence in the Third World cannot but lead to contempt, humiliation, and ultimate strangulation for the West. Aside from terrorist acts against Western embassies and officials, consider the composition and conduct of the United Nations, increasingly dominated by communist-supported regimes hostile to the republican form of government.* There, the multitudinous and swelling Afro-Asian bloc of states, some of which still traffic in chattel slavery, are making it ever more difficult for the remaining handful of republics or free states to preserve their independence. In other words, as the number of peo-

---

*Of the 47 nations of the Organization of African Unity, 43 are either military or civilian dictatorships. Such regimes are in fundamental conflict with the principle of self-determination articulated in the Declaration of Independence, concerning which, see below, pp. 165-166.

7

ple living in servitude increases, the scope of liberty and civility which the West formerly enjoyed decreases. Like any organism, a republic requires a favorable environment. It cannot long survive in an environment of communist or communist-manipulated states. With equal reason, however, a communist regime cannot long survive in an environment of republics, that is, of republics animated not by the "spirit of Helsinki", but by the "spirit of '76". For as its very location signifies, the spirit of Helsinki is pedagogically neutral toward Communism. Its practical teaching to the world at large—certainly to the people of Eastern Europe—is not very different from the teaching of those ante-bellum pragmatists who did not care whether slavery was voted up or voted down in the territories of the United States. Consequently, that teaching will incline more and more men to tolerate the extension of Communism in the territories of the Third World, *and perhaps elsewhere as well.* To be sure, the spirit or teaching of Helsinki is one of peace, but peace primarily understood as the avoidance of conflict. That teaching, to repeat Professor Kissinger's warning, can only encourage aggression by the most ruthless member of the international order. It can only eventuate in self-abasement and servility. The "spirit of '76" yields a different teaching, that genuine peace can exist only among just men and just regimes. The peace envisioned by the Declaration of Independence is that rich feeling of mutual trust and confidence among men who enjoy republican liberty, equality, and civility. This kind of peace goes beyond détente and ought to be the avowed goal of American foreign policy.

Such a peace cannot be achieved without wholehearted dedication, the kind evoked by those statesmen of '76 who, in the peroration of the Declaration, pledged their lives, their fortunes, and their sacred honor. But wholehearted dedication could hardly have been forthcoming had not that revolutionary generation believed in the intrinsic justice of their cause, hence in the power of reason to apprehend moral and political truths of universal significance, those embodied in the preamble of the Declaration. It was not a pragmatic but a philosophic reason which enabled the statesmen of the Declaration to articulate those truths or "Laws of Nature and of Nature's God" from which they deduced the principles of republican government. For upon reflection, the laws of nature and of nature's God point to the very qualities which distinguish the human from the sub-human. I mean not only the

8

power of reason, but that civilizing power of self-restraint which alone justifies the right to life, liberty, and the pursuit of happiness on the one hand, and government by the consent of the governed on the other. Here, then, were universal standards by which to judge whether the acts of any government dignified or debased human nature, or whether one form of government was just or unjust. And it was these standards that enabled the statesmen of the Declaration to inspire the American people: to unite reason to their passion for justice, and their passion for justice to their sense of honor. They did not commit the error of pragmatists who underestimate the importance of *publicly* articulated principles of morality. Nor did they commit the error of moralists who underestimate the necessity of force in defense of morality.

I contend that recent American statesmen have in large measure abandoned the teachings of the Declaration or have failed to grasp the subtle interplay of reason, force, and morality exemplified in the statesmanship of the founding fathers. Perhaps they lack the founders' confidence in the power of the human intellect to comprehend truths of universal significance. Or, lacking the founders' oratorical skills, perhaps they believe that the elucidation of foreign policy in the light of those truths would arouse violent passions. Whatever the case, it is important to state here what shall be shown later, namely, that the principles of the Declaration constitute what Whitehead termed a "genial orthodoxy" as much opposed to dogmatism or doctrinairism as to skepticism or moral indifference. That genial orthodoxy, adjusted to the nuclear age, can restore the confidence of the American people and facilitate the development of an American foreign policy which unites principle and prudence, and which therefore can foster Republicanism in the world at large while avoiding armed conflict with the Soviet Union.

To admit the need of restoring the confidence of the American people is to acknowledge the need to restore their common faith, and this means their ancient faith. Not the "spirit of Helsinki," but the revolutionary "spirit of '76" alone can compete with the revolutionary spirit of Communist Russia. The contest is between a genial orthodoxy and a tyrannical orthodoxy. That genial orthodoxy has enriched the lives of countless millions. That tyrannical orthodoxy has impoverished and destroyed the lives of millions more. The reason is incredibly simple: the one is consistent with human nature; the other is a violation of human nature. The one pays a decent respect to the opinions of mankind and thus points to government by consent, which in turn requires truth and candor. The other, steeped in pseudo-scientism and self-righteousness, is contemptuous of mankind's opinions, and so eventuates in government by compulsion, which requires mendacity and secrecy. But all this reveals another simple truth: In comparison with a nation governed by a tyrannical orthodoxy, one governed by a genial orthodoxy has a greater variety of intellectual and moral resources which the wise statesman can harness, hence should be far more capable of persevering in a protracted conflict with a tyranny whose people live in darkness and in fear.[16]

Unfortunately, and occasional utterances to the contrary notwithstanding, the genial orthodoxy of which I have been speaking has in fact been largely forsaken by those who now determine the course and character of American foreign policy. As a result, whereas Communists confidently believe in the moral superiority of their system of government over ours, fewer and fewer Americans, thanks to the doctrine of relativism, confidently believe or express belief in the moral superiority of our system over theirs. This asymmetry is simply indicative of the West's declining confidence in the power of reason to apprehend moral and political truths or standards by which to determine whether one form of government is better than another. We are witnessing the eclipse of philosophic reason. A truncated, pragmatic reason now dominates political mentality with the consequence that the United States is now suffering from a perilous decline in statesmanship. Without the promptings of philosophic reason, statesmen lower their sights and standards; their political understanding diminishes; their intellects become preoccupied with comfort and security. And what of our people? Lacking a genial orthodoxy they cannot but lack genuine statesmen; they cannot but falter, not knowing whither they are going. Such a people can hardly persevere in a protracted conflict with an implacable foe. What, then, is to be done?

The chief resource of the United States, indeed, of any republic, is an enlightened and public-spirited citizenry. What must they be enlightened about? But I have already answered this question. For the American people must be enlightened about that genial orthodoxy which alone constitutes them a people rather than a mere aggregation of individuals and groups pursuing their own private interests. At the same time, they must be enlightened about the tyrannical orthodoxy of the Soviet Union. Hence this book is also an inquiry into the *foundations* of American and Soviet foreign policy. Those foundations comprise the two orthodoxies in question. Only by the elucidation of those orthodoxies will it be possible to formulate an American foreign policy, one that transcends both moralism and pragmatism.

II

Because of the diverse and alternating influence of moralism and pragmatism, American foreign policy has lacked clarity and consistency of purpose. Clarity is needed because of the ambiguous and shifting character of Soviet foreign policy. Consistency is needed because of the pluralistic and shifting character of American domestic politics. Let us briefly consider these two factors which complicate the formulation and conduct of American foreign policy.

The Soviet Union pursues what may be termed an "octangular" strategy of protracted war, a strategy which may be illustrated as follows:

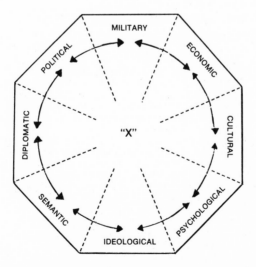

The Soviet Octangular Strategy of Protracted War

These eight overlapping and sometimes indistinguishable operational factors of protracted conflict are synchronized to produce on the targeted country ("X") increasing pressure which, reaching unbearable levels, eventually brings about its disintegration and collapse. The method, in the words of a recent Soviet handbook, "is the uninterrupted attack; its means, prolonged operational pursuit, which avoids pauses and stops, and is attained by a succession of consecutive operations, each of which serves as the transitional link toward the ultimate goal," which is "the complete annihilation of the vital forces of the enemy."* As we shall see in Chapter 6, "détente" is but a "transitional link" or operational factor intended to hasten that goal. Each factor, itself an ensemble of sub-factors, is varied in intensity depending on what strategists in the Politburo call the "correlation of forces" within the target area. Military capabilities and economic conditions; party rivalry and class antagonisms; racial and group conflict; divisions among elites, that is, between opinion-makers and policy-makers—these and other "contradictions" are weighted and correlated in the process of orchestrating the strategy of octangular war. And the orchestration is facilitated by the highly centralized, disciplined, and unrestrained power of an oligarchy acting under the secrecy of a closed society.[17]

In contrast, American foreign policy is now vitiated by the fragmented power of an amorphous aggregation of men subject to the vicissitudes and publicity of an open society. Inter-agency rivalry

---

*Cited in Richard Pipes, "Some Operational Principles of Soviet Foreign Policy", in Michael Confino & Shimon Shamir (eds.), *The U.S.S.R. and the Middle East* (New York: John Wiley & Sons, 1973), p. 7. This perceptive essay provides a number of concrete illustrations of Soviet tactics, of which the following is an example. According to international practice, the peace settlement following any war usually involves concessions to the victor by the vanquished, sometimes territorial ones. This is dictated by logic as well as by the interests of the countries concerned. As Professor Pipes notes, international practice was not followed in the Arab-Israeli War of 1967, first, because Egypt refuses to recognize the existence of Israel as a sovereign state, and second, because the Soviet Union supports the Egyptian position. He continues: "The peculiar feature of this conflict is that whereas the real issue at stake is negotiation between belligerents, Soviet propaganda has managed to make the main issue appear Israeli withdrawal from territories occupied in the course of the war. Thus, a matter which should be part of the final settlement of the conflict becomes a precondition of negotiations leading to a settlement." Professor Pipes concludes by saying: "Whatever one's feelings about the substance of the Israeli-Egyptian dispute, one cannot but admire the adroit use of an intellectual confidence trick to turn the tables on an opponent and shift the burden of recalcitrance from onself to the other party" (p. 20). The word used by both politicians and by the press to describe what was preventing the conclusion of the Middle East accords of 1975 was Israeli "intransigence." (See below, p. 171†.) Other examples of semantic and psychological subversion will be discussed in Chapter 6.

within the Executive branch; congressional restrictions on Executive power; media criticism of the administration; electoral and partisan politics; the competing demands of a welter of groups within society at large—all these fragment the formulation and enervate the conduct of American foreign policy. In all fairness it must be said that our chief foreign policy-makers are under a perpetual state of siege. Policy, instead of being optimized vis-à-vis the strengths and weaknesses and shifting tactics of the Soviet Union, is a result of a domestic cold war called a "consensus", a consensus influenced by groups having little or no competence in foreign affairs. Of course, the perennial problem of democracy is how to reconcile consent with wisdom. But so precarious and complex is the character of contemporary international relations that, in a democracy lacking statesmen with wisdom, consent itself hangs in the balance. Let me explain.

Formerly, when military aggression was rendered unambiguous by armies crossing international borders, democratic statesmen might readily galvanize public opinion against the aggressors merely by appealing to principles of international law and morality. Not that legal considerations and abstract notions of right or justice alone determined democratic foreign policy. Economic interests (to say nothing of geopolitical concerns), were also at work, but it was deemed unnecessary or imprudent to make these an explicit part of publicly announced policies. Truth to tell, there has long been a moralistic aversion to defending foreign policy on economic grounds (despite the preoccupation of domestic politics with economic interests). Attributable, perhaps, to the Christian contempt for worldly goods and the feeling of guilt resulting from the common disregard of that pious sentiment, American statesmen have been reluctant to inform the public that material abundance is a precondition for the pursuit of happiness in a commercial society dedicated to *equality of opportunity*. (In fact, given the increasing secularization of modern life and the elimination of rigid class distinctions, modern democracies require more and more material goods the more they are committed to equality.) The foreign policy of such a democracy must therefore be vitally concerned with securing foreign markets and sources of energy and raw materials—and not simply for the sake of maximizing wealth, but for extending equality and the blessings of liberty to all its citizens. Regard for economic interests may thus be perfectly compatible with

13

moral purpose, indeed, with the cultivation of human excellence. Now, unless statesmen publicly acknowledge the interdependent relationship between material and moral interests, not only will foreign policy continue to be distracted by pragmatism and moralism, but fewer and fewer citizens will be willing to support any policy which entails some sacrifice of immediate comforts for the sake of ultimate values. But to make that interdependent relationship explicit in terms of foreign policy, the statesman will have to reveal the geopolitical objectives of the Soviet Union: he will have to show how the rulers of that regime have long sought to gain political and military primacy in areas the control of which would enable Moscow to deprive the United States of vital forces of energy and raw materials, thereby undermining not merely the material well-being of this country, but its very capacity to survive as an independent republic dedicated to liberty, equality, and civility.* Stated another way, precisely because Soviet Russia has rendered international relations highly complex and ambiguous by its strategy of octangular warfare—a strategy which enables the Kremlin to pursue its objectives not by marching Russian armies across international frontiers, but by such indirect means as subversion and the arming of clients or "proxies"—it has become all the more necessary for American statesmen to speak candidly to the American people, appealing not only to moral principles, but to material interests. In no other way will it be possible to win their *informed* consent and *sustained* dedication. But precisely because much more candor, especially about the tactics and intentions of the Soviet Union, is indispensable for the effective conduct of American foreign policy, there arises the danger of arousing untoward passions. Hence it will also be necessary for the statesman to enlighten the people about our own principles of representative government and statesmanship, of civility and magnanimity, for which purpose he could do no better than to recur to the political thought of America's founding fathers. Accordingly, we turn now to Washington's Farewell Address.

---

*British Admiral of the Fleet Sir Peter Hill-Norton, chairman of NATO's Military Committee, has warned that units of the Soviet fleet are now deployed in strength in the South Atlantic and the Indian Ocean. "Their newly acquired bases on the east and west coasts of Africa provide them with the capability of mounting sea and air attacks on our supply routes, and at any time of their choosing they could effectively disrupt the essential supplies of oil and other raw materials on which not only our fighting capacity but our economy and indeed our lives depend." *Los Angeles Times*, June 11, 1976, Pt. I, p. 5.

CHAPTER 2

THE CENTRAL PROBLEM
OF AMERICAN FOREIGN POLICY:
THE ORIGINAL QUEST FOR NATIONAL UNITY

The only remedy [for the problem of democratic tyranny] is to enlarge the sphere [of government], and therefore divide the community into so great a number of interests and parties, that in the first place, a majority will not be likely at the same moment to have a common interest separate from that of the whole or of the community; and in the second place, that in case they should have such an interest, they may not be apt to be united in the pursuit of it.

—James\ Madison

I have heretofore proposed to the consideration of Congress, the expediency of establishing a National University. . . . Among the motives to such an Institution, the assimilation of principles, opinions and manners of our Countrymen, by the common education of a portion of our Youth from every quarter, well deserves attention. The more homogeneous our Citizens can be made in these particulars, the greater will be our prospect of permanent Union; and a primary object of such a National Institution should be the education our Youth in the science of Government.

—George Washington

The first thematic paragraph of the Farewell Address, in which Washington reveals with subtlety and magnanimity the tribulations of his presidency of the United States, begins as follows:

In looking forward to the moment, which is intended to terminate the career of my public life, my feelings do not permit me to suspend the deep acknowledgment of that debt of gratitude which I owe to my beloved country, for the many honours it has conferred upon me; . . . If benefits have resulted to our country from [my] services, let it always be remembered to your praise . . . that, under circumstances in which the Passions agitated in every direction were liable to mislead, amidst appearances sometimes dubious, vicissitudes of fortune often discouraging, in situations in which not unfrequently want of Success has countenanced the spirit of criticism, the constancy of your support was the essential prop of the efforts, and the guarantee of the plans by which they were effected. Profoundly penetrated with this idea, I shall carry it with me to my grave, as a strong incitement to unceasing vows that Heaven may continue to you the choicest tokens of its beneficence; that your Union and brotherly affection may be perpetual; that the free Constitution, which is the work of your hands, may be sacredly maintained; that its Administration in every department may be stamped with wisdom and Virtue; that, in fine, the happiness of the people of these States, under the auspices of liberty, may be made complete, by so careful a preservation and so prudent a use of this blessing as will acquire to them the glory of recommending it to the applause, the affection, and adoption of every nation which is yet a stranger to it.[1]

That Washington should emphasize the theme of unity is understandable; party and sectional rivalry had wracked his two administrations on both domestic and foreign policy—and this, during the very first eight years of the Republic and its still precarious Constitution. Of course, a country living "under the auspices of liberty", where citizens may freely criticize the policies of government, will be especially prone to faction. As Madison points out in *Federalist* 10: "Liberty is to faction what air is to fire."[2] And in a letter to Jefferson written the month before *Federalist* 10 was published, Madison confided:

In all civilized societies, distinctions are various and unavoidable. A distinction of property results from the very protection which a free Government gives to unequal faculties of acquiring it. There will be rich and poor, creditors and debtors; a landed interest, a monied interest, a mercantile interest. . . . However erroneous or ridiculous these grounds of dissention and faction may appear to the enlightened Statesman or the benevolent philosopher, the bulk of mankind who are neither Statesmen nor philosophers, will continue to view them in a different light.[3]

To rescue from mutual obstruction and to bring into coördination the welter of interests, passions, and opinions displayed in a free society would tax the wisdom of a Solomon. But such is the task of *any* President of the United States. For Washington the task was infinitely greater. To appreciate this fact let us consider why Washington's administration was especially troubled by "circumstances in which the passions [of the American people] agitated in every direction" or by "situations in which not infrequently want of success ha[d] countenanced the spirit of criticism."

The Presidency has often been said to represent the unity of the nation. Yet who can appreciate, who can feel more than its incumbent, how fragile is that unity? A nation can hardly be called a *nation,* can hardly enjoy unity, unless its citizens tacitly acknowledge commonly shared values of paramount significance, values rendered more or less immune from questioning by being embodied in well-established traditions. But this country was born in revolution, a revolution unique in recorded history. The statesmen of that revolution undertook the unprecedented task of constructing a government based primarily on *rational* as opposed to *customary* foundations, and according to an explicit body of principles themselves subject to critical analysis. Hamilton was not exaggerating when he wrote in *Federalist* 1: "It has been frequently remarked that it seems to have been reserved to the people of this country, by their conduct and example, to decide the important question, whether societies of men are really capable or not of establishing good government from reflection and choice, or whether they are forever destined to depend for their political constitutions on accident and force." Or consider *Federalist* 14 where Madison proclaims:

> But why is the experiment of an extended republic to be rejected, merely because it may comprise what is new? Is it not the glory of the people of America, that, whilst they have paid a decent regard to the opinions of former times and other nations, they have not suffered a blind veneration for antiquity, for custom, or for names, to overrule the suggestions of their own good sense, the knowledge of their own situation, and the lessons of their own experience? . . . Happily for America, happily, we trust, for the whole human race, they [the

17

leaders of this country] . . . accomplished a revolution which has no parallel in the annals of human society. They reared the fabrics of governments which have no model on the face of the globe.

This revolution bore with it profound problems. When Washington assumed office his authority was circumscribed by a newly written Constitution. Unlike the founders of regimes in antiquity, the authors of that Constitution could not claim divine sanction. And what men could make, men could unmake. Also, the Constitution placed under a single and supreme authority thirteen hitherto sovereign but still rivalrous states. Furthermore, the strongest opposition to ratification came from state office-holders whose power and prestige would be significantly diminished by the establishment of a national government. As Hamilton remarks in *Federalist* 1: "Among the most formidable of the obstacles which the new Constitution will have to encounter may readily be distinguished the obvious interest of a certain class of men in every State to resist all changes which may hazard a diminution of the power, emolument, and consequence of the offices they hold under the State establishments." Ratification did not put an end to this source of divisiveness. Meanwhile, many citizens of each State retained their local loyalties and thought of themselves more as "Virginians", for example, than as Americans. Finally, when one considers the enormous problem of organizing and staffing a new government and its various departments, of formulating a variety of programs and policies concerning domestic and foreign affairs, of responding to a welter of conflicting needs and wants from the diverse parts of the country—inevitably disappointing the hopes and expectations of some, arousing the fears and hostility of others—when all these factors are taken into consideration, it can be said that no other President, perhaps not even Lincoln, had so crushing a burden as Washington's: the burden of creating, as it were, a national character, of endowing a people with a sense of national unity and purpose. No wonder Washington was the object of unrestrained criticism, nay, of vilification. (That he should nonetheless express gratitude for the "constancy" of popular support when, in fact, that support was less than constant is, of course, a rhetorically permissible, indeed required, exaggeration on the one hand, but also a mark of Washington's magnanimity on the other.) Still, in view of the bitter attacks on his

18

administration, it is also no wonder that Washington was more than ready to retire to his beloved Mount Vernon.

Perhaps no one today can fully appreciate the magnitude of the problem confronting the founders of the first "extended republic". The wisdom, the fortitude, the magnanimity required to rule, let alone to establish, such a republic probably surpasses that required of any other kind of regime. Certainly the knowledge and virtue needed to be the ruler of a free and civilized society excels that demanded of any primitive society, or of any modern tyranny for that matter. It is one thing to rule men bound by toil, with simple wants, ignorant of sophisticated arts and sciences. It is another and a more noble thing to rule free men, men who must be persuaded more by reason than by superstition or by fear, men who are themselves capable of exercising political rule.[4] But reason is not always persuasive, even among civilized men. Hamilton candidly avers, again in *Federalist* 1: "So numerous indeed and so powerful are the causes which serve to give a false bias to the judgment, that we, upon many occasions, see wise and good men on the wrong as well as on the right side of questions of the first magnitude to society." Moreover, seldom is there simply a right and wrong side on any major public issue. As Whitehead points out in reference to Plato: "The moral of his writings is that all points of view, reasonably coherent and in some sense with application, have something to contribute to our understanding of the universe, and also involve omissions whereby they fail to include the totality of evident fact."[5] But since it is virtually impossible to accommodate all points of view, especially on the pressing problems of political life, any public policy is bound to offend and perhaps even alienate various groups or individuals. The tragic, hence ineluctable truth is that no act of government is ever simply just or perfectly consistent with distributive justice. And so criticism of government is unavoidable and frequently justifiable. On the other hand, it is also true that the "bulk of mankind, who are neither Statesmen nor philosophers," are too often preoccupied with rather narrow and immediate interests, as a consequence of which they may readily become, or may readily be made, impatient with government policies which, however just, fail to exhibit quick and tangible results. Few if any problems of the first magnitude to society are likely to be resolved during the period between presidential elections, perhaps not even in a generation. Madison puts the problems this way in *Federalist* 63:

> The objects of government may be divided into two general classes: the one depending on measures which have simply an immediate and sensible operation; the other depending on a succession of well-chosen and well-connected measures, which have a gradual and perhaps unobserved operation. The importance of the latter description to the collective and permanent welfare of every country needs no explanation.

It should be noted that in *Federalist* 63 Madison is defending the six-year term prescribed for the Senate. As I have elsewhere shown, one of the intended functions of the Senate was to facilitate the exercise of presidential leadership, especially in the domain of foreign affairs.[6] Also, the reason why the President was originally made eligible for re-election an indefinite number of times was, as Hamilton comments in *Federalist* 72, "to prompt a man to plan and undertake extensive and arduous enterprises for the public benefit, requiring considerable time to mature and perfect." Such long-term enterprises would often "have a gradual and perhaps unobserved operation"—unobserved by the ordinary citizen. Thus, if the ordinary citizen is not to succumb to the impatience which is so characteristic of a free society, he must be willing to give the long-range wisdom of his government the benefit of his short-range doubt. But precisely because long-term policies seldom yield immediate and conspicuous results, the ordinary citizen will be susceptible to the manipulations of politically ambitious men. Any administration which desires to undertake farsighted objectives thus exposes itself to partisan criticism and risks the déterioration of popular support. This dilemma can be avoided to some extent by advancing a variety of relatively minor programs well calculated to produce immediate public benefits, thereby winning the public confidence needed to undertake a really important long-term policy whose benefits may not become visible to the electorate during a single term of office. Obviously, the task is infinitely more difficult for the statesman charged, like Washington, with organizing a government *de novo* than it is apt to be for his successors. In short, "to establish a more perfect Union" is one thing; to preserve that more perfect union, once established, is another.

Now, at the conclusion of the first thematic paragraph, it will have been noticed that Washington identified the good of the American people with the good of mankind—just as Hamilton had done in *Federalist* 1 and Madison in *Federalist* 14. Let the United States only pursue its "own" interests and it will have thereby promoted the interests of mankind. Assuredly, the United States would have to understand what constitutes its "own" interests (which is why "its administration, in every department, m[ust] be stamped with wisdom and Virtue"). But how are we to explain this supposed identity between the interests of the United States and mankind? What are the underlying assumptions of such an identity?

Strange and yet obvious as it may seem in the saying, it nonetheless needs to be said that for there to exist an identity of interest between the United States and mankind in general, two preconditions must obtain: (1) mankind itself must constitute a single species, and (2) the principles of American government must be intrinsically conducive to the perfection of that species, that is, to the fullest development of that which distinguishes the human from the sub-human. That mankind constitutes a single species is implied in the teaching of the Declaration of Independence that all men are created equal. In the order of nature, men do not stand to each other as they stand to beasts, as superior to inferior creatures. This is why *all* men are endowed with the unalienable rights to life, liberty, and the pursuit of happiness. As for that which distinguishes the human from the sub-human, the answer has already been anticipated but may be further elucidated by asking *What kind of being is man that he, unlike all other creatures, should be endowed with the unalienable rights to life, liberty, and the pursuit of happiness?* Elsewhere I have written:

> Surely a being thus endowed must be potentially capable of governing himself without impairing the unalienable rights of others. Presumably, such a being would have the capacity to distinguish between his immediate wants and his long-range interests. He would have to understand how the pursuit of his own interests may affect the well-being of others and how the wants and interests of others may affect his own. To this end he would have to be considerate of the claims advanced by others. . . . Finally, he and his fellows would have to know how to bring into mutual adjustment their competing

21

claims and interests if the so-called rights to life, liberty, and the pursuit of happiness are to be something more than a façade for foolishness and petty egoism.[7]

From the preceding passage two principal qualities may be inferred which distinguish the human from the sub-human. One may now be described as the discriminating and synthesizing power of reason. The other may now be called "civility", with the understanding that it issues from intellectual as well as moral virtues. On the one hand, civility presupposes the power to appreciate diverse points of view. On the other hand, it presupposes moderation or self-restraint, hence the power to control those passions which sometimes obscure the differences between men and brutes. Thus, only if man is understood as *homo rationalis et civilis*, and further, only if American government is rooted in these two qualities of human nature, can there possibly obtain an identity of interest between the United States and mankind.

Consistent with the preceding, we have seen that American government, as envisioned by its founders, was to be based on "reflection and choice" as opposed to accident and force. Or as *Publius* declares in *Federalist* 49: "[I]t is the reason, alone, of the public, that ought to control and regulate the government. The passions ought to be controlled and regulated by the government." About the principle of civility, surely this was exemplified in *Federalist* 1, where Hamilton urbanely admitted that, oftentimes, there are "wise and good men on the wrong as well as on the right side of questions of the first magnitude to society." Also, in *Federalist* 14, Madison spoke of "a decent regard to the opinions of former times and other nations"—thus recalling the civility of Jefferson in the Declaration, which speaks of "a decent respect to the opinions of mankind".

Now it goes without saying that every government, like every individual, is fallible, or more or less deficient in wisdom and virtue, to which extent it will pursue various policies discordant with the interests of mankind as a whole, and therefore to its own ultimate detriment. In other words, just as the individual may mistake his apparent for his real interests, so too may a nation. Conversely, just as one individual is more civilized than another—more considerate and moderate in his dealings with his fellows—so may one nation be more civilized than another. This is but to acknowledge the palpable truth

22

that just as there are small- and large-souled men, so there are small-
and large-souled nations. Let us put away obscurantism, cynicism,
and sentimentalism and admit that magnanimity is not possessed
equally by all nations, no more so than by all individuals—and the inequality is not to be attributed solely to unequal material resources.
But what allows us to make such comparisons is the principle that
mankind forms a single species comprehensible in terms of some
standard of perfection against which one can measure individuals as
well as nations, a standard which is immanent in human nature and
which distinguishes men from beasts. Given the unity of human nature
and the definition of man as *homo rationalis et civilis,* a nation may
indeed be magnanimous, such that in pursuing its "own" interests it
cannot but promote the good of mankind. At the same time, however,
unless that definition of man is implicitly understood by the American
people, then Washington's declared wish "that [their political] union
and brotherly affection may be perpetual" was without rational foundation.

So, two levels of unity confront us: the unity of man as a species
and the unity of men as a particular society or people. We have now to
explore in greater detail what constitutes and yet disturbs and en-
dangers the unity of the American people.

In Washington's view (contrary to Tocqueville), liberty (and not
equality) appears to be the supreme value of Americans. He says:
"Interwoven as is the love of liberty with every ligament of your
hearts, no recommendation of mine is necessary to fortify or confirm
the attachment." But liberty, we have seen, is one of the fundamental
causes of faction, hence, of disunity. Why is this the case? To answer
this question, let us return to *Federalist* 10 where Madison expands
upon the causes of faction:

> As long as the reason of man continues fallible, and he is at liberty to
> exercise it, different opinions will be formed. As long as the connec-
> tion subsists between his reason and his self-love, his opinions and his
> passions will have a reciprocal influence on each other; and the
> former will be the objects to which the latter will attach themselves.
> The diversity in the faculties of men [such as judgment, desire, voli-
> tion, memory, and imagination] from which the rights of property
> originate, is not less an insuperable obstacle to a uniformity of in-
> terests. . . .
> The latent causes of faction are thus sown in the nature of man;

and we see them everywhere brought into different degrees of activity, according to the different circumstances of civil society.

So here we see that it is not merely the *differences,* but the *natural inequality* among men—the inescapable fact that men are born unequal in their intellectual and moral endowments—which is the ultimate cause of faction. And needless to say, these intellectual and moral differences and inequalities will manifest themselves in various ways: "A zeal for different opinions concerning religion, concerning government . . . [or] an attachment to different leaders ambitiously contending for pre-eminence and power . . . have, in turn, divided mankind into parties [and] inflamed them with mutual animosity. . . . But the most common and durable source of factions has been the various and unequal distribution of property."

Various derivative causes of faction may here be distinguished and may even be included among the principal causes of international conflict. The first concerns *opinions,* more precisely, conflicting ideas of justice or of how men should live. The second concerns men's *passions.* One is the passion of *ambition* or the inordinate desire for power. Another is *avarice,* but also the poor man's *envy:* in either case an inordinate desire for wealth. Interestingly enough, in *Federalist* 6, where Hamilton discusses the causes of hostility among nations, he includes "the love of power or the desire of pre-eminence and dominion—the jealousy of power, the desire of equality and safety." When to this he adds "avarice" or the "love of wealth", it appears that the causes of international conflict are very much the same as the causes of domestic faction. Nor should this be surprising, inasmuch as the ultimate cause of faction is rooted in human nature. Nevertheless, and as Madison has indicated, "the different circumstances of civil society" will affect the degree in which factional conflict manifests itself. Of decisive importance will be the form of government.[8] Such is the design of American government that a considerable degree of faction is not only inevitable, but tolerable. Madison acknowledges this in *Federalist* 10: "The regulation of . . . various and interfering interests forms the principal task of modern legislation, and involves the spirit of party and faction in the necessary and ordinary operations of the government." Given the circumstances and purpose of the Farewell Address, Washington takes a dimmer view of faction, warning against "the baneful effects of the spirit of party, generally."

There is an opinion that parties in free countries are useful checks upon the Administration of the Government and serve to keep alive the spirit of Liberty. This within certain limits, is probably true, and in Governments of a Monarchical cast, Patriotism may look with indulgence, if not with favour, upon the spirit of party. But in those of the popular character, in Governments purely elective, it is a spirit not to be encouraged. From their natural tendency, it is certain there will always be enough of that spirit for salutary purposes.

Perhaps anticipating the Civil War, Washington was especially concerned about and attempted to guard against, the formation of parties based "on geographical discrimination" which, he foresaw, would turn one part of the country against another and even foment insurrection.

Lest we misconstrue their intentions or their expectations, it should be noted that neither Washington nor Madison had in view *party* government, that is, government by nationally organized political parties. "Party" conflict was to be resolved within the government itself, more particularly, within Congress. To recur again to *Federalist* 49: "the passions ought to be controlled and regulated by the government", meaning that the government was intended to control and regulate the multifarious interest groups which are bound to proliferate in a free society. Indeed, the most obvious aspect of the Madisonian solution to the problem of faction—there are less obvious ones—is to control the *effects,* as opposed to eliminating the *causes,* of faction, which necessarily requires positive or constructive statesmanship.[9] Leaving this issue aside, however, the mere fact that American government was designed, in part, to tolerate a considerable degree of faction within society should dispose its citizens to being tolerant of a considerable degree of international diversity. On the other hand, lest tolerance degenerate into moral indifferentism, the American people will have to be imbued with a high sense of national unity, purpose, and character. This is the architectonic function of the national government.

The control and regulation of faction necessitates "unity of government", that unity of government, Washington said, which constitutes the American people one people and not a welter of self-seeking groups and individuals. But surely Washington must have primarily in mind the Executive, who alone can endow the government as a whole with unity.[10] And surely only a powerful Executive could

25

possibly endow the American people with a sense of national unity, purpose, and character. As Hamilton says in *Federalist* 70: "Energy in the Executive is a leading character in the definition of good government. It is essential . . . to the security of liberty against the enterprises and assaults of ambition, of faction, and of anarchy."[11] Admittedly, Washington was accused of being a "monocrat". Although there is some truth to this partisan exaggeration, it merely confirms the intentions of those who designed the Constitution, especially the institution of the Presidency.

After all, it is the President, more than any Senator or Representative, who is the guardian of the Constitution. He alone has a constitutionally prescribed oath of office, namely, "I do solemnly swear (or affirm) that I will faithfully execute the Office of President of the United States, and will to the best of my Ability, preserve, protect, and defend the Constitution of the United States." It were as if the President, in some sense, stands above the Constitution, and must if he is to be its guardian. Indeed, it is no accident that, of the three branches of government, only the executive power *per se* is unqualified. The Constitution prescribes that "The executive power shall be vested in a President of the United States." In contrast, "All legislative powers *herein granted* shall be vested in a Congress of the United States", and we know that there are explicit exceptions to the legislative power. Meanwhile, the appellate jurisdiction of the Supreme Court is controlled by Congress, so that as an unshared function, the executive power alone is not explicitly delimited.[12] (It would appear from the preceding that the doctrine of implied powers applies especially to the Presidency.) From this it follows that the notion of three co-equal branches of government is a half-truth, and less than that during periods of national crisis. Unity of government, certainly national unity, cannot exist without the architectonic power of the Presidency. Or to put the matter another way: Without presidential leadership, the tendency of American society would be to degenerate into a phantasmagoria of petty, self-seeking interest groups. Only an energetic Executive can possibly rescue those groups from their self-defeating particularity and, in the process, coördinate their interests so as to advance the common good.

Unlike the distraught statesmen of today who merely call for national unity, Washington again and again emphasizes the specific blessings which unity actually confers upon the American people. "It is", he points out, "a main Pillar in the Edifice of your real independence, the support of your tranquillity at home, your peace abroad, of your safety, of your prosperity, of that very liberty which you so highly prize." But the mere statement of these blessings of unity is not enough. In exemplary rhetorical fashion, Washington proceeds to engender or reinforce the belief in the value of national unity by associating it with, and by appealing to, the three motivating factors of human nature, namely, sentiment, interests, and ideas or principles. Thus, after warning the American people against "every attempt to alienate any portion of our country from the rest, or to enfeeble the sacred ties which now link together the various parts", he continues:

> For this you have every inducement of sympathy and interest. Citizens by birth or choice, of a common country, that country has a right to concentrate your affections. The name of AMERICAN, which belongs to you, in your national capacity, must always exult the just pride of Patriotism, more than any appellation derived from local discriminations. With slight shades of difference, you have the same Religion, Manners, Habits and political Principles. You have in a common cause fought and triumphed together. The independence and liberty you possess are the work of joint councils, and joint efforts; of common dangers, sufferings and successes.

But Washington knows that appeal to common sentiments—to the "mystic chords of memory"—is not sufficient to unite men. Hence the appeal to interests, that is, to the present and prospective material advantages of union:

> The *North,* in an unrestrained intercourse with the *South,* protected by the equal Laws of a common government, finds in the productions of the latter, great additional resources of Maritime and commercial enterprise and precious materials of manufacturing industry. The *South* in the same intercourse, benefitting by the Agency of the *North,* sees its agriculture grow and its commerce expand. . . . The *East,* in a like intercourse with the *West,* already finds, and in the progressive improvement of interior communications, by land and water, will more and more find a valuable vent for the commodities which it brings from abroad, or manufactures at home. The *West* derives from the *East* supplies requisite to its growth and comfort, and what is perhaps of still greater consequence, it must of necessity owe the *secure* enjoyment of indispensable *outlets* for its own

productions to the weight, influence, and the future Maritime strength of the Atlantic side of the Union, directed by an indissoluble community of interest as *one Nation.*

To the economic advantages or mutual enrichment facilitated by union, Washington adds the greater security against external danger as well as "an exemption from those broils and Wars between themselves, which so frequently afflict neighbouring countries, not tied together by the same government; which their own rivalships alone would be sufficient to produce, but which opposite foreign alliances, attachments and intrigues would stimulate and embitter." But just as the appeal to sentiment is insufficient, so too is the appeal to interests, and for the following reason.

Mere sentiment, including patriotic feeling, is not self-sustaining. This is why the statesman who would persuade diverse men to a common course of action must also show how his proposals are conducive to their material well-being and safety. But to sustain men's passions and, at the same time, to enlarge their interests, the statesman must also appeal to commonly accepted though not necessarily well-understood principles. These principles must be made vivid by relating them to men's sentiments and interests, hence by showing how they justify the statesman's objective, here national unity. In other words, the statesman must articulate those principles in such a way as to modulate and render coherent the mutually obstructive opinions, passions, and interests of his audience. Finally, and of decisive importance, *only by the articulation of such principles can the statesman pursue comprehensive and long-range policies without having constantly to defend himself against inevitable critics.* Bearing this in mind, let us see how Washington proceeds to educate his audience.

> To the efficacy and permanency of Your Union, a Government for the whole is indispensable. No alliances however strict between the parts can be an adequate substitute. They must inevitably experience the infractions and interruptions which Alliances in all times have experienced. Sensible of this momentous truth, you have improved upon your first essay [the Articles of Confederation] by the adoption of a Constitution of Government, better calculated than your former for an intimate Union, and for the efficacious management of your common concerns. This government, the offspring of your own choice . . . adopted upon full investigation and mature deliberation, completely free in its principles, in the distribu-

28

tion of its powers, uniting security with energy, and containing within itself a provision for its own amendment, has a just claim to your confidence and your support.

Again Washington identifies the Constitution as the work of the American people. This is not to be construed simply as democratic rhetoric. Rather, it is the use of democratic language for the sake of promoting the ends of a Constitution which is not simply democratic.[13] Be this as it may, if the Constitution is the handiwork of the American people, might they not then feel perfectly free to change it? Anticipating this question, Washington responds by saying of the government established under the Constitution:

> Respect for its authority, compliance with its Laws, acquiescence in its measures, are duties enjoined by the fundamental maxims of true Liberty. The basis of our political system is the right of the people to make and to alter their Constitutions of Government. But the Constitution which at any time exists, until changed by an explicit and authentic act of the whole People, is sacredly obligatory upon all. [Or as Hamilton says in *Federalist* 78: "Until the people have, by some solemn and authoritative act, annulled or changed the established form, it is binding upon themselves collectively as well as individually; and no presumption, or even knowledge, of their sentiments, can warrant their representatives in a departure from it, prior to such an act."] The very idea of the power and the right of the People to establish Government presupposes the duty of every Individual to obey the established Government.

This is clearly an argument against civil disobedience. In fact, civil disobedience is based on the principle underlying *secession,* since it substitutes the judgment of a part for that of the whole. Thus Lincoln argued in his First Inaugural:

> If the minority will not acquiesce, the majority must, or the government must cease. . . . If a minority, in such case, will secede rather than acquiesce, they make a precedent which, in turn, will divide and ruin them. . . .
> Plainly, the idea of secession [and, indeed, of civil disobedience], is the essence of anarchy. A majority, held in restraint by constitutional checks, and limitations, and always changing easily, with deliberate changes of popular opinions and sentiments, is the only true sovereign of a free people. Whoever rejects it, does of necessity, fly to anarchy or to despotism. Unanimity is impossible; the rule of a minority, as a permanent arrangement, is wholly inadmissible, so

that, rejecting the majority principle, anarchy, or despotism in some form, is all that is left.[14]

On its face, any act of civil disobedience involves the substitution of the rule of men for the rule of law. As Harry Jaffa has pointed out, "The idea of the rule of law rejects the notion that any individual or any group has sufficient wisdom and virtue to be trusted with the decision of individual cases on their own merits, without regard to general rules established by and through the authority of the whole community."[15] Washington was well aware that various groups, "under whatever plausible character", would seek, from time to time, to thwart the authority of government, perhaps most often in the name of "popular ends" or causes. He therefore warns the American people that attempts to obstruct "wholesome plans digested by common councils" subvert the very principles of popular government.

But the authority of government can be undermined not only from without, but from within, that is, by "innovation upon its principles". Says Washington:

> One method of assault may be to effect, in the forms of the Constitution, alterations which will impair the energy of the system, and thus to undermine what cannot be directly overthrown.

No doubt Washington has especially in mind attempts which may be made to sap the power of the Executive branch, and most likely via encroachments by the Congress.[16] And so, he continues:

> In all the changes to which you may be invited, remember that time and habit are at least as necessary to fix the true character of Governments, as of other human institutions; that experience is the surest standard, by which to test the real tendency of the existing Constitution of a country; that facility in changes upon the credit of mere hypotheses and opinion, exposes to perpetual change, from the endless variety of hypotheses and opinion.[17] And remember, especially, that for the efficient managment of your common interests, in a country so extensive as ours, a Government of as much vigour as is consistent with the perfect security of Liberty is indispensable. Liberty itself will find in such a Government, with powers properly distributed and adjusted, its surest Guardian.

This recalls Hamilton's remark in *Federalist* 1 that "the vigor of government is essential to the security of liberty", as well as Madison's more elaborate statement in *Federalist* 37:

Among the difficulties encountered by the [Constitutional] convention, a very important one must have lain in combining the requisite stability and energy in government, with the inviolable attention due to liberty and to the republican form. . . . Energy in government is essential to that security against external and internal danger, and to that prompt and salutary execution of the laws which enter into the very definition of good government. Stability in government is essential to national character. . . . An irregular and mutable legislation is not more an evil in itself than it is odious to the people . . . . On comparing, however, these valuable ingredients [of energy and stability] with the vital principles of liberty, we must perceive at once the difficulty of mingling them together in their due proportions.

This means that the Constitution was not established to maximize liberty. As already suggested, the fundamental problem confronting the founders was to design political institutions that would facilitate the development of a *national* character—which is but another way of saying "a more perfect Union". This is perhaps the major reason why the Senate was invested with a six-year term of office. "[T]he utility of a senate", says Madison in *Federalist* 63, "is the want of a due sense of national character." Obviously these are not democratic considerations. To the contrary, the Senate was established as "an anchor against popular fluctuations", meaning as a check against democratic liberty. "Liberty", writes Madison in *Federalist* 53, "lies within extremes, which afford sufficient latitude for all the variations which may be required by the various situations and circumstances of civil society." Recall that liberty is precisely what makes faction possible. Hence the need to place liberty under proper restraints, the restraints of moderate laws. But laws are not self-enforcing. "It is essential to the idea of a law", says Hamilton in *Federalist* 15, "that it be attended with a sanction; or, in other words, a penalty or punishment for disobedience. If there be no penalty annexed to disobedience, the resolutions or commands which pretend to be laws will, in fact, amount to nothing more than advice or recommendation." If the laws are to be attended with a sanction and, at the same time, if their enforcement is to promote national unity, there must obtain a system of federal courts which, under the Supreme Court, will provide uniformity in the interpretation of the national laws. Accordingly, "the Judicial power of government", Hamilton notes in *Federalist* 80, "[will have to be] coextensive with its legislative [power]". But "the judiciary is

beyond comparison the weakest of the three departments of power."
Its judgments are not self-executing. Or as Hamilton says of the
judiciary in *Federalist* 78, "It may truly be said to have neither
FORCE nor WILL, but merely judgment; and must ultimately depend upon the aid of the executive arm even for the efficacy of its
judgments." Once again we see the need for a powerful Executive. Not
that the President is constitutionally bound to enforce the judgments
of the Supreme Court, as many have only recently come to believe.
For if this were the case, the Supreme Court, far from being the
weakest, would be the strongest branch of government. At the same
time, such an interpretation of the proper relationship between the
judicial and executive branches could not but undermine the power of
the Presidency, if only because the Court is hardly in the position to
act with the "decision" and "dispatch" required of the Executive.[18]
The point is that, unlike the other members of government, the President must possess considerable discretionary power, especially in the
domain of foreign affairs or national security. Thus, in the very case
establishing judicial review, *Marbury v. Madison*, Chief Justice
Marshall, speaking for a unanimous Court, declared that "By the constitution of the United States, the president is invested with certain important political powers, in the exercise of which he is to use his own
discretion, and is accountable only to his country in his political
character and to his conscience. . . . [W]hatever opinion may be enter-
tained of the manner in which executive discretion may be used, still
there exists, and can exist, no power to control that discretion. The
subjects are political: they respect the nation, not individual rights,
and being entrusted to the executive, the decision of the executive is
conclusive."[19] Marshall's respect for presidential prerogatives must be
understood not only in relation to national crises or emergencies, but
also in the light of the central problem of the founding, the problem of
endowing a diverse people with a sense of national unity, a problem
which concerns the Presidency more than any other branch of
American government.

Returning, however, to the theme of law, I suggested a moment
ago that the uniform administration and enforcement of the laws require a powerful executive. Yet, the very extent to which the executive
must enforce the laws itself indicates a lack of national unity,
patriotism, or dedication to the common good. The truth is that the

more unified a nation, or the more patriotic its citizens, the less need is there for the exercise of governmental power. John Stuart Mill put it this way:

> [A] people must be considered unfit for more than a limited and qualified freedom, who will not co-operate actively with the law and the public authorities in the repression of evil doers. . . . [Taught] to regard the law as made for other ends than their own good, and its administrators as worse enemies than those who openly violate it . . . [they] cannot be governed with as little power exercised over them as a people whose sympathies are on the side of the law, and who are willing to give active assistance in its enforcement.[20]

Thus, while law imposes certain limits on freedom, respect or reverence for law is indispensable for the preservation and even the extension of freedom. But respect for law requires, in the first place, continuity in the laws themselves, especially as concerns the fundamental law, the Constitution. This is why Washington cautions against innovations "in the forms of the constitution". *Federalist* 49 provides the profoundest insights into this problem. There it is argued that frequent changes of the Constitution would

> . . . deprive the government of that veneration which time bestows on every thing, and without which perhaps the wisest and freest governments would not possess the requisite stability. If it be true that all governments rest on opinion, it is no less true that the strength of opinion in each individual, and its practical influence on his conduct, depend much on the number which he supposes to have entertained the same opinion. The reason of man, like man himself, is timid and cautious when left alone, and acquires firmness and confidence in proportion to the number with which it is associated. When the examples which fortify opinion are *ancient* as well as *numerous,* they are known to have a double effect. In a nation of philosophers, this consideration ought to be disregarded. A reverence for the laws would be sufficiently inculcated by the voice of an enlightened reason. But a nation of philosophers is as little to be expected as the philosophical race of kings wished for by Plato. And in every other nation, the most rational government will not find it a superfluous advantage to have the prejudices of the community on its side.

This is without doubt the boldest passage of *The Federalist*. Unlike the philosopher, the average man is not governed by "enlightened reason". The philosopher would revere the laws insofar as they were consistent with reason. The average man reveres the laws because they are old and revered by the rest of the community. Now, if the laws are frequently changed, they cannot become old and venerable; and the general run of men will not respect laws made yesterday and which they are free to change today. This applies *a fortiori* to the Constitution. Frequent disputes about the Constitution necessarily encourage divergent and conflicting opinions about its principles and purposes, shattering the community consensus about this fundamental and paramount law. The average man will not respect a Constitution about which there is a welter of conflicting interpretations. Reverence for the Constitution is based on general agreement about its meaning; but such agreement requires a stable body of opinion about the Constitution which is not disturbed too often. Only if there prevails the salutary prejudice of the average man, who reveres things because they are old and revered by the community—who identifies the good with what is ancient, and the true with what is commonly believed—only then can "rational governments" exist or be effective.[21]

Here we see why the wise founder will emphasize the ingredient of stability and will try to introduce that ingredient into every institution of government. Without stability, nothing great can be accomplished.

Admitting that stability and energy in government, or that continuity in the laws and efficient law-enforcement, are essential to liberty and national unity, still, according to Washington, the efficacy of law and the achievement of national unity ultimately depend on religion and morality. Here is what Washington says in the Farewell Address:

> Of all the dispositions and habits which lead to political prosperity, Religion and morality are indispensable supports. In vain would that man claim the tribute of Patriotism, who should labor to subvert these great Pillars of human happiness, these firmest props of the destinies of Men and citizens. . . . Let it simply be asked where is the security for property, for reputation, for life, if the sense of religious obligation *desert* the oaths, which are the instruments of investigation in Courts of Justice? And let us with caution indulge the supposition, that morality can be maintained without religion. Whatever may be conceded to the influence of refined education on minds of peculiar structure, reason and experience both forbid us to

34

expect that National morality can prevail in exclusion of religious principle.

The theme of religion (the root meaning of which is to tie, fasten, or bind) lends itself well to the theme of unity (as does morality to the related theme of patriotism). For religion—and Washington surely has in mind the Christian religion—emphasizes the brotherhood of man under one God. Religion moreover restrains the divisive passions of men: it teaches moderation and concern for the well-being of others. Finally, religion fosters respect for authority and, by so doing, conduces to the growth of a more perfect union.[22]

And so, by teaching the people some of the fundamental principles of American government, Washington facilitates the very exercise of presidential leadership. Only if the people understand those principles can they be a people at once free and united. Accordingly, Washington urges statesmen to "Promote . . . as an object of primary importance, Institutions for the general diffusion of knowledge. In proportion as the structure of government gives force to public opinion, it is essential that public opinion should be enlightened". To this end Washington proposed, in his last State of the Union Message, the establishment of a national university, reference to which appears in the second epigraph of this chapter. His rationale is worth recalling:

> Among the motives to such an Institution, the assimilation of principles, opinions and manners of our Countrymen, by the common education of a portion of our Youth from every quarter, well deserves attention. The more homogeneous our Citizens can be made in particulars, the greater will be our prospect of permanent Union; and a primary object of such a National Institution should be the education of our Youth in the science of *Government*. . . . [W]hat duty [is] more pressing on its Legislature, than to patronize a plan for communicating it to those who are to be the future guardians of the liberties of their country?[23]

Madison, too, formally proposed the establishment of a national university when he became President; and, like Washington, he recommended that the university be located in the nation's capital, the better to promote not only the science of government, but "those national feelings, those liberal sentiments, and those congenial manners which contribute cement to our Union and strength to the great political fabric of which that is the foundation."[24] Again and again we behold the theme of unity or union. On the one hand, Washington warned (1) against the spirit of party or faction; (2) against precipitous innovations in the Constitution; and (3) against the impairment, explicitly, of energetic government, but implicitly of presidential power. On the other hand, Washington appealed (1) to shared sentiments, the sufferings and struggle of the American people for independence; (2) to the economic interdependence and material advantages of union; (3) to the fundamental principles of American government especially those concerning respect for lawful authority; and (4) to the importance of morality, religion, and education—the bases of republican government.

Finally, it should be reiterated that for Washington unity is rooted in the truth of America's founding principles: Only if those principles possess universal validity can Washington be justified in saying to the American people that their success in the experiment of republican government "will acquire to them the glory of recommending it to the applause, the affection, and adoption of every nation which is yet a stranger to it." Only if American foreign policy is based upon those principles can the interests of the United States coincide with the good of mankind. Those principles will now be elucidated.

CHAPTER 3

SOURCES AND CRITERIA
FOR AN AMERICAN FOREIGN POLICY

When in the Course of human events, it becomes necessary for one people to dissolve the political bands which have connected them with another, and to assume among the powers of the earth, the separate and equal station to which the Laws of Nature and of Nature's God entitle them, a decent respect to the opinions of mankind requires that they should declare the causes which impel them to the separation.—We hold these truths to be self-evident, that all men are created equal, that they are endowed by their Creator with certain unalienable Rights, that among these are Life, Liberty and the pursuit of Happiness.

—The Declaration of Independence

I am convinced man has no natural right in opposition to his duties . . . [and that] questions of natural right are triable by their conformity with the moral sense and reason of man.

—Thomas Jefferson

You will find among [the American people] . . . some politeness, but more civility.

—John Adams

To preserve a nation's unity, the statesman must pursue a foreign policy whose principles or purposes are visibly consistent with those governing his country's political institutions and way of life. For if a nation's foreign policy conflicts with its domestic policy, public confusion will occur, followed by weakening of the social bonds. At this

37

point of our inquiry, therefore, it will be necessary to make explicit the original principles of the American republic in order to grasp the intended character of American foreign policy. These original principles will be outlined in Part I of this Chapter. Part II will relate these principles to the second half of the Farewell Address where Washington discusses the operational and moral standards intended to govern American foreign policy. Part III will then consider some of the difficulties confronting any statesman attempting to apply these standards today, especially vis-à-vis the Soviet Union, and what must be done to overcome those difficulties.

I

It may well be argued that the American polity is ultimately based on the principle that all men are created equal. Contrary to universally accepted opinion, however, this principle, far from being wholly democratic, is the precondition for any genuine aristocracy. Needless to say, so shocking or paradoxical an assertion requires supportive argument, for which purpose I must refer to my work *On the Silence of the Declaration of Independence.*

Viewed within the proper political context, the statement of the Declaration that all men are created equal was intended to inform mankind in general, and the British government in particular, that Americans belong to the same species as Englishmen, hence that they are endowed by *nature* with certain unalienable rights peculiar to that species. These rights constitute an *unalienable* possession because man is a created being who did not create himself. More precisely, inasmuch as man did not create his own nature, he did not create the rights he possesses in virtue of his nature. In consequence of this he cannot be justly divested of those rights so long as he does not violate his nature or the distinction between men and beasts.[1] In short, only because man is *homo rationalis et civilis* does he possess (or can he reasonably claim) the unalienable rights to life, liberty, and the pursuit of happiness.

Notice, however, that while the statesmen of the Declaration claimed that the Americans possess these rights *as species*, they were being prevented from fully exercising those rights *as individuals*. This implicit distinction between the *possession* and *exercise* of rights is of profound significance. For nothing in the Declaration suggests that *all* men *as individuals* are entitled to the actual exercise of their rights without qualification. In proof of this it is sufficient to point out that the preamble of the Declaration or its equivalent was incorporated into most of the state constitutions, many of which prescribed property and other qualifications for voting and for office. An implicit distinction was therefore made between men's rights and their privileges. Whereas the rights men possess *as species* are defined by nature, the privileges they exercise *as individuals* are defined by law, whether written or customary. Accordingly, the equality spoken of in the Declaration does not extend to privileges. Nevertheless, and strange as it may seem, the notion of privilege is a logical consequence of the Declaration's principle of equality. For the principle that all men are created equal should be understood as a moral prohibition against any and all privileges based on race, nationality, class, or parentage. The only moral title to any privilege which society may confer must be based on *individual* merit. In other words, what the equality of the Declaration requires is that no person be precluded by law from earning any established privilege on the basis of factors extrinsic to human nature or to those intellectual and moral qualities which distinguish the human from the sub-human. Examined in this light, the principle that all men are created equal—which does *not* mean they are born equal in their intellectual, moral, and physical endowments—may be regarded as the precondition of any aristocracy. As Jefferson wrote to John Adams: "I agree with you that there is a natural aristocracy among men. The grounds of this are virtue and talents. . . . The natural aristocracy I consider as the most precious gift of nature for the instruction, the trusts, and government of society."[2]

It thus appears that the American polity had its origin in a synthesis of democratic and aristocratic principles. This synthesis is consistent with the notion of government based on the consent of the governed, provided the governed consist of an enlightened and public-spirited body of citizens—citizens who possess the capacity to discern, select, and defer to men of merit. With one qualification to be discussed in a moment, this democratic-aristocratic synthesis underlies *The Federalist* and is most clearly evident in its recurring theme of deference to merit. In *Federalist* 36, Hamilton declares: "There are strong minds in every walk of life that will rise superior to the disadvantages of situation, and will command the tribute due to their merit, not only from the classes to which they particularly belong, but from society in general. The door ought to be equally open to all." To be sure, Madison admits in *Federalist* 10 that "Enlightened statesmen will not always be at the helm"; nevertheless he expects popularly elected representatives will more often than not be of such caliber as "to refine and enlarge the public views", representatives "whose wisdom may best discern the true interest of their country, and whose patriotism and love of justice will be least likely to sacrifice it to temporary or partial considerations." As for the (original) Senate, inasmuch as the "State legislatures who appoint the senators, will in general be composed of the most enlightened and respectable citizens, there is reason to presume," says Jay in *Federalist* 64, "that their attention and their votes will be directed to those men only who have become the most distinguished by their abilities and virtue, and in whom the people perceive just grounds for confidence." Finally, in *Federalist* 68, after analyzing the advantages of the electoral college method of choosing a President, Hamilton concludes with these words: "It will not be too strong to say, that there will be a constant probability of seeing the station filled by characters preëminent for abilities and virtue." Thus do we see, even in this brief sketch, institutions designed to render the consent of the governed a rational principle of political life.[3]

One other principle of the American polity needs to be emphasized, and that is the principle of private property. This "oligarchic" principle, insofar as it fosters diversity—and not only economic diversity—prevents the stultifying uniformity engendered by the egalitarian principle of democracy. Stated another way, private property (which does not preclude government regulation), makes possible the development of many different "oligopolies" of economic power preventing, in the process, any concentration of political power in the hands of a tyrannical majority. These "oligopolies", notwithstanding certain contrary tendencies (of which, more later), may thus contribute to the preservation of liberty and, given the diverse and unequal faculties of men, to the achievement of distributive justice.

And so, as I have argued more fully in my earlier works on the founding, the republic established under the American Constitution synthesizes democratic and oligarchic, as well as aristocratic principles. Let us say, therefore, that the ends of American government, hence the ends of American foreign policy, include (1) the promotion of *justice* (meaning arithmetical *and* proportionate equality); (2) the augmentation of *wealth* or material abundance; (3) the encouragement of *peace*; (4) the protection of *liberty*; and (5) the advancement of *reason* and *civility*. These ends or values are implicitly and explicitly affirmed in the Farewell Address to which I again turn.

II

Consider this key paragraph in which Washington commences his teaching regarding the principles which ought to govern American foreign policy:

> Observe good faith and justice towards all Nations. Cultivate peace and harmony with all. Religion and morality enjoin this conduct; and can it be that good policy does not equally enjoin it? It will be worthy of a free, enlightened, and, at no distant period, a great Nation, to give to mankind the magnanimous and too novel example of a People always guided by an exalted justice and benevolence. Who can doubt that in the course of time and things the fruits of such a plan would richly repay any temporary advantages which might be lost by a steady adherence to it? Can it be, that Providence has not connected the permanent felicity of a Nation with its virtue? The experiment, at least, is recommended by every sentiment which ennobles human Nature. Alas! is it rendered impossible by its vices?

This paragraph requires extended commentary. The phrase "observe good faith" recalls the statement, "let it simply be asked, where is the security for property, for reputation, for life, if the sense of religious obligation *desert* the oaths, which are the instruments of investigation in Courts of Justice?" This emphasis on good faith, meaning, in particular, the fulfillment of agreements and contracts, is to be expected in a commercial society. (In the paragraph preceding the one just cited, Washington also speaks of why it is important to "cherish public credit" and to avoid "the accumulation of debt.") The oligarchic bias is evident, but no more so than a motif peculiar to aristocracy. For to fulfil one's commitments is also a matter of personal honor (which recalls Washington's association of reputation and adherence to religious oaths). The same principle, that men should honor their promises, underlies the obligation of contract clause appearing in the Constitution. "This principle", I have written, "is the basis of mutual trust and confidence. It is the basis of friendship and community. Above all, it is the affirmation of man as that earthly being who alone regards the *word* as the external sign of a commitment to truth, a commitment which transcends the here and now and so unites the generations of mankind."[4] To observe good faith, therefore, is not only essential to domestic tranquillity, but to international peace and harmony.

Notice, too, how Washington brings to the support of these national objectives the teachings of religion and morality, by which he means, once again, the teachings of Christianity. And well he might. For Christianity holds that mankind comprises a single species subject to the same moral law before which all men are equal. Consequently, nations do not stand to each other as superior and inferior species, where the inferior may be exploited for the advantage of the superior. Instead, we are morally obliged to observe "justice towards *all* nations", the weak as well as the powerful. To say, however, that a universal moral law renders all men equal is not to say that all nations are equal, or rather, that their forms of government are equally just or equally conducive to domestic felicity or to international peace and harmony. To the contrary, a universal moral law is a political standard in terms of which one may judge whether the way of life of one nation is preferable to that of another. And as we have seen, only if the form of American government is itself rooted in principles of universal validity could Washington reasonably speak of recommending it to the adoption of every nation. Here the uniqueness of the American Constitution should be reiterated, I mean the fact that it prescribes a government based primarily on rational foundations. It is precisely in virtue of the rationality of the Constitution that one may speak of its universality or the universal applicability of its basic principles. Of course, to recommend those principles to the adoption of other nations is to suggest the inferiority if not the non-rationality of other existing regimes. Few if any statesmen of the West would have the inclination, let alone the courage, to suggest such a thing today. And yet the truth will out. For Western statesmen, along with cultural relativists and other commentators, will refer to certain nations as "underdeveloped", a diplomatic way of calling them more or less uncivilized. (What is all the more remarkable is that Washington, and the founding fathers in general, could insinuate that Europe was politically "backward" when, in many respects, it was culturally superior to the United States. Would that we had such supremely self-confident statesmen today. But bear in mind that this self-confidence was rooted in the conviction that human reason was capable of apprehending universal truths concerning how man should live.)

Despite, or really because of, his confidence in its moral superiority, Washington, like Hamilton and Madison, regarded the Constitution of the United States as a model not to be imposed upon other nations, but rather one which other nations might imitate or seek to approximate once they became familiar with its principles and advantages. Those principles do not require the United States to reform mankind, but rather to "give mankind the magnanimous and too novel example of a people always guided by an exalted justice and benevolence." This teaching has remarkable implications.

Again we see the need for an enlightened people: to whom the Declaration of Independence is addressed and to whom its basic principles primarily apply. Such a people would surely have to be animated by the teachings of religion and morality. (Recall Washington saying that "virtue or morality is a necessary spring of popular government.") No other kind of people could "give to mankind the magnanimous and too novel example . . . of always [being] guided by an exalted justice and benevolence." But what is it that renders this projected foreign policy so novel? As already anticipated, simply this: Here, perhaps for the first time in human history, a government was established whose foreign policy was to be guided by the universal and harmonizing principles of reason and civility intended to govern its own people.[5] Whether we go back to such antithetical regimes as Athens and Sparta, or to republican or imperial Rome, the primacy of force, as opposed to the primacy of persuasion, generally governed the relations between states. Were the United States to follow such a policy vis-à-vis other nations, then, apart from unavoidable wars, it would make a mockery of the Declaration of Independence, especially of the truth that all men are created equal, from which follows the principle of government based on the consent of the governed. Moreover, a foreign policy based on the primacy of force could not but erode the principles of reason and civility intended to govern domestic affairs.

But notice Washington's vision of America becoming "at no distant period, *a great nation*". Hitherto, every great nation has abused its power, has looked upon the less powerful as fit objects for domination or exploitation. And this means that, hitherto, there has always been a conflict of interest between the powerful and the weak. In contrast, even when it becomes a mighty nation, America is not to imitate the powerful nations of the past. Rather, it must be guided by an exalted justice and benevolence. And yet, it would be perfectly consistent with justice and benevolence for the United States to make clear that it will not hesitate to use force, if necessary, in defense of its rights and interests. How else may the enemies of republican government—regimes based on the primacy of force—be rendered more just and benevolent? This, then, is America's historic purpose: to pursue a foreign policy which, like its domestic policy, is to be governed by a politics of magnanimity.

Behold a pluralistic society where men of diverse ethnic background, of diverse opinions, passions and interests, live in peace and friendship. Consider the political institutions of this society. These are deliberative institutions designed to facilitate the peaceful resolution of differences, to bring into coördination and mutual intensification the diverse aims and interests of men. Hence it is misleading to call this a pluralistic society. For what the citizens of this society have in common is more important than their differences: an abiding commitment to reason and truth, a cultivated disposition to civility and justice. This is the example which America is to present mankind: the magnanimous capacity to accommodate and synthesize diverse points of view within the limits prescribed by the definition of man as *homo rationalis et civilis*. It should be noted, however, that this is not simply an example to be imitated by other nations severally considered. Rather, it is an example which mankind as a whole is to emulate. For considered as a whole (apart from the sovereignty of each nation), mankind is but a vast, multiform "society" which, not unlike the United States envisioned by Washington, might someday be governed by the disposition of *homo rationalis et civilis*. The historic mission of the United States is to foster that disposition among the nations, which it can only succeed in doing if its own people are governed by the politics of magnanimity.

Only a powerful nation can pursue such a politics, can be animated by "every sentiment which ennobles human nature" without itself being subjugated by powerful nations motivated by the desire for conquest or dominion. And America must become a powerful nation if it is to be an effective example for mankind. Not the "arrogance of power", but the magnanimity of power should characterize American foreign policy.[6] Only then can the interests of the United States coincide with the good of mankind.

Now, to avoid misunderstanding, what I have called the politics of magnanimity must be further distinguished from moralism. The tendency of most moralists, as argued in Chapter 1, is to commend a foreign policy the primary motive of which is the good of others. This is equivalent to a politics of altruism or of compassion. In contrast, the politics of magnanimity is primarily concerned with the enhancement of one's own self—only the "self" is to be conceived not as consuming but as overflowing, not as small-souled, but as large-souled, embracing in its largeness the good of others. The significance of this difference between altruism and magnanimity is not to be minimized.

A foreign policy based on altruism or compassion imposes upon the powerful a moral obligation to alleviate the sufferings of the unfortunate. The politics of magnanimity denies the existence of such an obligation so long as the powerful have not themselves been the cause of those sufferings. Nevertheless, depending on the extent of its own resources, the powerful, out of magnanimity or a sense of honor, will in fact seek to relieve the distress of others. In contrast, many moralists display a strong tendency to be distrustful of power. They usually believe that right cannot remain right when invested with might, or that the use of force on behalf of justice makes one morally suspect. Such moralists tend to identify with the weak. To the contrary, the politics of magnanimity looks upon power, in one respect, as indicative of certain virtues. I have especially in mind technological skills and the discipline required for their development. In other respects, power is to be regarded as morally neutral, a mere instrument either for good or for evil, depending upon the character of the agent. Few things noble, however, can be accomplished without great power—although it may also be argued that if power is measured in terms of the duration and extent of its influence, then great power cannot be achieved unless directed toward the noble. Considering, therefore, the historic purpose of the United States, it is the noble which is to animate American foreign policy insofar as it is based on the policies of magnanimity.

To sum up this portion of the discussion on American foreign policy as envisioned by Washington, it may be said that given the monarchic and oligarchic character of regimes contemporaneous with the founding of the American republic, the historic purpose of this republic could not be achieved unless it pursued *greatness*. Once again, the United States could hardly set an example for mankind—the example of a government based on the definition of man as *homo rationalis et civilis*—unless it commanded the esteem of other nations, which it could only do by being not only a just nation, but a powerful one. This quest for greatness (so prominent in the thought of Hamilton) could thus be conceived as a moral imperative, but may more accurately be designated as characteristic of a foreign policy rooted in magnanimity.[7] Of course, only a nation with great pride and self-confidence could pursue such a goal. But again that pride and self-confidence requires a healthy belief in the universal validity of the founding principles. And lest that universalism degenerate into doctrinaire democratism, I emphasize that this republic was never intended to be a democracy, hence was never intended to pursue a democratic foreign policy.

But what, precisely, are the character and aims of a *purely* democratic foreign policy? To answer this question it will first be necessary to explicate the two cardinal principles of democracy, namely, "freedom" and "equality". In advanced democratic societies, far removed in time from aristocratic oligarchies (as well as from the constraints of religion), freedom is understood to mean "doing as one pleases" as opposed to acting in accordance with insight or *informed* conscience. In other words, democratic freedom is rooted in the passions rather than in reason (or in moral intuition). As for equality, democracies worship equality based on numbers (arithmetic equality) rather than equality based on merit or dessert (proportionate equality). Finally, in common with commercial oligarchies, democracies have an inordinate desire for material well-being; only whereas such oligarchies encourage accumulation and the passion for economic adventure, democracies encourage consumption and the passion for security and comfort. These democratic values of "freedom" and "equality", along with security and comfort, determine the character of any democratic foreign policy.

On the one hand, democratic regimes obviously prefer democratic neighbors, the better to secure their own freedom while avoiding foreign influences which might reinforce any domestic oligarchic faction. On the other hand, the egalitarianism of democratic societies engenders a vulgar relativism—one nation's way of life is deemed as valid as another's—which tends to render democratic foreign policies ethically neutral. To be sure, the bias of democracies (and, in the twentieth century, of doctrinaire liberals) in favor of the poor incline them to be less hostile to communist than to fascist regimes because of the former's egalitarian pretensions.[8]* (Conversely, the bias of doctrinaire conservatives in favor of the rich disposes them to be less hostile to fascist than to communist regimes because of the former's state-sanctioned inequalities.) Still, the decisive intellectual factor affecting democratic foreign policy is relativism. Since this doctrine reinforces the notion of freedom as living as one pleases—and one man's pleasure is said to be as valid as another's—democratic statesmen derive their prestige by pursuing a foreign policy that will maximize "freedom" together with security and comfort. Such a foreign policy will emphasize the value of "peace" above justice and honor, and for two related reasons. First, both justice and honor involve constraints or impose limits on "living as one pleases". Whereas justice requires us to act out of motives larger than our own pleasure or advantage, honor requires us to risk death rather than act basely or ignobly. In other words, neither justice nor honor is compatible with the democratic tendency to regard comfortable self-preservation as the highest good, or violent death as the greatest evil. (After all, considerations of justice and honor may themselves require us to wage war.) Second, relativism denies the power of human reason to apprehend universal standards by which to determine what is just or unjust, honorable or dishonorable. Besides, the very notion of honor, in its relation to the noble, is an aristocratic value.[9] In sum, it may be said that peace, meaning the absence of strife, is the highest aim of a

---

*Notice the media's favorable coverage of Chou En-lai and their hostile coverage of Franco upon the deaths of those two tyrants. Yet, in comparison with the enormities of Chou, Franco was an angel of mercy. See below, p. 97n.

democratic foreign policy insofar as it serves the highest aim of democracy itself, which is the life of ease and comfort.[10]

Peace may also be said to be the highest aim of the Farewell Address; but *this* peace is not to be pursued at the expense of justice and honor. True, Washington cautions his countrymen that

> *permanent, inveterate* antipathies against particular Nations and *passionate* attachments for others should be excluded; and that in place of them just and amicable feelings towards all should be cultivated. The Nation, which indulges towards another an *habitual* hatred, or an *habitual* fondness, is in some degree a slave. It is a slave to its animosity or to its affection, either of which is sufficient to lead it astray from its duty and its interest.

Here the aloof Washington had especially in mind the impassioned divisions in America occasioned by the outbreak of war between France and England and by his own proclamation of neutrality in 1793. It is in this light that we are to understand his repeatedly emphasizing the need to pursue a policy of peace and harmony with all nations. Yet the words I have italicized in the above passage signify the obvious qualifications of such a policy. No less than domestic policy, foreign policy must be the result of "reflection and choice", must issue from considerations of duty and interest, rather than from the impulses of passion or from mere habit. It is perfectly rational, however, to show affection toward one nation, *so long as* it is just, while showing hostility toward another, *so long as* it is unjust. The latter is not contradicted by the fact that Washington urges a foreign policy "always guided by an exalted justice and benevolence". In the first place, that he should speak of justice *and* benevolence indicates that justice and benevolence are not identical. Furthermore, a foreign policy guided by benevolence is to be understood simply as the antithesis of one guided by *malevolence*. The latter, in effect, is precisely what Washington cautions against in decrying "*permanent*, inveterate antipathies against particular nations", suggesting that enemies in the past may become friends in the future. (This recalls the magnanimous words of the Declaration of Independence, "Enemies in War, in Peace Friends.") Now, inasmuch as justice is not identical with benevolence, but rather involves the notion of proportionality, it may be right to show affection for one nation and hostility toward another in the present, and the very reverse in the future. But consider another alternative already alluded to.

If a nation's foreign policy were to be ethically neutral, if it were to make no distinction between just and unjust regimes, that is, if it were to treat both equally, extending its friendship to one no less than to the other, the result would be moral confusion and apathy at home, and a mixture of contempt and hostility abroad. The impact of such a foreign policy on friends and enemies is pointedly drawn by Ibn Hazm of Cordova (994-1064):

> He who befriends and advances friend and foe alike will only arouse distaste for his friendship and contempt for his enmity. He will earn the scorn of his enemy, and facilitate his hostile designs; he will lose his friend, who will join the ranks of his enemies.
>
> The height of goodness is that you should neither oppress your enemy nor abandon him to oppression. To treat him as a friend is the work of a fool whose end is near.
>
> The height of evil is that you should oppress your friend. Even to estrange him is the act of a man who has no sense, for whom misfortune is predestined.
>
> Magnanimity is not to befriend the enemy, but to spare them, and to remain on your guard against them.[11]

For a nation not to distinguish between friend and foe, far from being a mark of magnanimity, is rather indicative of a a lack of national pride or honor. Or what is to say the same, apart from extreme circumstances,[12] to befriend and advance friend and foe alike is symptomatic of a foreign policy infected by moral relativism or decadence.[13]

But how is a republic to conduct its relations with nations which are not republics, indeed, when it is the only republic of its kind on the face of the earth? Says Washington:

> The Great rule of conduct for us, in regard to foreign Nations is in extending our commercial relations to have with them as little *political* connection as possible. So far as we have already formed engagements let them be fulfilled, with perfect good faith. Here let us stop.

Apart from certain circumstances, for a republic to enter into a political alliance with a regime which is not republican would tend to dignify the latter and degrade the former. It could obscure in the minds of its own citizens the moral difference between a government based primarily on reflection and consent as opposed to those based primarily on custom or on force. It may be argued, however, that the same public confusion would result from the establishment of commercial relations between the United States and non-republican regimes. To some extent the objection is valid. Nevertheless, until recently, commercial relations between nations were not visible to the general public, so that the danger in question was rather remote. On the other hand, the establishment of commercial relations between nations can contribute to peace so long as the nations concerned are not animated by imperialistic ambitions. By providing for those necessities which each nation cannot provide for itself, international trade can be a substitute for war. But here one should recall the warning of Hamilton in *Federalist* 6. To the contention that "the spirit of commerce has a tendency to soften the manners of men, and to extinguish those inflammable humors which have so often kindled into wars," Hamilton replies:

> Is it not . . . the true interest of all nations to cultivate the same benevolent and philosophic spirit? If this be their true interest, have they in fact pursued it? Has it not, on the contrary, invariably been found that momentary passions, and immediate interests, have a more active and imperious control over human conduct than general or remote considerations of policy, utility, or justice? . . . Has commerce hitherto done any thing more than change the objects of war? Is not the love of wealth as domineering and enterprising a passion as that of power or glory? Have there not been as many wars founded upon commercial motives since that has become the prevailing system of nations, as were before occasioned by the cupidity of territory or dominion? Has not the spirit of commerce, in many instances, administered new incentives to the appetite, both for the one and for the other? Let experience, the least fallible guide of human opinions, be appealed to for an answer to these inquiries.

Complicating the problem for the United States, especially in Hamilton's time, was that it had to conduct commercial relations for the most part with monarchic regimes animated not only by the "spirit of commerce", but by "cupidity of territory or dominion". Yet the prejudice concerning the pacific consequences of international commerce—of "intermeshing" or interdependent national economies —prevails to this very day.[14] Those who place so much faith in the salutary effects of expanding trade between the United States and the Soviet Union overlook the fact that trade frequently generates friction and conflict even among friends, and that Germany was the largest trading partner of Russia before each of the two World Wars.[15]

Even though foreign trade requires peace, it does not follow that militant and imperialistic powers will give up their militant character and imperialistic objectives for the sake of foreign trade.[16] The love of gain (or of ease and comfort) is not in all cases the strongest passion of the human heart. (It would be ironic indeed for a non-Marxist society to be guided by a foreign policy based on para-Marxist assumptions, forgetting that ideas, to say nothing of the love of power, may sometimes hold an imperious sway over the conduct of men and nations.) This, of course, is not an argument against trade with the Soviet Union, so much as a warning against the naïve and historically myopic expectations of so many of its proponents. But to this must be added the warning alluded to earlier, that under ordinary circumstances, commercial relations between a just and an unjust regime (whether communist or fascist) may confuse and divide the public and undermine confidence in the moral integrity of one's own political institutions.[17]

By no means do I wish to suggest, however, that only republics are just regimes. Certainly this is not the teaching of the Declaration of Independence which, in saying "That whenever *any* Form of Government becomes destructive of [men's unalienable rights], it is the Right of the People to alter or abolish it"—implies that limited or constitutional monarchies may be just forms of government.[18] Accordingly, commercial relations with such regimes would not have the pernicious consequences mentioned above. Nevertheless, Washington urges his countrymen "to have with them as little *political* connection as possible." He continues:

> Europe has a set of primary interests, which to us have none, or a very remote relation. Hence she must be engaged in frequent controversies, the causes of which are essentially foreign to our concerns. Hence therefore it must be unwise in us to implicate ourselves, by artificial ties, in the ordinary vicissitudes of her policies, or the ordinary combinations and collisions of her friendships, or enmities . . . . Why, by interweaving our destiny with that of any part of Europe, entangle our peace and prosperity in the toils of European Ambition, Rivalship, Interest, Humour or Caprice?

Clearly, Washington is alluding especially to *dynastic* ambitions which, in addition to commercial rivalry, can only increase the likelihood of war. Here, by the way, is the problem of the Monroe

Doctrine. For when President Monroe declared, in his State of the Union Message of 1823, "that the American continents . . . are henceforth not to be considered as subjects for future colonization by any European powers," he was simply recognizing the fact that "The political system of th[ose] powers is essentially different . . . from that of America". Precisely because monarchies tend to be animated by "cupidity of territory or dominion", which is to say imperialism, their colonization of Latin America would constitute an ever-present threat to the United States. Or as the Monroe Doctrine also implies, because the governments of Europe were not then founded on republican principles, in particular, on the consent of the governed, their establishment of non-republican regimes in proximity to the United States would have tended to undermine the foundations of American liberty.

As noted in Chapter 1, a republic, or any regime seeking to develop parliamentary institutions, requires a favorable environment, an environment conducive to government based on the consent of the governed. For example: if any form of tyranny with imperialistic ambitions were to gain a foothold in Mexico, it would seek to foment internal divisions within the United States. It would appeal to two types of men found in any society, namely, those who desperately wish to rule, and those who desperately wish to be ruled. Confronted by the danger of subversion within aided by the encroaching enemy without, the United States would have to place more or less stringent limits on freedom of speech and press, to say nothing of greatly increasing the size of its standing armies. Government by the consent of the governed can hardly succeed or prosper under such conditions.[19] The same conclusion appears in the Farewell Address where Washington, having said that the American people would "derive from Union an exemption from those . . . Wars . . . which so frequently afflict neighboring countries not tied together by the same government," goes on to point out that "likewise they will avoid the necessity of those overgrown Military establishments, which under any form of Government are inauspicious to liberty, and which are to be regarded as particularly hostile to Republican Liberty."

So we see in the Farewell Address principles anticipating the Monroe Doctrine, according to which it was the policy of the United States to disengage European powers from the Western hemisphere. It was *this* disengagement that enabled the American republic to prosper and develop into a great continental power—say rather a more perfect union of free states relatively immune from the imperialistic ambitions of European despotism. It would be a grave mistake, however, to understand the Farewell Address as advocating a policy of isolationism. Says Washington:

> 'Tis our true policy to steer clear of *permanent* Alliances with any portion of the foreign world. . . .
> Taking care always to keep ourselves, by suitable establishments, in a respectably defensive posture, we may safely trust to *temporary* alliances for extraordinary emergencies. (Italics added.)

This is not a policy of isolationism. Political or diplomatic relations between the United States and foreign nations will exist if only to sustain commercial intercourse. And, in "extraordinary emergencies", the United States will form temporary military alliances with various powers to secure its own safety and welfare. What Washington is trying to teach the American people is that they should be more concerned with internal perfection than the external glory. Indeed, the very principle of republican self-government, consistent with the teachings of religion and morality, preclude an imperialistic foreign policy, one aimed at the conquest and subjugation of other nations. Moreover, only by the pursuit of internal perfection—by presenting mankind the example of a virtuous nation—can the American people achieve true glory, "the glory of recommending [republicanism] to the . . . adoption of every nation which is yet a stranger to it." Unlike the autocracies of Europe ever embroiled in territorial conflicts,

> Our detached and distant situation invites and enables us to pursue a different course. If we remain one People, under an efficient government, the period is not far off, when we may defy material injury from external annoyance; when we may take such an attitude as will cause the neutrality we may at any time resolve upon to be scrupulously respected; when belligerent nations . . . will not lightly hazard the giving us provocation; when we may choose peace or war, as our interest guided by justice shall Counsel.

There is something providential in "our detached and distant situation". It enables us to pursue the experiment of liberty, of government based on reflection and choice. Free from the proximity of powerful neighbors animated by territorial ambition, we need not maintain large standing armies, themselves a potential threat to liberty. Nevertheless, we must not encourage, through weakness, the designs of imperialistic powers.[20] Despite the strategic importance of the Atlantic Ocean, a defensive military posture, sufficiently respectable to deter would-be aggressors, will be necessary for the preservation of republican liberty, the more so in a world hostile to the republican form of government. In such a world it may be necessary for the United States to ally itself temporarily with non-republican regimes either to prevent the outbreak of war or to bring it to a successful conclusion. This, of course, is no less true today when vast oceans have lost their original significance in the face of intercontinental and submarine-launched ballistic missiles.

Nor should it be thought that our rather permanent alliance with the members of the North Atlantic Treaty Organization is incompatible with the principles and long-range objectives of the Farewell Address.

Recalling its very first thematic paragraph, there Washington evidently envisions an international environment conducive to the development of republican institutions, institutions which enable men to resolve their differences by means of rational persuasion rather than by force. But in 1796, the United States was the only genuine republic, the preservation of which might depend, from time to time, on *temporary* alliances. That Washington should disapprove of *permanent* alliances is therefore to be understood precisely (though not exclusively) in terms of the non-republican character of eighteenth-century Europe. For reasons discussed earlier, permanent alliances with a non-republican regime would tend to undermine the moral and political cohesion of this country. But suppose there came a time when Europe itself consisted for the most part of republics? Against the unremitting threat of Soviet imperialism it would be perfectly consistent with the principles of the Farewell Address to form a more or less permanent alliance with those European republics, which alliance need not undermine the moral and political integrity of the United States. Now, the fact that certain members of NATO are not republics is politically insignificant, and for two reasons: first, because the regimes in question are themselves politically insignificant, meaning that their form of government does not materially affect the character of the alliance, which is overwhelmingly republican; and second, because the political differences between those regimes and the United States are trivial in comparison with the ideological conflict between this country and the Soviet Union. Nevertheless, it is incumbent upon statesmen to educate the American people to the *moral* necessity of an alliance with those non-republican regimes, lest the counterfeit morality of moral purism take the place of moral judgment—that comprehensive form of judgment which, attentive to long-range as well as immediate consequences, ever seeks to balance good against evil, maximizing the one while minimizing the other. Finally, to appreciate the contingent nature of Washington's disapproval of permanent alliances, we ought to remember that, in 1796, the United States was not a powerful nation, let alone a very cohesive one. Thus, to understand the Farewell Address we must focus not on its policy of non-entangling alliances, but rather on the underlying motives and ultimate objectives of such a policy. Says Washington:

> With me, a predominant motive has been to endeavour to gain time to our country to settle and mature its yet recent institutions, and to progress without interruption, to that degree of strength and consistency, which is necessary to give it, humanly speaking, the command of its own fortunes.

Were we to have allied ourselves with a considerably more powerful nation, our foreign policy would have been more or less determined by the interests of our ally (which recalls the major political problem of NATO). Not until this pluralistic society had become a more perfect as well as more powerful union could we have afforded to play a more significant if not central role in world affairs. Only then could we "choose peace or war, as our own interest guided by justice [should] counsel." Far from being intrinsic to the founding of this republic, the so-called policy of isolationism was originally conceived as a tactical means of enabling the young regime to develop and consolidate its strength, the strength necessary to fulfil its historic purpose, that of providing mankind "the magnanimous and too novel example of a [powerful nation] always guided by an exalted justice and benevolence."

III

Having elucidated the basic principles of the Farewell Address, the time has come to apply them critically to the conduct of American foreign policy in the twentieth century, with particular reference to the Soviet Union. Two things, however, must be borne in mind throughout the following discussion. First, the fundamental task of any statesman is to secure and strengthen the bonds of his community—those internalized persuasions or unquestioned beliefs and sentiments which enable otherwise diverse individuals to be fellow-citizens. Second, the task of securing and strengthening the bonds of a society accustomed to freedom is infinitely more difficult than it is for a society accustomed to servitude.

Free societies, recall, are especially prone to the spirit of party or faction. This spirit of party, says Washington,

> . . . exists under different shapes in all Governments, more or less stifled, controlled, or repressed; but, in those of the popular form it is seen in its greatest rankness, and is truly their worst enemy. . . .
> It opens the door to foreign influence and corruption, which find a facilitated access to the government itself through the channels of party passion. Thus the policy and the will of one country, are subjected to the policy and will of another.

The truth of these words is evident to careful students of the Vietnam War.[21] We know—or at least some of us know—how the North Vietnamese as well as the Soviet Union were able, in the language of the Farewell Address, "to tamper with domestic factions; to practice the arts of seduction; to mislead public opinion; [and thereby] to influence or awe the public councils."[22] One hundred and fifty years after these words were written, George Kennan sent the following warning about the intention of the Soviet Union to undermine the political and strategic potential of the Western powers:

> Efforts will be made in such countries to disrupt national self-confidence, to hamstring measures of national defense, to increase social and industrial unrest, to stimulate all forms of disunity. All persons with grievances, whether economic or racial, will be urged to seek redress not in mediation and compromise, but in defiant violent struggle. . . . Here poor will be set against rich, black against white, young against old. . . .[23]

Precisely because public opinion is a powerful force in a republic, it is absolutely essential for statesmen to thwart the attempts of hostile powers to influence or divide public opinion against the policies of government. Censorship being out of the question, then, as Washington points out, "In proportion as the structure of government gives force to public opinion, it is essential that public opinion should be enlightened." This requires that the American people be adequately informed' of the character of our enemies: their political institutions, their way of life, their ultimate international objectives, their methods of pursuing those objectives. As Mr. Kennan urged in his telegraphic message from Moscow in 1946:

> We must see that our public is educated to realities of Russian situation. I cannot overemphasize the importance of this. Press cannot do this alone. It must be done mainly by government, which is necessarily more experienced and better informed on practical problems involved. In this we need not be deterred by ugliness of the picture. I am convinced that there would be far less hysterical anti-Sovietism in our country today if the realities of this situation were better understood by our people. There is nothing as dangerous or as terrifying as the unknown.[24]

Clearly, this advice was not intended to encourage the government to engage in propaganda or to inflame public passions against the Soviet Union. Such a policy would not only be an insult to the intelligence and character of the American people, but it would diminish the government's own range of options in the conduct of foreign affairs. Instead, the immediate objective should be to anticipate and refute the propaganda of our enemies, or of those whom they have influenced or corrupted, and, by so doing, to uphold the authority of reason and truth over against passion and falsehood. In no other way can the statesman rightly counter the enemy's strategy of *divide et impera*. This is but to say that, in a society based on the notion of *homo rationalis et civilis*, truth and counsels of moderation must be the principal means by which the statesman seeks to achieve national solidarity. However, simply to tell the truth about the nature and ultimate objectives of one's enemy can inflame the passions. Hence the need for statesmen to remind their fellow-citizens about the principles of a truly civilized society, a society where moral fervor is under the governance of moral judgment.

Unfortunately, with the much heralded "end of ideology" and with the concomitant ascendency of anti-anticommunism, it will not be easy for an American statesman to reveal the truth about Soviet designs on the United States. Here I touch upon a decisive turning point in American history, one having the gravest consequences for Western Civilization.

Like the so-called "end of ideology", the failure of American statesmen during the last two decades to reveal the truth about the ultimate intentions of the Soviet Union is symptomatic of something more profound. As previously suggested, no longer do those who shape American foreign policy *wholeheartedly* believe, as their predecessors believed, that the fundamental principles upon which this government was established can be recommended as an example or model for mankind. They no longer possess such wholeheartedness because they no longer regard those principles as universally valid; and they no longer believe with genuine conviction in the universal validity of those principles because, having been more or less influenced by relativism, they have lost confidence in the power of reason to apprehend universal and immutable truths concerning how men should live. Life has thus become meaningless, a ceaseless quest for paltry pleasures and security. As Nietzsche predicted, relativism has engendered in the West a paralysis of the will, the will to greatness.[25] With the "end of ideology" no cause is worth fighting and dying for.[26] The eclipse of truth has therefore magnified the fear of violent death into a first principle, the paramount principle of politics.[27] Not that an American statesman, who dares to reveal the truth about the intentions of the Soviet Union, need fear that such a revelation would exacerbate U.S.-Soviet relations and thereby increase the possibility of nuclear war. As Kennan has urged—and, as we shall see, this applies even during a period of nuclear parity: "*Do not be afraid of unpleasantness and public airing of differences* [with the Soviet Union]," in explanation of which, he continues:

> The Russians don't mind scenes and scandals. If they discover that someone else does mind them and will go out of the way to avoid them, they will use this as a form of blackmail in the belief that they can profit from the other fellow's squeamishness. If we are to reestablish our prestige with the Soviet government and gain respect in Russia we must be prepared to undertake a "taming of the shrew"

> which is bound to involve a good deal of unpleasantness. On the
> other hand, we need not fear that occasional hard words will have
> permanent bad effect on our relations. The Russian is never more
> agreeable than after his knuckles have been sharply rapped.[28]

Their cynicism unsurpassed—for they have made an art of appearing
as the aggrieved party in the very midst of vilifying their op-
ponents—the leaders of the Soviet Union would not in the least feel
personally offended should American statesmen criticize the Soviet
regime or communist thought and practice.[29] Indeed, the failure of
American statesmen (to say nothing of the mass media) to expose
communist tyranny for fear of arousing the passions—a fear which
betrays not only their own lack of oratorical skill and wisdom, but
their lack of confidence in the good sense and moderation of the
American people—that failure has only served the communist policy
of *divide et impera* employed with devastating effectiveness during the
Vietnam War.[30] All the more need, therefore, to inform the American
people of the methods and strategic objectives of the Politburo.
Unless public opinion is enlightened by American statesmen (as Kennan suggests), but above all by the President of the United States, the
public will be divided and demoralized by communist propaganda
deceptively appealing to our own values, using such slogans as
"peace", "national liberation", and "self-determination".[31] The question is, from what sources may the American people best learn the
truth about the fundamental principles and purposes of the Soviet
Union?

CHAPTER 4

SOURCES OF SOVIET FOREIGN POLICY: THE MEANING OF MARXISM

In direct contrast to German philosophy which descends from heaven to earth, here we ascend from earth to heaven. That is to say, we do not set out from what men say, imagine [or] conceive . . . in order to arrive at men in the flesh. We set out from real, active men, and on the basis of their real life-process we demonstrate the development of the ideological reflexes and echoes of this life-process. The phantoms formed in the human brain are also, necessarily sublimates of their material life-process. . . . Morality, religion, metaphysics, all the rest of ideology . . . no longer retain the semblance of independence.

—Karl Marx and Frederick Engels

[C]riticism is not the passion of the head but the head of a passion. It is not a lancet, it is a weapon. Its object is an enemy *it wants not to refute but to* destroy. . . .*[It] is no longer an* end in itself *but simply a* means. *Its essential pathos is* indignation, *its essential task*, denunciation.

—Karl Marx

My words were calculated to evoke hatred, aversion and contempt . . . not to convince but to break up the ranks of the opponent, not to correct an opponent's mistake, but to destroy him. . . .

—V.I. Lenin

[N]ot criticism, but revolution is the driving force of history. . . .
—Karl Marx and Frederick Engles

Addressing a group of young Communists, the principal founder of the Soviet Union saw fit to declare: "we reject any morality based on extra-human and extra-class concepts. . . . We say that our morality is entirely subordinated to the interests of the proletariat's class struggle."[1] This means that "everything is moral which is necessary for the annihilation of the old exploiting order."[2] No leader of Communist Russia has rejected this teaching of Lenin. None has renounced or deviated from the intention of bringing about, through deception, subversion, and violence, the disintegration and destruction of nations which, whether "capitalist" or "socialist", have retained parliamentary institutions wherein men may resolve their differences by means of rational persuasion and compromise. No Soviet leader, in other words, has ceased to be animated by a "permanent, inveterate antipathy against particular nations" whose way of life is based on the principle of *homo rationalis et civilis*. What is more, and as I shall presently show, no regime can cease to be so animated as long as it derives its inspiration from the teachings of Karl Marx. If, therefore, an American statesman is to tell his fellow-citizens the truth about the fundamental principles and purposes of the Soviet Union and, at the same time, to remind them of the fundamental principles and purposes of their own society, he could hardly do better than to contrast the teachings of the Declaration of Independence with those of the *Communist Manifesto* and certain earlier writings of Marx. I single out the *Manifesto* not only because it embodies, like the Declaration, a unique doctrine of revolution, but again like the Declaration vis-à-vis the United States, it is in fact the original source and reveals the animating spirit of Soviet foreign policy.[3] In comparing these two revolutionary documents, I shall focus on their different conceptions of human nature, primarily with a view to elucidating their respective teachings regarding the role of reason and force in human affairs.

What most distinguishes the Declaration of Independence from the *Communist Manifesto* is that the former affirms, while the latter denies, the power of reason to apprehend trans-historical truths—those "Laws of Nature and of Nature's God" in terms of which men may criticize the character of their own class or the values of their own society. This architectonic principle of the Declaration implies the possibility of intellectual detachment or independence, which means that our thoughts concerning justice, for example, are not wholly determined by non-rational or by sociological forces. In other words, the statesmen of the Declaration presuppose the possibility of moral *insight*, which in turn presupposes the freedom of the intellect from external compulsion. It is this intellectual freedom that makes revolution possible; it is moral insight which alone can render revolution justifiable: insight into the disparity between the actual and the potential, between the historical and the trans-historical—again those laws of nature and of nature's God. As previously noted, these laws are constitutive of man's very being; they are the very norms which distinguish the behavior of men from that of beasts.[4] Consequently, to understand the laws of nature and of nature's God is to understand how men should live and how society should be governed. Let us call those laws what they were once understood to be, the moral law.

Because the moral law distinguishes the conduct of men from that of beasts, no group of men may rule other men like chattel or as an inferior species. Before a universal moral law all men are equal. Furthermore, because the moral law is eternal and immutable, all the generations of mankind are equal. Not "History", not some privileged class or millennial epoch, but again the laws of nature and of nature's God—therein are the ultimate foundations of government and of men's unalienable rights to life, liberty, and the pursuit of happiness.

The Declaration thus posits nature as the norm and man as a part of nature. The norm, the moral law, is not made by men, precisely because man is not the maker of his own nature. Man is rather a created being, the only created being endowed with insight, that is, with the power to understand his own nature. That power has its source in the philosophic, but which I shall now call the metaphysical, function of reason which, unlike reason's pragmatic function—the two, though distinct, are inseparable—is not preoccupied with spatio-temporal interests. It is the metaphysical reason that renders man the *meta*-physical animal, the only animal that goes beyond the physical. Again, the metaphysical reason is the critic of the actual, of existing human institutions, laws, and purposes. It may therefore engender or counsel reform or revolution. This means that reason is a persuasive agency cognizant of the limits of persuasion. In this light are we to understand those words of the Declaration, "let Facts be submitted to a candid world". The very statement of those facts—that list of grievances against the British government set forth to *justify* a revolution—is testimony of the primacy of reason over force. For inasmuch as the acts of the British government "evince[d] a design to reduce [the American people] under absolute Despotism", to submit to those acts without struggle would be to accept, in effect, the status of an inferior species, something repugnant to the metaphysical reason (so closely allied with man's self-respect or sense of honor). What we see here is the rebellion of the metaphysical reason against its own violation, the violation of that which distinguishes the human from the sub-human. The primacy of reason is thus evidenced in the very act of rebellion, as may be seen in the following passage of the Declaration:

> In every stage of these Oppressions We have Petitioned for Redress in the most humblest terms: Our repeated Petitions have been answered only by repeated injury. . . . Nor have We been wanting in attentions to our British brethren. . . . We have appealed to their native justice and magnanimity, and we have conjured them by the ties of our common kindred to disavow these usurpations. . . . They, too, have been deaf to the voice of justice and of consanguinity. We must, therefore, acquiesce in the necessity, which denounces our Separation, and hold them, as we hold the rest of mankind, Enemies in War, in Peace Friends.

Despite the resort to force, the primacy of reason could hardly be stated more eloquently.

By the primacy of reason I do not mean that men's opinions, say about justice, are unaffected by their economic interests. Still, even ordinary men will sometimes adhere to their opinions knowing that by so doing they will suffer economic loss.[5] Perhaps this is why "a decent respect to the opinions of mankind" requires that we regard men's opinions as articulations of *thought* rather than of material interests. Indeed, only if opinions are regarded as articulations of thought does it make any sense to criticize them. (Otherwise, our criticism may be deemed a mere "rationalization" of our own economic interests.) If criticism is not to be an *argumentum ad hominem,* it must appeal to men's reason, and its ultimate object must be the establishment of truth. This is precisely what is implied in those words of the Declaration, "let *Facts* be submitted to a *candid* world". Candid men are open to the truth, whatever be their interests or the interests of their particular class or society. This openness to the truth is but the freedom and civility of the soul, of the metaphysical reason prompting man to transcend the interests of time and place, such that his good may encompass the good of others. It was the vision of a comprehensive or common good—which is but the aim of justice or morality—that made it possible for the statesmen of the Declaration to pledge to each other their lives, their fortunes, and their sacred honor.

Consider, now, the *Communist Manifesto*, written by Marx and Engels in 1848 when Marx was thirty years old. The first thing to be noted is that the *Manifesto* denies the existence of a common good, a comprehensive good transcending the interests of any particular class of society. This is the meaning of those words which occur at the very outset of Part I of the *Manifesto*, namely, "The history of all hitherto existing society is the history of class struggles."[6] Of course, and as Marx explains in *The German Ideology* written two years earlier, "each new class which puts itself in the place of one ruling before it, is compelled, merely in order to carry through its aim, to represent its interest as the common interest of all the members of society, put in an ideal form; it will give its ideas the form of universality, and represent them as the only rational, universally valid ones."[7] In other words, such notions as the "common good", "justice", and "morality" are merely articulations of the material interests of the ruling class.

The second point to be noted is this. If the history of all hitherto existing society is the history of class struggles, then the fundamental fact about human society is *conflict*, class conflict. This means that *force*, not reason, is the dominant principle of human history. Indeed, as we learn from the *Manifesto*, reason is itself a product of history, or rather of the flux of history:

> Does it require deep intuition to comprehend that man's ideas, views, conceptions, in one word, man's consciousness, changes with every change in the conditions of his material existence, in his social relations, and in his social life?
>
> What else does the history of ideas prove than that *intellectual* production changes its character in proportion as *material* production is changed? The ruling ideas of each age have ever been the ideas of its ruling class.[8]

Here the *Manifesto* merely reiterates the teaching of *The German Ideology*, wherein Marx maintained that "the 'inward nature' of men, as well as their 'consciousness' of it, 'i.e.' their 'reason', has at all times been an historical product." Furthermore the "inward nature" of men, as well as their understanding of their nature, has always corresponded to "external compulsion", whether economic or social.[9] This means that, at least until Marx, men have never possessed genuine insight or intellectual detachment; they have never been capable of transcending the ideas or interests of their particular class or society.[10] Hence it would be foolish to appeal to men's reason over against their interests. Not that reason is utterly impotent. It is simply that ideas can only be effective when they correspond to or reinforce the actual or historical interests of men, meaning the interests of their particular class. This is why the *Manifesto* is addressed to the proletariat:

> Let the ruling classes tremble at a communistic revolution. The proletarians have nothing to lose but their chains. They have a world to win. WORKINGMEN OF ALL COUNTRIES, UNITE!

It would be a mistake to think, therefore, that Marx intends the *Communist Manifesto* to create any tension between men's opinions and interests by appealing to men's reason. The appeal is primarily to men's *passions*, wherefore the *Manifesto's* scathing denunciation and vilification of bourgeois society:

> The bourgeoisie, wherever it has got the upper hand, has put an end to all feudal, patriarchal, idyllic relations. It has pitilessly torn asunder the motley feudal ties that bound man to his "natural superiors," and has left remaining no other nexus between man and man than naked self-interest, than callous "cash payment." . . . In one word, for exploitation, veiled by religious and political illusions, it has substituted naked, shameless, direct, brutal exploitation.[11]

This vilification of the bourgeoisie—and I have only chosen one of many equally inflammatory passages—stands in striking contrast to the Declaration's denunciation of the British king, a denunciation which, though impassioned, is encompassed by a preamble and a peroration cast in the language of civility and even of reverence. The explanation has already been suggested: (1) The Declaration affirms the primacy of reason; the *Manifesto* the primacy of force. (2) The Declaration acknowledges the existence of universal moral standards to which one may appeal over against conflicting class interests. The principles of the Declaration thus allow for the possibility of diminishing or transcending class conflict by replacing "class consciousness" with the consciousness of a common or more comprehensive good—this, to be achieved through moral suasion. In contrast, the *Manifesto* seeks to replace consciousness of a common good (which it identifies as the intellectual production of the ruling class) with class consciousness, more precisely, with proletarian class consciousness, in order to intensify class conflict to the point of revolutionary violence. This helps to explain the inflammatory rhetoric of the *Manifesto* vis-à-vis the urbane rhetoric of the Declaration. But there is more.

It would be a grave error to regard the *Communist Manifesto* as a philosophical critique of bourgeois society, a critique animated by a quest for truth. Were that the case, the *Manifesto* would have been intended to change men's ideas or consciousness through criticism. But as Marx wrote in *The German Ideology*, "all forms and products of consciousness cannot be dissolved by mental criticism [such as by appeals to universal ideals or moral principles] . . . but only by the practical overthrow of the actual social relations which gave rise to the idealistic humbug; . . . not criticism but revolution is the driving force of history. . . ."[12] The purpose of criticism is not to correct error or to dissuade men from persisting in the doing of injustice (as was the case of those petitions for redress mentioned in the Declaration). To the contrary, Marxist criticism—and this is true of communist criticism today—is a weapon of class war. Taking up the second headnote of this chapter, it was a "young" Marx who wrote in 1843, this time in his *Critique of Hegel's Philosophy of Law:*

> criticism is not a passion of the head but the head of a passion. It is not a lancet, but a weapon. Its object is an *enemy* it wants not to refute but to *destroy*. . . .[It] is no longer an *end in itself* but simply a *means*. Its essential pathos is *indignation*, its essential task, *denunciation*.[13]

This suggests that the *Communist Manifesto*, unlike the Declaration of Independence, is not truth-oriented. Rather, it is a polemic primarily intended to inflame the passions. This is further borne out in the *Critique of Hegel's Philosophy of Law*, where Marx writes:

> Material force must be overthrown by material force. But theory

also becomes a material force once it has gripped the masses. Theory is capable of gripping the masses when it demonstrates *ad hominem*, and it demonstrates *ad hominem* when it becomes radical.[14]

Needless to say, this is far from showing "a decent respect to the opinions [i.e., the reason] of mankind". But then, Marxist rhetoric is addressed not to mankind, but to the "masses". Addressed to the masses Marxist theory demonstrates *ad hominem* when it appeals to men's passions and interests rather than to their intellect or reason. What is more, Marxist theory becomes radical when it incites the masses to revolutionary violence, for then it confirms the doctrine that "revolution is the driving force of history". Marxism is thus to be understood as a self-fulfilling theory animated *not* by the will to truth, *but by the will to man's supremacy over truth*. It is in this light that we are to understand Marx's statement that "Criticism is no longer an *end in itself* but simply a *means*." Viewed in context, this is equivalent to saying that truth is no longer an end in itself but simply a means, a means of destroying, not merely the existing political and economic order, but the inverted *epistemological* order dominating men's consciousness. Again:

> In direct contrast to German philosophy which descends from heaven to earth, here we ascend from earth to heaven. That is to say, we do not set out from what men say, imagine [or] conceive . . . in order to arrive at men in the flesh. We set out from real, active men, and on the basis of their real life-process we demonstrate the development of the ideological reflexes and echoes of this life-process. . . . Morality, religion, metaphysics, all the rest of ideology and their corresponding forms of consciousness, thus no longer retain the semblance of independence. They have no history, no development; but men, developing their material production and their material intercourse, alter, along with this their real existence, their thinking and the products of their thinking. Life is not determined by consciousness, but consciousness by life.[15]

Under the old (and then still existing) epistemological order, it was believed that the mind could apprehend eternal and immutable truths, could discover the laws of nature and of nature's God. Accordingly, men objectified or reified their ideas about nature and God as self-subsisting entities ruling over them, dictating their economic and social relationships. Now the purpose of the *Communist Manifesto* (or of the communist movement) is to revolutionize men's consciousness through revolutionary *activity*. This it can only do by bringing the existing consciousness of the proletariat into conflict with their material interests, that is, by showing that their moral and religious ideas merely serve the interests of those who are exploiting them, the bourgeoisie. Since those ideas are nothing more than the "ideological reflexes" of capitalist modes of production, the destruction of capitalism will put an end to the rule of those ideas—indeed, to all ideology—hence the false consciousness under which the proletariat have lived. A new consciousness will then have to be created to take the place of the old. Therein is the great, interminable, and deadly problem of Marxism.

Imagine a nation ruled by men who know what men never knew before, that "intellectual production [regarding metaphysics, morality, religion, etc.] changes its character in proportion as material production is changed." Their task is to create a new mode of thought or consciousness, one which is independent of the "external compulsion" of material forces. Around what principle will the new consciousness be constructed? What logic will govern men's thought? What will be the criterion of truth and falsity? What will be the criterion of good and bad? And once these criteria structure consciousness, will they not thereby become habits of mind (without which communication and coöperative endeavor would be impossible)? Will the rulers of this nation be free to restructure men's consciousness in response to the "external compulsion" of bourgeois nations? But wait. New modes of thought cannot be established overnight, not even in one or two generations. Hence there will have to be a succession of rulers consistently guided by the same long-range project of shaping anew the consciousness of men around the same principles. Of course, these rulers, having learned from the *Communist Manifesto* that "Law, morality, religion are . . . so many bourgeois prejudices, behind which lurk . . . as many bourgeois interests,"[16] will not be affected by the prejudice that truthfulness is a matter of personal honor. Nor will they be constrained by such "bourgeois" notions as the dignity of the individual and the sanctity of his conscience. Having learned that God is dead, they will also have learned that everything is permitted. They will have been taught by Lenin that

"Everything is moral which is necessary for the annihilation of the exploiting order." This doctrine has a deeper significance.

First, we must take this teaching seriously, no less seriously than did Alexander Solzhenitsyn in *The Gulag Archipelago*. Here is what Solzhenitsyn says of the founder of the Soviet Union:

> In his essay "How to Organize the Competition" (January 7 and 10, 1918), V.I. Lenin proclaimed the common, united purpose of "purging the Russian land of all kinds of harmful insects." And under the term *insects* he included not only all class enemies but also "workers malingering at their work". . . . And then again: "In what block of a big city, in what factory, in what village . . . are there not . . . saboteurs, who call themselves intellectuals?" True, the forms of insect-purging which Lenin conceived of in this essay were most varied: in some places they would be placed under arrest, in other places set to cleaning latrines; in some, "after having served their time in punishment cells, they would be handed yellow tickets"; in others, *parasites would be shot.* . . .[17]

But Lenin was simply the disciple—one of the truest disciples—of Marx, the *distinctive* Marx, not the so called "young" or "early" Marx who of late has been tendentiously transformed into an innocuous humanist.[18] What is most distinctive of Marx, so evident in the very violence of his rhetoric (the principles of which are studiously employed by communist leaders today), is the doctrine of revolution, of economic class conflict, meaning civil war, as the propelling and even progressive force of history.[19] Stated another way: what constitutes Marx's unique contribution to the history of political thought is that he incorporated into a philosophy of history the Machiavellian principle of the primacy of force over persuasion in human affairs. It is to this doctrine of force or violence that we must trace the subordination of, indeed, the contempt for truth in Marxist rhetoric, and, with the contempt for truth, the cynical use and abuse of morality.*

Not that Marx denies morality. Unlike most contemporary social or behavioral scientists (whose reductionist mode of thought may be traced, in part, to Marx), he knows there is good and bad, better and worse. But like Machiavelli, Marx did not think morality an end-in-

---

*Referring to Arthur Koestler's *Darkness at Noon*, Orwell notes that, even though innocent of the crimes he is accused of during the Soviet purge trials, "Rubashev ultimately confesses because he cannot find in his own mind any reason for not doing so. Justice and objective faith have long ceased to have any meaning for him." (*Essays*, III, 239.)

itself, no more than he thought truth an end-in-itself. From what we have already learned of his understanding of the purpose of criticism, Marx would certainly have subscribed to this cardinal teaching of Machiavelli: "therefore it is necessary for a prince, who wishes to maintain himself, to learn how not to be good, and to use this knowledge and not use it, according to the necessity of the case."[20] Because men are governed by hopes and fears, rulers must know how and when to appear as doves, and how and when to appear as hawks, relaxing tensions at one time, increasing them at another.[21] Or as Lenin has written: "the strictest dedication to the ideas of communism must be combined with the ability to make all the necessary compromises, to 'tack,' to make agreements, zigzags, retreats, and so on."[22] In short, rulers must be above good and evil (as well as above truth and falsity) if they are to secure and extend their power. In this light are we to understand that lecture on morality which Lenin delivered to future rulers of the Soviet Union. Thus instructed, they too could exterminate men like insects, and with a good conscience.[23]

That Lenin should have regarded certain Russian workers and intellectuals as insects itself suggests that Marxism may not be compatible with the notion that mankind constitutes a single species subject to the same moral law, before which all men are equal. Such appears to be the case, as may be seen in Marx's criticism of French socialists. What most concerned those socialists, according to the *Manifesto*, was "not the interests of the proletariat, but the interests of human nature, of man in general, who belongs to no class, has no reality, who exists only in the misty realm of philosophical fantasy."[24] The notion of man *sub specie aeternitatis*, or of man governed by "eternal laws of nature and reason", is a mere fiction.[25] Again, what those socialists failed to comprehend is that "the 'inward nature' of men, as well as their 'consciousness' of it, i.e., their 'reason', has at all times been an historical product" based on the prevailing mode of material production. But inasmuch as there is a multiplicity of modes of material production varying from country to country and from epoch to epoch, there must be a corresponding multiplicity of "human" species each with a different "inward nature".

A similar but more radical conclusion follows from Marx's doctrine of political society as the historical battleground for class warfare. This doctrine, as noted earlier, entails the denial of a common good, meaning that, in any non-communist society, the good of one class is obtained at the expense or injury of the other. In this "zero-sum" relationship, each class may be said to be a distinct species, such that the members of one species may (and necessarily will) treat the members of the other as inferior creatures, as mere work-animals, just as the bourgeoisie, according to Marx, treated the proletariat as "a commodity, like every other article of commerce".[26] How, then, might an ascendant proletariat, inflamed by Marxist rhetoric, treat his former bourgeois oppressors? There is not a note of sentimentality in Marx's ominous answer: "The proletariat of each country must, of course, first of all settle matters with its own bourgeoisie."[27] The bourgeoisie and the proletariat are thus comparable to two species which, vis-à-vis each other, are beyond morality. This is why Lenin could say that morality is subordinate to class war, in view of which he and his successors could feel justified in exterminating millions of Russians as so many insects.

Now just as it would be folly to condemn wolves for devouring sheep, so it would be folly to condemn the bourgeoisie for exploiting the proletariat. In the absence of a common good, moral preferences can only be arbitrary, mere *non sequiturs.* Yet Marx himself takes the side of the underdog, of those he calls the oppressed, and denounces their oppressors.[28] As we have seen, however, denunciation is the "essential task" of Marxist criticism. That criticism is philosophically armed propaganda designed to inflame the proletariat by demonstrating, *ad hominem,* that their ideas and values are nothing more than the ideas and values of their oppressors, that those ideas and values serve only the "selfish" interests of the bourgeoisie to the detriment of the proletariat's own class interests. Here Marx poses as a moralist precisely because the proletariat are themselves moralists. He uses morality to overthrow morality. Or what is to say the same, he turns the language of morality against itself (just as communist leaders turn the language of democracy against itself). Not for a moment, however, is Marx unaware of the paradoxical nature of his denunciation of bourgeois oppression—paradoxical if only because oppression is of the very essence (the propelling force) of history.[29] Thus, in the preface to the first edition of *Capital* (1867), Marx cautioned his readers by saying:

I paint the capitalist and landlord in no sense *couleur de rose*. But here individuals are dealt with only in so far as they are the personifications of economic categories, embodiments of particular class-relations and class-interests. My stand-point . . . can less than any other make the individual responsible for relations whose creature he socially remains, however much he may subjectively raise himself above them.[30]

That the individual may subjectively raise himself above his class appears to contradict the "early" Marx of *The German Ideology*, where, as we have seen, men's consciousness was said to be, at all times, an historical product based on external compulsion. But the decisive point is that human reason has no initiatory power or independent agency, which is why men ought not be held morally responsible for their conduct. This means that the phenomenon of oppression is not a reflection on "human nature" so much as on nature in general or on history. Given the Marxist view of history, a moralistic attitude toward the universality of oppression might lead to the conclusion that to oppress is to be human, which is equivalent to saying that to be human is to be evil or malevolent. But unlike Machiavelli, Marx did not regard malevolence as something intrinsic to men's "inward nature". Rather, it was a consequence of the penury of external nature: Nature at large did not of itself provide for men's needs, the satisfaction of which necessitated a division of labor which in turn engendered class antagonism and oppression. Thanks to modern science, however, and to the technological and industrial accomplishments of bourgeois society, the penury of nature was in process of being overcome, and would finally be overcome under the dispensation of a communist society. That overcoming would mark man's total conquest of nature, including himself as part of nature.

Therein, I believe, is the root of Marx's criticism of those French socialists who were more concerned about "human nature" than about the proletariat. What they failed to understand is that man has no "nature". Indeed, it is the nature of man to have no nature, no fixed or permanent nature. Man is to be defined not as *homo sapiens* but as *homo faber*,[31] and in the most radical sense. For man is his own maker and will consciously become his own maker in complete freedom from morality or from the laws of nature and of nature's God. What takes the place of morality (in which Marx sees the traditional tension between the individual and society) or what takes the place of the laws of nature and of nature's God (in which Marx sees the alienation of man from himself), is "History", the termination of which in Communism will issue in "the complete and conscious restoration of man to himself":

> This communism as completed naturalism is humanism, as completed humanism it is naturalism. It is the *genuine* resolution of the antagonism between man and nature; it is the true resolution of the conflict between existence and essence, objectification and self-affirmation, freedom and necessity, individual and species. It is the riddle of history solved and knows itself as this solution.[32]

Until that final but distant stage of history, when man achieves *"generic consciousness"*[33] or becomes a fully "conscious species-being, that is, a being which is related to its species as to its own essence or is related to itself as a species-being"[34]—until then, I must conclude, perhaps to the consternation of neo-Marxists, men will be less than men, will be less than human. But this means that in the name of an incredibly remote if not impossible humanism, Marx degrades and dehumanizes men of the past, of the present, and, for that matter, of the foreseeable future. This is the inevitable consequence of dialectical materialism or historicism which is at once progressivist and eschatological. As such, Marxism disposes men to look with contempt (not to say with hatred and resentment) upon all that is well-established, since all human accomplishments are destined to obsolescence by the "progressive" forces of history. Profound and perpetual discontent (not to say self-contempt) issues from this teaching. It is discontent with existence, with the present existence. For what is the present but a period of transition having no intrinsic value? And of we who live in this transition—what are we, even if we choose to be among the vanguard, but pawns of a cruel history, the witting or unwitting instruments of historical "progress"? Here we see why Marxism justifies the ruthless sacrifice of men living today—men who, at this stage of history, are only partly human—for the sake of those wholly humanized or species-oriented men of the future.

Given Marx's historicism, consider his statement in the *Communist Manifesto*, "In bourgeois society . . . the past dominates the present; in communist society the present dominates the past."[35] Two correlative meanings emerge from this statement. On the one hand, to say that in communist society the present dominates the past suggests that the records of what men have said and done in the past must be interpreted or reinterpreted in such a way as to serve the interests of the present. It means that the living have a license to rewrite history. (And how often has the Communist Party of the Soviet Union rewritten its own history!—knowing, in the words of Orwell, that "he who controls the past controls the future.") On the other hand, inasmuch as Communism, as projected by Marx, remains eschatologically a thing of the future, to say that in communist society the present dominates the past is to say that until such a society comes into existence, the future must dominate the present. Lenin was therefore correct in regarding Marxism as a "panegyric on violent revolution".[36] For despite if not because of Marx's eschatology, his dialectical and materialistic philosophy of history is, for all practical purposes, a doctrine of *permanent* revolution, a doctrine which cannot but result in periodic violence, terror, and tyranny.[37]

Finally, to say as Marx does that "man is the highest essence of man"[38] is not only to deny that man is created in the image of God. It is to deify man. But inasmuch as the essence of this deified man, his species-consciousness, will not come into existence until the end of history, then, at least until that far-off time, Marxist rulers, conscious that man is his own maker, may make and dispose of men as they will, unbound by any law.[39] Lenin spoke as a true disciple of Marx in saying: "The scientific concept, dictatorship . . . means neither more nor less than unlimited power resting directly on force, not limited by anything, not restrained by any laws or any absolute rules. *Nothing else but that.*"[40] In Marx and in Lenin we are at the opposite pole from the statesmen of the Declaration of Independence, nay more, from the fundamental principles of Western Civilization.

Summary and Conclusion

If it now be asked, Does Marxism animate Soviet foreign policy today?—I answer most emphatically *Yes*, provided we focus on the distinctive Marx: (1) the Marx who was not a sentimentalist, a mere social critic or bourgeois reformer, but a tough-minded thinker, a harsh if not cynical polemicist, a bold and brilliant revolutionary; (2)

the Marx who taught men that violence, not reason, is the propelling and progressive force of history; (3) the Marx who taught that history is but the history of class oppression, of irreconcilable class conflict, rather than an adventure revealing the coöperation as well as the conflict between persuasion and force; (4) the Marx who thereby denied the existence of a common good or of any moral norms uniting and binding upon mankind; (5) the Marx who thereby armed a portion of mankind, the vanguard of the proletariat, with a doctrine that placed them beyond good and evil, and with a rhetoric that placed them beyond truth and falsity; (6) the Marx who thereby fashioned the teachings of Machiavelli into an instrument of world-wide revolution—say rather of international civil war. This is the Marx that guides the destiny of the Soviet Union. This is the Marx that confronts the destiny of the United States. The remaining chapters will substantiate this conclusion.

CHAPTER 5

DETENTE 1933:
AMERICAN RECOGNITION OF THE SOVIET UNION

The recognition of one government by another is not a mere courtesy. It is an act having a specific meaning, and involves an acceptance by the recognizing government of the principles, purposes and avowed intentions of the recognized government as being in conformity of civilized nations toward each other.

—*Elihu Root*
Secretary of State (1905-09)

The Bolsheviks . . . openly propose to excite revolutions in all countries against existing governments; they are as hostile to democracy as they are to autocracy. If we should recognize them in Russia, we would encourage them and their followers in other lands. . . . To recognize them would give them an exalted idea of their own power, make them more insolent and impossible, and win their contempt, not their friendship. . . . As to Lenin and Trotsky I am in doubt. . . . For national and personal honor, for truth and for the individual rights of life, liberty and property they seem to have no regard.

—*Robert Lansing* (1917)
Secretary of State

[T]he existing regime in Russia is based upon the negation of every principle of honor and good faith, and every usage and convention, underlying the whole structure of international law; the negation, in short, of every principle upon which it is possible to base harmonious and trustful relations, whether of nations or of individuals.

—*Bainbridge Colby* (1920)
Secretary of State

The American government . . . is not prepared to barter away its principles. . . . If the Soviet authorities are ready to repeal their decrees repudiating Russia's obligations to this country and appropriately recognize them, they can do so. It requires no conference or negotiations to accomplish these results which can and should be achieved at Moscow as evidence of good faith. . . . Most serious is the continued propaganda to overthrow the institutions of this country. This Government can enter into no negotiations until these efforts directed from Moscow are abandoned.

—Charles Evans Hughes (1923)
Secretary of State

The experiences of various European Governments which have recognized and entered into relations with the Soviet regime have demonstrated conclusively the wisdom of the policy to which the Government of the United States has consistently adhered. Recognition of the Soviet régime has not brought about any cessation of interference by the Bolshevik leaders in the internal affairs of any recognizing country, nor has it led to the acceptance by them of other fundamental obligations of international intercourse.

—Frank B. Kellogg (1928)
Secretary of State

Russia is (a) inclined to a more reasonable attitude towards nations that have not accorded the recognition she seeks than towards those that have, and (b) after eagerly seeking and obtaining recognition she becomes more indifferent to her obligations than theretofore.

—R. Walton Moore (1933)
Assistant Secretary of State

The case [of the Soviet Union] is without precedent, for there has never before in the history of civilization been a government which on the one hand openly proclaimed its intent and purpose to be the overturning and destruction of the social and political institutions and the economic systems of other nations, while on the other hand it demanded that the governments of those other nations accord it recognition as a friendly power, grant it diplomatic privileges and advantages which are universally reserved for friendly powers and universally withdrawn from any power which commits unfriendly acts. It is futile and vain to argue the matter; recognition of Soviet Russia would be shameful self-abasement.

—John Spargo (1930)
Socialist Party of America

If it is true, as the preceding chapter indicates, that the teachings of Marx and Lenin concerning the role of reason, force, and morality in political life are fundamentally opposed to the teachings of the American founding fathers, then, insofar as the Soviet Union was and continues to be governed by Marxist and Leninist principles, thoughtful Americans, unawed by the weight of the past or by prevailing opinions and practices, will candidly face the question whether it was in the best interest of the United States to have accorded Communist Russia diplomatic recognition in 1933 and, having done so, whether subsequent international developments require this country to have diplomatic relations with such a regime today. I shall argue, in this and in the next chapter, that while it may have been unwise to recognize the Soviet Union initially, continued diplomatic relations, if not based on the democratic relativism which now governs American foreign policy, could advance the cause of genuine peace and once more enable the United States "to give mankind the magnanimous and too novel example of a people always guided by an exalted justice and benevolence." But first a word of caution.

As noted earlier, justice and benevolence are not identical. Unlike justice, benevolence or good will may sometimes diminish our moral sensibilities, may undermine our capacity for indignation. It may even close our eyes to evil or to injustice. Such is the tendency of benevolence, which must never be confused with magnanimity. For while it is true that the magnanimous man will not harbor ill will or resentment even toward those who have wronged him, he will never be indifferent to evil or to injustice. If he can, he will try to correct both, and less from a sense of moral obligation than from his sense of honor, his love of what is fine or noble. This said, let us begin our inquiry into "Détente 1933" by way of a digression.

I

In his "Open Letter to Kuznetsov",[1] Andrei Amalrik reproaches Western "progressive" intellectuals for their "dishonesty towards us"—their dishonesty toward those Russian dissidents who, like Amalrik, have spoken out against the tyranny of the Soviet Union. He writes:

I speak of dishonesty because it is dishonest, when one enjoys complete freedom of speech and other freedoms in one's country . . . to collaborate in any way with a regime which deprives its citizens of these freedoms. . . .[2]

What Amalrik terms dishonesty may well be indicative of the profoundest crisis of Western Civilization.

Generally speaking, American intellectuals have applauded writers like Pasternak and Solzhenitsyn.[3] The courage of these men, adorned by the nobility of their thought, has endowed freedom of expression with a grandeur which, in the mundane world of politics, we Americans have yet to experience among ourselves. We have yet to witness the likes of their courage because we live in a regime whose founders, unlike those of the Soviet Union, were inspired, to no small extent, by the tragedy of Socrates. "What bitter anguish would not the people of Athens have often escaped if their government had contained so provident a safeguard [as a "select" body like the Senate] against the tyranny of their own passions. Popular liberty might then have escaped the indelible reproach of decreeing to the same citizens the hemlock on one day and statues on the next." Thus wrote Madison in *Federalist* 63—Madison, the author of the First Amendment. It should be noted, however, that Athens was an urbane democracy, one may fairly say the birthplace of that freedom of speech which democracies so highly prize. All the more remarkable, therefore, to find men of Socrates' courage and intellectual independence in the Soviet Union, an oppressive tyranny.

So American intellectuals have good reason to admire and praise those Russian heroes of freedom. But to praise their heroic freedom is tacitly to condemn as evil the communist tyranny under which they live. How is it, then, that the most "progressive" elements among American intellectuals, the most ardent defenders of freedom of expression, have been and remain the most committed defenders of American collaboration with that communist tyranny? Moreover, these same American intellectuals would be among the first to condemn American collaboration with fascist or non-communist tyrannies infinitely less repressive than the Soviet Union.[4] Perhaps Amalrik would have explained this curious phenomenon somewhat as follows:

Of course, you American intellectuals are always talking about freedom. Hence it would seem you are opposed to tyrannies of the left as well as to tyrannies of the right. But you are well aware that only communist tyrannies possess thermonuclear weapons. (And so you can be more or less honest and speak out against your government when it collaborates with military dictatorships—think of Chile—although I wonder why you utter not a word of protest when your government woos such military dictatorships as Egypt and Syria? Were you wholeheartedly devoted to freedom, you would condemn one tyranny as well as the other, and ours even more so, it being the more oppressive.) Still, that you should condemn petty dictatorships and not the government of the Soviet Union suggests that you respect Soviet power, which means you are cowed by the fear of nuclear war. So it is not the love of freedom that animates your bourgeois souls so much as the *fear of violent death*. This is why you are so ardent for détente, for collaboration with a regime that uses fear to suppress freedom, not only the freedom of its own people, but now your own freedom as well. For what is it but fear that prevents you from speaking freely about the crimes of the Soviet Union? What is it but fear that keeps you silent about its evil designs upon the Western world?

But what does it mean to be silent about evil while speaking all the time as you do about freedom? Simply this. All your freedom talk is talk about external freedom, freedom without moral content. About inner freedom you say nothing, that freedom by which tyrants are powerless to deprive a man of his moral values.[5] This inner freedom you have lost; it has succumbed to the fear of violent death. To this extent you are now on a convergence course with the bulk of the Russian people whose instincts for self-preservation, along with the desire for material well-being, has taken possession of their souls. No longer do they live by any moral criteria such as 'honorable' and 'dishonorable', 'right' and 'wrong'.[6] And you too, having surrendered to fear, have forsaken what is right and honorable by appeasing a regime rotten to the core!

So might Andrei Amalrik—released in 1975 after five years of imprisonment in Siberia for "anti-Soviet conduct"—so might this man for all seasons have reproached those of us who uncritically approve of American collaboration with the Soviet Union. And it is well that we take such a reproach seriously lest we become so benighted or complacent as to believe that the policy of "détente", exemplified at Helsinki in 1975, does not entail any pernicious and perhaps perilous consequences for free men everywhere. Indeed, as we shall soon see, insofar as "détente" serves to silence criticism of the Soviet Union and to obscure its geopolitical objectives, it cannot but undermine the survival of the United States as a free and independent nation. But to comprehend the grounds of contemporary American foreign policy, we must inquire into "Détente 1933", when the United States accorded diplomatic recognition of the Soviet Union.

II

The arguments then advanced in favor of American recognition of the Soviet Union may be divided into three categories: legal, economic, and geopolitical. Consider, first, the legal argument regarding the recognition of new governments. It was maintained by legal realists that not until the administration of Woodrow Wilson had this country withheld recognition of any government on *de jure* as opposed to *de facto* considerations. The mere fact that the Bolshevik government had been in control of Russia since 1917 was said to be sufficient to warrant official recognition. Aside from oversimplifying the traditional recognition policy of the United States (of which, more in a moment), this argument suffers from a number of defects.

To begin with, any political act, such as a decision to extend or withhold diplomatic recognition, is intended to serve some good, at least for the recognizing or non-recognizing government. It would therefore be inadequate to say, for example, that Russia exists, that it has been recognized by other nations; that Russia's population and its vast territory and natural resources render it (potentially, at the time in question) one of the most powerful nations in the world, and that it has long been under the unchallenged rule of its present government. All this is not an *argument* for official recognition of the Soviet Union if only because these facts do not of themselves indicate wherein recognition would serve either the immediate or long-range interests of the United States. But let us consider some of these facts.

That the Soviet Union exists, no one ever denied. But the contention that its mere existence requires automatic and unconditional recognition by other governments, has no warrant in international law.[7] If this were not the case, the severance of diplomatic relations would be inexplicable. Nations enter into diplomatic relations to facilitate, among other things, commercial and political intercourse. Such intercourse will necessarily implicate not only the economic interests but the civil and religious rights of countless individuals; and

82

the protection of their rights and interests will very much depend on the political character of the recognized government. By refusing to recognize the Soviet Union prior to 1933, the United States was not only expressing disapproval of that communist form of government; it was also proclaiming, in effect, that such a government could not be depended upon to respect and protect the rights of American nationals residing in or doing business with Russia. Consistently therewith, the State Department warned individuals and corporations dealing with the Soviet Union that they did so on their own responsibility and at their own risk.

True, the Soviet regime had been officially recognized by other governments. But this merely indicates that those other governments then thought recognition of Russia would be good for them; it does not follow that recognition would be good for us. Besides, there is the question of whether any government, after recognizing the Soviet Union, did in fact benefit from its relationship with that regime. For example, Britain, having recognized Russia in 1924, when a minority Labor Party was in power, completely severed diplomatic relations in 1927 after three years of Conservative trials, only to resume diplomatic relations when Labor returned to power in 1929. Like France (which recognized the USSR in 1925), Britain's post-recognition efforts at a Russian debt settlement proved fruitless. And while it is true that her export trade to the Soviet Union increased, it is also true that recognition brought with it an increase in communist propaganda and espionage, so that it is by no means clear whether the country *as a whole* benefited from its Russian connection.

Finally, the fact that Russia was then potentially one of the most powerful nations in the world only rendered more serious the issue of whether its despotic and militant government should be accorded official recognition. Unless there was good reason to believe that recognition would conciliate its reigning tyrant or dampen Russia's imperialistic ambitions, now rendered infinitely more dangerous by a revolutionary ideology, one could as well argue, as had Secretary of State Lansing, that recognition would only tend to make the tyrant more insolent and more contemptuous of the West. Also, it would increase his domestic as well as international prestige and power, thereby facilitating his world-historical objectives.

Be this as it may, *de facto* considerations are not self-justifying. A decision to grant or refuse recognition involves moral judgment. It has nonetheless been argued that recognition is a morally neutral act, that "the establishment of diplomatic relations with a government never was formerly supposed to imply approval either of its form or of its acts."[8] This view is contradicted, however, by Secretary of State Elihu Root, as may be seen in the first headnote of this chapter. Besides, to say that recognition does not imply approval is a legalistic distinction which, for most people, makes little more sense than the converse claim that a refusal to establish (to say nothing of severing) diplomatic relations with a government does not "imply" *disapproval* either of its form or of its acts. The question is, *imply for whom?* Legalists overlook the obvious fact that recognition (or non-recognition) is not only a legal but, above all, a *political* act. It is an act which shapes public opinion. Thus, in 1935, when the Soviet Union convened the Seventh Congress of the Communist International (with Americans actively participating in violation of the Roosevelt-Litvinov pre-recognition agreements of 1933,[9] various organs of American public opinion, including Congress (by means of a joint resolution), called upon the President to sever diplomatic relations with Russia. When such action was not forthcoming, *Time* magazine expressed regret that the Russian people would not have the opportunity to learn that Franklin Roosevelt had "withdrawn the moral approval which 165,000,000 Russians were happy to think he extended when he recongized the Soviet Union."[10] Clearly, the ordinary man, unless otherwise instructed, does not distinguish between recognition and approval. (This is why it is necessary for the statesmen of a republic that enters into diplomatic relations with a non-republican regime to educate their fellow countrymen, showing them how such a relationship, under certain circumstances, is morally justifiable or consistent with republican principles.)[11]

A second defect of the legal argument is that it is based on the narrowest understanding of the general recognition policy of the United States. The principles of that policy were enunciated by Assistant Secretary of State Alvey A. Adee in 1913 and cited approvingly by Secretary of State Henry L. Stimson while addressing the Council on Foreign Relations in 1931:

> Ever since the American Revolution entrance upon diplomatic intercourse with foreign states has been *de facto*, dependent upon the

existence of three conditions of fact: [1] the control of the administrative machinery of the state; [2] the general acquiescence of its people; and [3] the ability and willingness to discharge international and conventional obligations. The form of government has not been a conditional factor in such recognition; in other words, the *de jure* element of title has been left aside.[12]

Now, given the openly hostile intentions of the Soviet Union and, consistent with those intentions (1) its repudiation of its debts to the United States; (2) its expropriation without compensation of American-owned property in Russia; and (3) its relentless efforts, through the Comintern and other communist organizations, to undermine the political institutions of this country—given these facts, the third prerequisite of the general recognition policy of the United States, again, "the ability *and* willingness to discharge international and conventional obligations", unambiguously argues against diplomatic recognition of the Soviet regime throughout (and for that matter since) the pre-recognition period. And, in fact, the State Department, specifically its then existing Division of East European Affairs, consistently opposed recognition. Nor is this all. While the recognition issue was being reconsidered by the new Roosevelt Administration, the State Department instructed its embassies abroad to inquire of their host countries whether the Soviet Union, having once been granted diplomatic recognition, had become a more trustworthy member of the international community. The conclusions of the inquiry appear in the penulitimate headnote of this chapter. They bear repeating. In October 1933, the month before the United States officially recognized the Soviet Union, Assistant Secretary of State R. Walton Moore informed Secretary of State Cordell Hull that "Russia is (a) inclined to a more reasonable attitude towards nations that have not accorded the recognition she seeks than towards those that have, and (b) after eagerly seeking and obtaining recognition she becomes more indifferent to her obligations than theretofore."[13]

At this point let us return to the general recognition policy enunciated by Assistant Secretary of State Adee in 1913 and reaffirmed by Secretary of State Stimson in 1931. According to Mr. Adee, hitherto, "The *form* of government has not been a conditional factor in . . . recognition". The trouble is that this disclaimer potentially conflicts with the third conditional factor which, it will be recalled, required a government's willingness to discharge its international and conventional obligations. For the very form of some governments, which is to say their very principles and purposes, may be such as to render them unwilling to discharge their conventional and international obligations. Precisely in this light are we to understand the *de facto* recognition policy of the United States, a policy which does in fact go back to the founding period. For that seemingly neutral policy would have been an absurdity had it not presupposed a classical tradition modulated by Christianity, a tradition which prompts diverse forms of government to acknowledge two of the cardinal principles of international relations—indeed, of civilized society. The first principle is honor, by which men are disposed to be truthful and to abide by their word; the second is civility, by which men are disposed to be friends despite their differences.[14] These principles are sometimes violated in practice; but their violation is hardly made a matter of principle. The point is: the disclaimer of 1913, that the form of government has not been a conditional factor in recognition, was rendered obsolete in 1917 with the advent of a Marxist regime whose leaders rejected the principles of honor and civility in the very process of declaring unlimited war on any parliamentary form of government.* In theory as well as in practice, the rulers of the Soviet Union have repeatedly made it clear that for them, "morality [hence the question whether one ought to be truthful or whether one ought to fulfill one's international obligations] is entirely subordinate to the interests of class war". The State Department, or the forerunners of those now called "Sovietologists", had taken the words and deeds of Marxist Russia most seriously. Having taken them seriously, they could not but conclude that recognition of that regime would not be in the best interests of the United States.† What happened, then, in 1933 to reverse this sixteen-year policy of non-recognition? Nothing whatever to suggest to serious students of Russia that the Soviet Union had changed, had become a more or less conventional regime willing to

---

*Consider, however, Berdyaev's contention that "the absence of an age of chivalry in Russia has been disastrous for the moral culture." Quoted in George B. de Huszar, *The Intellectuals* (Glencoe: The Free Press, 1960), p. 110.

†Recall U.S. non-recognition of the Obregon regime in Mexico from 1920-1923 over but one article of the Mexican Constitution, Article 27, that retroactively confiscated the property of American citizens in Mexico. Not until he agreed to respect U.S. titles to land prior to 1917 was he granted diplomatic recognition. This is but one example of the efficacy of non-recognition as a means of protecting American rights.

honor its international obligations by ceasing to interfere in the domestic affairs of other nations, dividing peoples from their governments, and promoting revolution or civil war. Not the Soviet Union but the United States had changed. But I am getting ahead of my story. We have now to consider the economic argument in favor of recognition.

It should first be noted that the American government had placed few restrictions on trade or on ordinary commercial financing with the Soviet Union since 1920. Admittedly, long-term credits were discouraged and no securities could be offered for sale to the American people. But such restrictions did not prevent the substantial trade which actually developed between the two countries after 1924.[15] Nevertheless, the American-Russian Chamber of Commerce, representing some of the largest corporations in the United States, pressed for recognition. It was argued that the establishment of diplomatic and consular relations (from which might follow the mutual adoption of most-favored-nation privileges) would augment and facilitate trade on the one hand, while serving to protect American industrial concessions and financial investments in Russia on the other. Needless to say, the Soviet Union encouraged such hopes and expectations. A concerted propaganda campaign was launched by various communist organizations, notably Amtorg, the principal Soviet-American commercial agency in the United States, claiming that recognition would result in billions of dollars in trade.[16] For a nation in the midst of a depression, with millions unemployed, this intoxicating news, though known by the Administration to be utter nonsense, was allowed to circulate unchallenged, presumably to arouse support for recognition.[17] Contrary to the predictions of businessmen, however, and even of some economists, the data on trade for the years 1921-1938 show that, on the average, American exports to the USSR fell off markedly *following* recognition.[18]

Whatever the explanation,[19] the Roosevelt Administration understood that whereas the Soviet Union could take advantage of the open and competitive market in the United States, American businessmen would have no such opportunity in Russia if only because Soviet foreign trade is a state monopoly. Not that American businessmen were incapable of making handsome profits from their Russian investments. But what is good for Occidental Petroleum is not necessarily good for the United States or for the American tax-payer who, incidentally, would have to pay for any failures of American capitalism in communist Russia. As already indicated, the State Department had for several years warned that individuals or corporations doing business with the Soviet Union did so at their own risk. As early as 1923 it was learned from a "confidential" report circulated by New Scotland Yard in London that

> Concessions are offered, and foreign capital is sought with the object of restoring the collapsed industries of Russia in the interest of the Communist State. It is calculated that in some years foreign industry and enterprise will have revived these industries which then, more firmly established and efficient than ever before, will revert to the State, which will then be able, fortified by experience and the method of foreign participants, to resume the Marxist experiment. Nor need one believe that any conditions subscribed to by the Soviet Government will be faithfully observed. The capitalist and the private owner have no inherent rights. Faith need not be kept with them. Cozened into the open by their capitalist greed they will be overwhelmed when the great advance is resumed.[20]

From this it should be apparent that the economic argument in favor of recognition, however true on the surface, is a trivialization of the recognition issue. The issue is not whether the establishment of diplomatic relations would facilitate trade between the United States and Marxist Russia—in principle it could. No, the fundamental issue is whether recognition would, in the long run, promote the cause of freedom and civility, or the cause of despotism and brutality. But even on the question of trade itself, the truth is that the Soviet Union, on ideological grounds alone, was not really interested in building up a large export-import trade.[21] Not only did it want to become as self-sufficient as possible, but it also wished to minimize or keep within manageable limits East-West contacts: (1) lest the Russian people learn some engaging truths about the United States, and (2) lest the American people learn some ugly truths about the Soviet Union. What the Soviets hoped to obtain by the lure of trade was large long-term credits at low interest rates. The purpose of such credits, as a recent study indicates, is

> . . . to finance the purchase of equipment and technology for the development of oil, natural gas and other mineral resources. Such assistance from the [United States] may not only increase Soviet overall economic strength, but it could also enable the Soviet government to engage in military spending on a scale which would

otherwise be impossible, given the competing claims of investment and consumption.

The . . . strategy of seeking large Western credits may thus bring not only enormous economic advantage to the Soviet Union internally, but also to Soviet military and foreign policies, particularly as it will tend to create groups in the West with vested interests in Soviet-derived profits and in the protection of Western loans. These groups can be politically manipulated . . . while the appetite for profits among businessmen is also easily exploitable.[22]

By reducing the recognition issue to one of trade, many businessmen were simply subordinating political to economic considerations (a tendency shared by some labor organizations, with the notable exception of the AFL). The effect was to minimize or obscure the differences between a just and unjust regime, or to reduce American-Soviet relations to a cash nexus—which is what Marx would have predicted of capitalists in general. It would be easy to say, of course, that these businessmen were motivated by class or material interests, rather than by a concern for a more comprehensive good. But they hardly understood their own interests, certainly not their long-range interests. Like so many others, they refused to consider seriously the long-range political objectives of the Soviet Union, an imperialistic regime dedicated not only to the destruction of capitalism, but of the very forms of government under which capitalism can thrive.[23] And so it should not be too shocking to learn, from an address lauding Roosevelt's recognition of the Soviet regime, that Thomas J. Watson, president of International Business Machines, asked "every one in the United States", in the cause of amicable relations with Moscow, to "refrain from making any criticism of the present form of government adopted by Russia."[24] Could it be, as one study has claimed, that the Russians exert "pressure on businessmen, who are interested in trade with the Soviet Union, to use their influence to prevent unwelcome criticism"?[25]

The President of IBM, like other capitalists, was advocating, so-to-speak, an international cover-up. And so indeed were many egalitarian intellectuals who felt compelled to cover up the nakedness of Communist Russia lest the crimes of that tyranny forever stigmatize socialism.[26] Thus, while many capitalists sacrificed principles for profit, many intellectuals merely sacrificed their intellects. Curious bedfellows! But all this was foreseen with uncanny insight by Lenin in 1921, when he wrote:

As a result of my own personal observations during the years of my emigration, I must say that the so-called cultural strata of Western Europe and America are not capable of understanding the contemporary state of affairs nor the actual alignment of forces; we must regard these strata as deaf mutes and act with respect to them accordingly. [Meanwhile] . . . the capitalists of the entire world, and their governments, in the rush of conquering Soviet markets, will close their eyes to the realities, and will thus become blind deaf mutes. They will open credits which will serve as a support for the Communist Party in their countries and will provide us with essential materials and technology thus restoring our military industries, essential for our future victorious attacks on our suppliers. Speaking otherwise, they will be working to prepare their own suicides.[27]

This recalls the words of George Orwell: "A generation of the unteachable is hanging upon us like a necklace of corpses."

Inasmuch as economic considerations do not seem to have influenced Roosevelt's decision to recognize Russia,[28] some writers have speculated that the major factor contributing to that decision was geopolitical. American recognition of the Soviet Union, some believed, would contribute to world peace: it would serve to restrain Japanese imperialism in the Far East, and German ambitions in Europe.[29] Without denying its relevance, the geopolitical explanation of recognition does not account for the fact that Herbert Hoover (who, as Secretary of Commerce, had directed the American Relief Administration which had provided some $60,000,000 of food, grain, and medical supplies to a starving and famine-ridden Russia in 1921-1923) refused, as President, to reverse the non-recognition policy of the previous fifteen years—and this, even though confronted by very much the same international and domestic problems inherited by his successor. What, then, was the decisive difference between 1932 and 1933? Surely it was the election of Franklin Roosevelt to the Presidency. *

*Before continuing, it should be noted that Hitler came to power on January 30, 1933 toward the very end of the Hoover Administration. (This was before the adoption, on February 6, 1933, of the Twentieth Amendment terminating the term of the Presidency on the twentieth of January rather than, as previously, on the fourth of March.) Now, a realistic politics takes ideology seriously, attempting to understand other nations as they understand themselves. But as we shall see in a moment, Roosevelt's understanding of geopolitics was markedly flawed in this respect. To Roosevelt, as his subsequent foreign policy with regard to Hitler indicates, Germany had simply changed governments. The fact that its leader had proclaimed, in Mein Kampf, the desire to subjugate the civilized world was, for all practical purposes, ignored. This should be borne in mind when examining Roosevelt's policy vis-à-vis Hitler's Russian counterpart.

Mr. Hoover, no less than Woodrow Wilson, had opposed recognition on grounds of prudence. The leaders of the Soviet Union (along with Communists throughout the world) had repeatedly expressed the intention of bringing about the destruction of free government. Mr. Hoover believed they were in earnest, the more so when their deeds were consistent with their words. By making a conspiratorial regime respectable, recognition would only facilitate its imperialistic ambitions. This was the position taken by the State Department, a position which Mr. Hoover saw no reason to ignore. Evidently, he did not regard the intentions of the Soviet Union as a mystery wrapped in a riddle inside an enigma. He, and no doubt Mr. Churchill, would have agreed with Walter Laqueur who recently said:

> I fail to [see] what is so difficult to understand about the Soviet Union. For someone who makes his home outside this country, American policy is in fact far more difficult to understand. Soviet policy is difficult only if one refuses to take seriously what Soviet leaders are saying and if one refuses to compare their sayings with their actions.[30]

The question of questions is: *Why did the United States fail to take the words and deeds of Soviet leaders seriously?* To answer this question is to explain, in large measure, "Détente 1933". But first I must ask the reader to indulge a personal digression.

Not until I read *The Gulag Archipelago* and attempted to see the world through the eyes of Alexander Solzhenitsyn did I begin to comprehend the deeper significance of the West's inability to take seriously the words and deeds of a Lenin or Stalin. Only then did I begin to see that this inability is nothing less than an escape from morality, a refusal to acknowledge evil and the enormous ambition of evil. Of course, we live in a sophisticated age when to many it will appear anachronistic to speak about evil. Could it be that we are silent about evil because we lack courage, the courage to bear the sacrifices which any honest struggle against evil entails? I shall come back to this question in a moment; but first I want to share those passages from *The Gulag Archipelago* which prompted me to pose that question. Here is the first passage:

> In keeping silent about evil, in burying it so deep within us that no sign of it appears on the surface, we are *implanting* it, and it will rise up a thousand-fold in the future. When we neither punish nor reproach evildoers, we are not simply protecting their trivial old age,

we are thereby ripping the foundations of justice from beneath new generations. It is for this reason, and not because of the "weakness of indoctrinational work," that they are growing up "indifferent." Young people are acquiring the conviction that foul deeds are never punished on earth, that they always bring prosperity.

It is going to be uncomfortable, horrible, to live in such a country![31]

Needless to say, the evil of which Solzhenitsyn speaks involved the class extermination of an estimated sixty-six (66) million people, myriads of whom were tortured and perished in the slave-labor camps mentioned earlier.[32] Solzhenitsyn attributes those monstrous crimes, as well as the silence which obscures them, to Marxist ideology. It was Marxism, he rightly claims, that made morality relative, relative to class. He recalls the time, before the Bolshevik Revolution, "when morality was not considered relative and when the distinction between good and evil was very simply perceived by the heart."[33] In those days, says Solzhenitsyn, "people still had their pride, and many of them quite failed to understand that morality is a relative thing, having only a class meaning. . . ." And so, in the first post-revolutionary decade, such people "dared to reject the employment offered them [of being informers], and they were all punished without mercy."[33] Presumably, their pride, their sense of honor, of right and wrong, enabled them to face torture and death. But only men who do not regard violent death as the greatest evil can confront or withstand evil, such as the evil of Bolshevism. Hence it may be that the failure of the West to take seriously the words and deeds of a Lenin or Stalin, its inability to acknowledge and condemn evil, is rooted in the fear of violent death which it deems, beyond servitude and shame, the greatest evil. Nor is this all. For let us never forget that evil is no petty thing with which to challenge petty men. It demands from us what most men fear in denying evil, namely, responsibility. This said, let us resume our inquiry into "Détente 1933", but from the perspective of Alexander Solzhenitsyn. I can imagine him saying something like this:

To begin with, let me remind you that your President Roosevelt, no ordinary man, not only accorded diplomatic recognition to a regime ruled by Stalin; he also maintained diplomatic relations with a regime ruled by Hitler.[34] In other words, just as he refused to take seriously Stalin's *Foundations of Leninism*, so did he refuse to take seriously Hitler's *Mein Kampf*. Of course, he was not alone in closing his eyes to evil. But he alone was President of the United States. He alone among the Western powers was the head of a stable government. He alone had at his command the array of evidence gathered by American embassies and intelligence agencies, evidence with which to enlighten the American people about the true character and hostile intentions of their enemies. He alone could have made the seemingly remote near, the obscure clear—I mean the danger which, if candidly and courageously brought home to the American people might have won their support for a principled and farsighted foreign policy. Instead, he dignified a tyranny of the left on the one hand, and a tyranny of the right on the other. To some, this may be regarded as a remarkable display of tolerance or of political impartiality. It needs to be emphasized, however, that such tolerance, to say the very least, did not prevent the bloodiest war in human history. But "Détente 1933" was not a display of tolerance—not of that manly tolerance which learns from the past and which holds fast to what is right and honorable. No, "Détente 1933" was symptomatic of the moral indifferentism or obscurantism of a thoroughly bourgeois foreign policy, the obscurantism one might expect of a democracy without moral convictions, a democracy under the influence of moral relativism.[35]

Now here I must interject to point out that President Roosevelt was not himself a relativist, not a knowing one. Furthermore, he was the democratic President of a democratic country steeped in isolationism, and suffering, at the same time, from a calamitous depression. And although the Democratic Party controlled the Congress, Democrats and Republicans alike regarded that depression as the country's first and foremost enemy. Accordingly, so preoccupied were we with our own domestic problems, that it would have been most difficult—I do not say impossible—for the President to have enlightened the public about those international developments which, step by step, were leading us into the Second World War. True, Roosevelt was an enormously popular and persuasive President. Still, it is questionable whether Congress could have been persuaded to increase defense expenditures even had Roosevelt urged such a course (which, incidentally, would not only have served to deter aggression in Europe, in Asia, and in Africa; it would also have contributed to economic recovery). At any rate, in August of 1935, Congress passed a neutrality act requiring the President, when he found a state of war existing anywhere, to prohibit the sale of munitions to the belligerents of either side. Two months later Mussolini attacked Ethiopia. Though

Roosevelt himself favored neutrality legislation, he had hoped that Congress would invest him with authority to embargo war supplies to any aggressor and permit their sale to the victim. The following year witnessed the outbreak of the Spanish Civil War. While Hitler and Mussolini, in violation of a non-intervention agreement, supplied arms to Franco, the United States, along with France and Britain, denied arms to the Spanish Republicans.[36] It was a case of Fascists, or unjust men, fighting for an unjust cause while just men refused to fight for a just cause.* Not that morality requires us to correct every injustice or to relieve sufferings which we ourselves have not caused. Men and nations are not obliged to act magnanimously, otherwise medals of honor would cease to have meaning. The law requires that we act justly; it cannot require us to act nobly. But when men and nations refrain from defending their own interests, when they are so shortsighted and so fainthearted as to prefer to wait and fight only when the enemy is at the gate rather than one or two or ten thousand miles away, then we ought not be surprised at the enemy's insolence, his daring, his step-by-step encroachments, his contempt for men of peace and good will.

And so October 1936 saw the formation of the Rome-Berlin Axis. Congress responded in January and in May of 1937 by enacting a second and third neutrality act. The Neutrality Act of May was so stringent as to relinquish American claims to freedom of the seas in wartime. Two months later, Japan, no doubt encouraged by this refusal of the United States to play a leading role in world affairs, launched a full-scale attack on China.[37] This time Roosevelt not only refrained from invoking the Neutrality Act, but in October he delivered his famous Quarantine speech which stressed the need for collective measures to halt aggression. It appears, however, that the President had nothing more in mind than a collective breaking off of diplomatic relations, rather than the imposition of economic or military sanctions.[38] Whatever the case, to have severed relations with Japan is one thing, to have done so with Nazi Germany is another. Besides, Roosevelt seemed more inclined to appease than to offend Hitler. On the heels of the Munich pact the President cabled Chamberlain just two words: "Good man." Needless to say, other statesmen offered congratulations no less laudatory, if not more elo-

---

*Consider, in this connection, Angola.

quent. Besides, it should be said in Roosevelt's defense that in 1939 he did attempt to persuade Congress to repeal the Neutrality Act which he regretted having signed two years earlier. The embargo, he argued, would merely encourage Hitler, and by preventing the shipment of arms to Britain and France, it could only undermine American security. Not until the actual outbreak of war in Europe did the Congress revise the statute to allow belligerents to purchase arms on a cash-and-carry basis. Of course, the war itself was precipitated by the signing of the infamous non-aggression pact between Hitler and Stalin.[39] But neither the Nazi-Soviet dismemberment of Poland which followed, nor the Russian invasion of Finland, moved Roosevelt to sever diplomatic relations with the aggressors, a course which an enlightened public might have supported. Time and again, however, the President had emphasized the theme of peace, as a consequence of which he could hardly complain if the Congress saw little reason to support a military posture capable of preventing war. In the summer of 1940, with the fall of France, and Britain imperilled, Roosevelt, without congressional approval, but simply by means of an executive agreement, gave the British fifty over-age destroyers in return for ninety-nine year leases on eight bases in the Atlantic. Not only was this, as Churchill later wrote, "a decidedly unneutral act"; it was also a belligerent act which, in the opinion of many, exceeded the President's constitutional authority. But again I have digressed from "Détente 1933"—this time with a view to qualifying the relativistic implications of Roosevelt's foreign policy.

I must confess, however, that the doctrine of moral relativism, which had then gained ascendency in American higher education, cannot but silence men about evil.[40] Henceforth the conduct of governments will virtually cease to be described in moral terms, which is to say that the language of political discourse will become ethically neutral. "Left" and "Right" will take the place of *right* and *wrong, honorable* and *dishonorable*. Gradually and almost imperceptibly, self-respect, national as well as individual, will decline as the public witnesses an increasing tendency among statesmen, scholars, and journalists to obscure the differences between just and unjust regimes. A "liberal" version of such obscurantism—there is also a "conservative" one—seems to have insinuated itself into the Teheran

95

Conference when, in a toast obviously intended for Stalin rather than for Churchill, Roosevelt compared the political coloration of the conference to a rainbow, saying:

> It has many varying colors, each different, but blending into one glorious whole. Thus with our nations. We have different customs and philosophies and ways of life. Each of us works our scheme of things according to the desires and ideas of our peoples. But we have proved at Teheran that the varying ideals of our nations can come together in a harmonious whole, moving unitedly for the common good of ourselves and of the world.[41]

To some this toast will appear politically naïve—and it is certainly true that Roosevelt was incredibly naïve about the Russians. But this naïveté is symptomatic of that sentimental humanism which has long concealed a diminished sense of right and wrong, indeed, an attenuated capacity to face harsh truths. It was not simply naïveté (nor was it mere tact or the exigencies of war) which prompted Mr. Roosevelt to say that "Each of us [including Joseph Stalin] works our scheme of things *according to the desires and ideas of our peoples.*"[42] Such a statement, by portraying the Soviet Union as some form of democracy, degrades democracy and elevates a tyranny whose leader was then known to have been responsible for the extermination of millions of his own people. But that levelling obscurantism was the cause and effect of "Détente 1933".

The same conclusion may be reached another way. Thus, by recognizing the Soviet Union while maintaining diplomatic relations with Nazi Germany, Roosevelt knowingly or unknowingly carried out the logical consequences of the doctrine of legal realism which has long dominated American law schools. Alluded to earlier, legal realism denies any distinction between the legal and the just. Justice is determined solely by law, that is, by those who make the law—be they the One, the Few, or the Many.

This means that there are no universal standards in terms of which one could rightly say whether a particular law is just or unjust, hence whether any regime is just or unjust. Clearly, legal realism is a relativistic doctrine diametrically opposed to the universalist principles of the Declaration of Independence and the Farewell Address.[43] But what is more to the point at issue is this: by denying the distinction between the legal and the just, legal realists dignify all forms of government, including a tyranny like the Soviet Union *along with its conquests.*[44] What is more, even if legal realism were rejected as immoral, the doctrine may be fostered merely by statesmen who refrain from condemning such tyrannies. By their silence they unwittingly propagate the unmanly principle that one must not protest against an evil which one cannot prevent. This principle insinuates another, that might makes right. It leads to the worship of mere power and to the sanctification of any success.* This is the fruit of relativism.

While the relativism emanating from the academy was facilitating recognition of the Soviet Union, another and more subtle form of relativism was contributing to the same end—I mean the relativism long implicit in American capitalism or in the practices of the commercial establishment.[45] Here I should point out that one, though not the only, redeeming feature of twentieth-century capitalism, which renders it infinitely preferable to Communism, is that it leaves space for freedom. But this freedom is an abstraction; it lacks moral content, to say nothing of honor.[46] Thus, just as one capitalist does not discriminate between the wants of different individuals, but rather seeks to gratify all wants, whether good or bad, refined or vulgar (as long as there is profit in their gratification), so another capitalist refrains from discriminating between the wants of different nations, but rather seeks to supply the wants of any nation be it just or unjust, democratic or tyrannical, dedicated to peace or devoted to the overthrow of his own government. It was not only greed, therefore, but the moral relativism or indifference implicit in economic laissez-faire that disposed, and continues to dispose, some of America's largest corporations and banking institutions—such as Ford, General Electric, Standard Oil of New Jersey, U.S. Steel, and the Chase National Bank—to prop up and facilitate the industrial and hence the military growth of Communist Russia. Indeed, according to one well-documented study covering the years 1917-1930, at least 95 per cent of the industrial structure of the Soviet Union received and was dependent upon Western technological aid.[47] From this study one could reasonably conclude that, were it not for the transfer of Western

---

*A recent example of this occurred upon the death of Chou En-lai. Responsible, with Mao, for the deaths of tens of millions of Chinese, that communist tyrant received the adulation and a-vowed friendship of an American Secretary of State, to say nothing of a largely uncritical if not laudatory press.

technology to the USSR, the regime might have collapsed from the weight of its own tyranny. The consequences of such a collapse for subsequent history stagger the mind. But here I am reminded of the prescient words of Vladimir Lenin who, in discussing the grave economic difficulties of the Soviet Union before the Central Committee of the CPSU, concluded by saying, "But comrades, don't let us panic. If we give the bourgeoisie enough rope they'll hang themselves." To this, Karl Radek, a member of the Committee asked, "But where are you going to get the rope to give the bourgeoisie?" To which Lenin replied, "From the Bourgeoisie."[48]

III

Once again I raise the question, Why did the United States recognize the Soviet Union in 1933, reversing the policy of no less than four Secretaries of State, including Robert Lansing and Charles Evans Hughes? Thus far I have argued that "Détente 1933" was an act of moral obscurantism, an inability to acknowledge and confront evil. (Thus Orwell's words, "a generation of the unteachable . . .") Moreover, I have argued that the West's silence about evil may be attributed to the cooperation of moral relativism, and to the fear of violent death. Now, as suggested earlier, the phenomenon of moral relativism is especially prevalent in democracies, where the principle of equality has gone so far as to invade the domain of the intellect. In advanced democracies one man's opinion—let him be of the meanest intellectual capacity—concerning what, is "right" and "wrong", "good" and "bad", "honorable" and "dishonorable", is thought as valid as anyone else's. This vulgar or democratic form of relativism (reinforced by the moral neutrality or indifferentism of twentieth-century capitalism) cannot but undermine wholehearted dedication to any cause. Relativism, by relativising one's own values, corrodes and eventually paralyzes the will. Who indeed would remain resolute in a long-drawn-out conflict unless he believes in the absolute worth of his cause? Modern man will fight and die for what he believes to be true. But only the deluded would presevere in a protracted struggle on behalf of a cause which cannot be shown to be morally superior to that of any nation which threatens his own. Democratic relativism thus reinforces the fear of violent death and even disposes men to regard violent death as the greatest evil.[49]

And so "Détente 1933" reflects more than a change in the foreign policy of the United States and more than a mere change of administration. Rather, it reflects a profound change in the political character of the American regime. In my *Discourse on Statesmanship*, which is subtitled *The Design and Transformation of the American Polity*, I advance the thesis that whereas the New Freedom of Woodrow Wilson witnessed the *intellectual* ascendency of democracy, that ascendency was brought to a *political* conclusion under Franklin Roosevelt and the New Deal.[50] Consistent therewith, "Détente 1933" may be regarded primarily as a democratic phenomenon. (Interestingly enough, Litvinov himself is reported to have attributed American recognition of the Soviet Union to the abandonment by the United States of its previous ideological position, which alone suggests that there had occurred a regime change of no ordinary significance when Roosevelt succeeded Hoover to the Presidency.)[51] Of course, political life is more complex than just suggested. No world-historical individual is likely to exhibit all the attributes of his society. Franklin Roosevelt may have brought Woodrow Wilson's democratic revolution to a political conclusion; but neither Roosevelt nor Wilson was for that very reason the product of a thoroughly democratic regime.

Finally, the question must be raised, Was it *honorable* for the United States to have accorded diplomatic recognition to a brutal tyranny, especially when the leaders of that tyranny had repeatedly expressed unmitigated hostility toward everything which this nation stands for or so highly values? The fact that the Soviet Union sought diplomatic recognition from the United States—meaning *amicable* relations with a regime it despised, hated, and intended to subvert—is a mark of its own lack of honor. But for the United States to have complied is, in the words of John Spargo, "shameful self-abasement."[52] No doubt considerations of honor on matters pertaining to international relations will be deemed quixotic by so-called realists. But only a very narrow and short-sighted realism will ignore one of the ruling passions of great statesmen. Realists in the field of international relations like to believe that their realism derives support from Alexander Hamilton. They flatter themselves. Hamilton had nothing but contempt for politicians who today would pass for realists or pragmatists. Consider, first, his opinion of Aaron Burr:

> But it is said (1) that he is *artful* and *dextrous* to accomplish his ends; (2) that he holds no pernicious theories, but is a mere matter-of-fact man. . . .
>
> I admit that he has no fixed theory. . . . But is it a recommendation to have no *theory*? Can that be a systematic or able statesman who has none? . . .
>
> Let it be remembered that Mr. Burr has never appeared solicitous for fame, and that great ambition, unchecked by principle or the love of glory, is an unruly tyrant, which never can keep long in a course which good men will approve. . . . Ambition without principle never was long under the guidance of good sense. . . . [Mr. Burr] is far more *cunning* than wise, far more dextrous than *able*.[53]

Notice that a man without principle, hence without honor, will not long be under the guidance of good sense. He may be cunning but not wise. This suggests that the sense of honor tends to enlarge the intellect, to render it more comprehensive and farseeing in its grasp of political reality. Unlike the pragmatist preoccupied with the immediate and with immediate results—the base path to popularity and prestige—the statesman who ventures on the more difficult path of honor and glory will be concerned about posterity. If he is to be celebrated by distant generations, his political thought and policies will have to be of universal significance as well as of enduring value.[54] At issue here is the distinction between the large- and small-souled statesman, to which corresponds a large- and small-souled realism.

Was it realistic to have recognized the Soviet Union in 1933? Those who claim it was bear the burden of showing wherein recognition contributed to the moral and material betterment of this country. Was the realism which led to the recognition of the Soviet Union consistent with the teachings of Washington and Hamilton? Not at all. For in a proclamation issued by Washington in April 1793 announcing the abolition of the French monarchy, the President informed the American people that, "Whereas every nation has a right to change and modify their constitution and Government, in such manner as they may think most conducive to their welfare and Happiness . . . they who actually administer the government . . . are by foreign nations to be regarded as its *lawful Rulers*, so long as they continue to be recognized and obeyed *as such* by the great Body of their people."[55] Clearly, this teaching, obviously rooted in the Declaration of Independence, does not support the recognition of the Soviet Union in 1933. Moreover, in a lengthy memorandum to Washington dated April 18, 1793 (four days prior to the issuance of the Neutrality Proclamation) Hamilton reaffirmed that teaching of the Declaration, but went on to say:

> ... it will by no means follow, that because a Nation has a right ... to make such changes in its political institutions as itself judges best calculated to promote its interests—that it has *therefore* a right to involve other nations ... in the consequences of the changes, which it may think proper to make. This would be to give to a nation or society, not only a power over its own happiness, but a power over the happiness of other Nations or Societies. It would extend the operations of the maxim, much beyond the *reason* of it—which is simply that every Nation ought to have a right to provide for its *own happiness*.[56]

Here Hamilton merely develops the rational limits of the principle of self-determination.[57] What is more to the point at issue, however, is that Hamilton also raised the question whether the United States should recognize the successors of the dethroned French monarch, that is to say, the government under the Directory. He advised Washington that, in addition to other considerations,

> The character of the United States may be also concerned in keeping clear of any connection with the Present Government of France. . . .
> A struggle for liberty is in itself respectable and glorious. When conducted with magnanimity, justice and humanity it ought to command the admiration of every friend to human nature. But if sullied by crimes and extravagancies, it loses its respectability. Though success may rescue it from infamy, it cannot in the opinion of the sober part of Mankind attach to it much positive merit or praise. But in the event of a want of success, a general execration must attend it. . . .
> Will it be well for the United States to expose their reputation to the *issue*, by implicating themselves as associates? Will their reputation be promoted by a successful issue? What will it suffer by the reverse? These questions suggest very serious considerations to a mind anxious for the reputation of the Country—anxious that it may emulate a character of sobriety, moderation, [and] justice. . . .[58]

If only because consideration of a nation's reputation or honor weighed heavily in Hamilton's political thought, I doubt whether that realist would have encouraged American recognition of the Soviet Union or "Détente 1933".[59]

CHAPTER 6

DETENTE VIA PEACEFUL COEXISTENCE: FROM KHRUSHCHEV TO KISSINGER

It would be to our great disadvantage if our neighbors were to perceive us more minutely and from a shorter distance. In the fact that, so far they have understood nothing about us, lay our great strength.

—Dostoevski

Words must have no relation to actions otherwise what kind of diplomacy is it? Words are one thing, actions another. Good words are a mask for bad deeds.

—Stalin

The wolf sheds his Coat once a Year, his Disposition never.

—Benjamin Franklin

I

The establishment of diplomatic relations between the United States and the Soviet Union in 1933 implied the possibility of peaceful coexistence between a capitalist and a communist regime. This is clearly evident in the previously mentioned Roosevelt-Litvinov pre-recognition agreement which declared, in part, that

... it will be the fixed policy of the Government of the Union of Soviet Socialist Republics:

103

1. To respect scrupulously the indisputable right of the United States to order its own life within its own jurisdiction in its own way and to refrain from interfering in any manner in the internal affairs of the United States, its territories or possessions.

2. To refrain, and to restrain all persons in government service and all organizations of Government or under its direct or indirect control . . . from any act overt or covert liable in any way whatsoever to injure the tranquillity, prosperity, order, or security of . . . the United States . . . and, in particular, from any act tending to incite or encourage armed intervention, or any agitation or propaganda having as an aim, the violation of the territorial integrity of the United States . . . or bringing about by force of a change in the political or social order of . . . the United States. . . .

4. Not to permit the formation or residence on its territory of any organization or group—and to prevent the activity on its territory of any organization or group, or of representatives or officials of any organization or group which has as an aim the overthrow or the preparation for the overthrow of, or the bringing about by force of a change in, the political or social order of . . . the United States, its territories or possessions.

These articles of the 1933 pre-recognition agreement with the Soviet Union seem to represent a complete renunciation of the *Communist Manifesto* which concludes by proclaiming that

. . . communists everywhere support every revolutionary movement against the existing social and political order of things.

In all these movements they bring to the front, as the leading question in each, the property question, *no matter what its degree of development at the time.*

Finally, they labor everywhere for the *union and agreement* of the democratic parties of *all* countries.

The communists disdain to conceal their views and aims. They openly declare that their ends can be attained only by the forcible overthrow of all existing social conditions. Let the ruling classes tremble at a communistic revolution. The proletarians have nothing to lose but their chains. They have a *world* to win.

WORKINGMEN OF ALL COUNTRIES, UNITE![2]

Nothing in the *Manifesto*, or in the early works of Marx discussed in Chapter 4, suggests the possibility of peaceful coexistence between capitalist and communist regimes. Does this mean that the rulers of the Soviet Union have renounced the principle of violence or tne primacy of force which, it was shown, is intrinsic to Marxism? Or is it possible that the Soviet policy of *"peaceful* coexistence", which shall here be deemed equivalent to "détente", is deliberately deceptive?

Consider, for example, Nikita Khrushchev's article "On Peaceful Coexistence" appearing in the October 1959 issue of *Foreign Affairs* (three years after his bloody suppression of Budapest). In that most prestigious and influential journal, Khrushchev taught his American readers that "peaceful coexistence"

> In its simplest expression . . . signifies the repudiation of war as a means of solving controversial issues. However, this does not cover the entire concept of peaceful coexistence. Apart from the commitment to non-aggression, it also presupposes an obligation on the part of all states to desist from violating each other's territorial integrity and sovereignty in any form and under any pretext whatsoever. The principle of peaceful coexistence signifies a renunciation of interference in the internal affairs of other countries with the object of altering their system of government or mode of life or for any other motives.

Here Khrushchev was merely reiterating the first article of the pre-recognition agreement of 1933. In the sequel, however, he dismissed the Western accusation "that peaceful coexistence is nothing else than a tactical method" which the Soviet Union employs as part of "an expansionist policy of conquest and an effort to subordinate other countries to their influence". He insisted that "the allegations that the Soviet Union intends to overthrow capitalism in other countries by 'exporting' revolution are absolutely unfounded". Nevertheless, Khrushchev made it very clear that "peaceful coexistence" does not mean the end of "ideological struggle" between the United States and Russia. *"The main thing"*, he emphasized, *"is to keep to the positions of ideological struggle, without resorting to arms in order to prove one is right."*

Having set forth the Soviet definition of "peaceful coexistence", the question arises as to whether it is compatible with "ideological struggle", especially if one ideology posits the primacy of force and justifies imperialistic objectives. In other words, can there be "peaceful coexistence" between the United States and Russia so long as the latter is governed by a Marxist ideology?

To clarify the issue, notice that American liberals and conservatives more or less enjoy peaceful coexistence because what they have in common is more important than their differences, an American philosophy of government ultimately rooted in the notion of *homo rationalis et civilis*. This common root enables them to resolve their differences through the method of consent or persuasion. Paraphrasing Jefferson, "we are all liberals, we are all conservatives" insofar as we adhere to and conserve the oldest liberal tradition, namely, that men can be friends despite their differences.[3] But Marxist ideology rejects this tradition. As a consequence, what Khrushchev refers to as the continuation of the "ideological struggle" involves a conflict between those who believe and those who do not believe that men can be friends despite their differences.[4] "Peaceful coexistence" must therefore harbor meanings for Communists and for Americans which do not entirely coincide. We must discover that those meanings are by philosophical analysis.

II

Consider, first, the term "peace". In its positive signification Whitehead defines peace as "that Harmony of Harmonies which calms *destructive* turbulence and completes civilization."[5] Thus understood, peace does not anesthetize men or even entail the elimination of all tensions. Rather, it only removes or requires the removal of those political, economic, and psychological obstacles or privations which thwart the development of our creative energies. The positive experience of peace is one of overcoming hindrances or difficulties; it is an experience of dynamic accomplishment, a feeling of progress toward fullness of being. Accordingly, for a nation to pursue a policy of peace is a magnificent adventure, the success of which involves a transition from the mutual obstruction toward the mutual intensification of the diverse aims, values, and relationships existing among mankind. This is not the policy of the Soviet Union. As Khrushchev wrote in his memoirs:

> It would be a betrayal of our Party's first principles to believe that there can be peaceful coexistence between Marxist-Leninist ideology

on the one hand and bourgeois ideology on the other. . . . I always said that there can be no such thing as ideological peaceful coexistence. I have always stressed that we would fight to the end, and that we were sure we would prevail.[6]

Turning to the negative meaning of peace, it is usually defined as the absence of conflict, or anesthesia. But surely anesthesia is not preferable to all forms or degrees of conflict. To rest content with a negative view of peace would condemn every revolution, our own and those directed against the tyranny of communist monotony. Besides, there are more or less benign as well as more or less malevolent forms of conflict. Of the latter, no less than three generic and interrelated types may be delineated: military, economic, and political, each of which may be subdivided into "direct" and "indirect" or "overt" and "covert" species, themselves not always distinguishable.[7] For example, as already noted, the transfer of fifty American destroyers to Britain in 1940 constituted, according to international law, a belligerent act. It was, in fact, an indirect attack by the United States against Nazi Germany. Germany thus had cause not only for breaking diplomatic relations, but for launching a direct military attack upon any part or possession of the United States. Now compare Soviet arming of North Vietnamese Communists against Americans when the latter were fighting in the South. This was nothing less than an indirect attack by Russia against the United States as well as against South Vietnam. Considering this act from a *conventional* view of law and morality, it could be argued that, just as Germany had grounds for severing relations with and attacking the United States, so this country had grounds for severing relations with and attacking the Soviet Union. To be sure, a profounder view of law and morality might result in a less drastic course of action.[8] Germany could not readily afford open war with this country in 1940. Probably the same may be said of the United States vis-à-vis the Soviet Union over Viet nam, but with this difference: During the Vietnam War, American statesmen refused to recognize or name the principal enemy, which is to say they failed to face the all-challenging truth that we were at war with Communist Russia.

But the point is that a nation can in fact, as well as in terms of law and morality, be at war without itself firing a single shot at its enemies. And so far am I from dismissing the ordinary understanding of law and morality as irrelevant to international relations and statecraft that, in opposition to "realists", I wish to emphasize this simple but no longer obvious truth: *It is precisely the ordinary understanding of law and morality which makes it possible for a people to recognize that their country can in fact be at war without its enemies firing a single shot.* Contrary to legalists and moralists, however, the recognition of that fact does not itself suffice to determine any specific course of action.[9] On the other hand, if the fact of war is not recognized, no people will support a realistic and morally defensible foreign policy. Stated another way: if it is not generally understood that the person who contracts a "hit man" is no less guilty of murder than the one who squeezes the trigger, the number of "contractors" and "contracts" will increase, as will the number of murders. Immune even from the threat of punishment, the wicked will multiply and violence will abound. Not to say that communist soldiers of North Vietnam were merely the "hit men" of the Soviet Union—some prefer to call them or their leaders Soviet "clients". But when tens of thousands of Americans are killed by bombs and bullets supplied by Soviet Russia, even to speak of a "*cold* war" between that communist regime and the United States is morally purblind. What, then, shall we say of the obfuscation of "peaceful coexistence"? Merely that we live in an Orwellian universe in which war is called peace.

In that universe there exists a species of indirect military conflict between the the United States and the Soviet Union but one step removed from the preceding, namely, where only the clients of each nation are engaged in direct military confrontation. Like the Arab-Israeli wars of 1967 and 1973 (of which, more later), the war between North and South Vietnam after the withdrawal of American forces is a case in point, and a most extraordinary one at that. No serious observer denies that the conquest of South Vietnam by communist North Vietnam was a serious defeat for the United States.* Yet few

---

*Indeed, as Professor Rood has pointed out to the author, "the loss of Vietnam may have rendered certain, either a Sino-Soviet War of incredible dimension, or a Sino-Soviet alliance aimed at the erasure of the United States—depending on whether the Soviet Union is convinced that the U.S. would stand aside for the destruction of China, and on whether China believes that the U.S. defeat in Vietnam is the final symptom of terminal impotence. A weak national policy does not keep a country out of war; it merely raises the price the citizenry will have to pay in

have the audacity to admit that the loss of South Vietnam was a profoundly significant victory for the Soviet Union whose expanding navy, with access to the strategically important American-improved facilities of Camranh Bay, can now penetrate the South China Sea and the South Pacific. As a consequence, the Russian navy is in a position to interdict the sea lanes between Japan and the American naval base at Subic Bay in the Philippines on the one hand, and the oil-rich Persian Gulf via the Indian Ocean on the other. Here we see how a proxy war can threaten free world energy sources—all this in the midst of "peaceful coexistence". Hence it would be more accurate to say that the communist conquest of South Vietnam represents not only a military but a political and even economic victory of the Soviet Union over the United States.[10]

Whereas Vietnam was the scene of a proxy war waged by means of arms, the Arab oil embargo of 1973 and the subsequent inflation of oil prices imposed on the West by the Organization of Petroleum Exporting Countries was a proxy war waged by means of economics. Four months prior to the outbreak of the Middle East War of that year, *Pravda* boldly made known that "To stop pumping Arabian Gulf oil in the present situation will be an economic earthquake to the entire capitalist economy."[11] Now, the oil embargo could hardly have been successfully orchestrated were it not for (1) Soviet leverage over its Arab clients in the form of long-standing military aid programs, and (2) Russia's predominance in the Eastern Mediterranean and its naval presence in the Indian Ocean, a predominance which renders it extremely difficult, as the Arabs well know, to loosen that stranglehold on the Free World's economy by military intervention, let alone by diplomacy. Of course the pawns were delighted, and for political as well as economic reasons. For by virtue of the oil embargo, or say by the threat of its subsequent employment, Moscow was able to blackmail the United States into compelling (or blackmailing) Israel to withdraw from territories in the Sinai.*

Although the motives and interests of the Soviet Union and such Arab states as Syria, Iraq, and Libya are not entirely consistent, they

---

order to prevent defeat. The choice is not between war and peace, but between war with victory and war with defeat and servitude."

*It should also be noted that the embargo has strained American relations with Western Europe. See William Schneider, *Food, Foreign Policy, and Raw Materials Cartels* (New York: Crane, Russak & Co., 1976), pp. 61-69.

converge on two objectives: to disengage the United States from the Middle East and to eliminate Israel as the West's only agent for liberalism: for democratic enlightenment and social progress. Here the despotic character of Arab regimes, more than any other single factor, enables Russia to fuel and exploit the Arab-Israeli conflict as a vehicle for becoming the dominant power in the area. But even in the absence of that conflict, Stalin pursued the same geopolitical objective in his secret pact of 1940 with Hitler, one provision of which described "the area south of Batum and Baku in the general direction of the Persian Gulf . . . as the center of the aspirations of the Soviet Union."[12] There is no sound reason to believe that Russia has abandoned this objective, hence that the Kremlin will cease to manipulate Israeli-Arab hostility. Indeed, in a speech delivered on April 22, 1974, Boris Ponomarev, a candidate member of the Politburo and perhaps the most authoritative spokesman on Soviet world strategy, had this to say to Russia's ruling hierarchy: "The Soviet Union will continue in the future to do everything necessary to defend the legitimate interests of the Arab countries, to make its contribution to the liquidation of the Near East crisis, and not to permit a 'settlement' which would in practice encourage the aggressor. That would damage both the cause of peace and the interests of the national liberation struggle. But it should not be so, and it will not be so."[12a] All this, however, is the inevitable consequence of the "ideological struggle" which Khrushchev (and his successors) would have us believe is compatible with peaceful coexistence.*

Finally, political conflict between the United States and Russia may be seen in (1) Soviet supported Afro-Asian bloc voting in the United Nations;[13] (2) Soviet efforts to divide NATO by means of bilateral agreements with one or another of its members; and (3) Soviet financed Communist Party activity in such countries as Italy, France, and Portugal (to say nothing of the espionage of the KGB in the United States). These overt and covert efforts of the Kremlin are among the milder elements of "ideological struggle" or protracted war. By Khrushchev's own admission, they are ultimately intended to

---

*By fostering the belief that ideological struggle or peaceful coexistence are compatible, the Soviets minimize, in the minds of the West, the overriding importance of ideology. At the risk of redundancy, it is worth emphasizing that "peaceful coexistence" is merely a disarming tactic aimed at buying time, with Western compliance, for the Russians to gain strategic nuclear superiority.

transform "peaceful coexistence" into "peaceful existence", i.e., the existence of a politically anesthetized or communist world.

Summing up this inquiry into the negative meaning of peace it may be said that "peaceful coexistence", in point of historical fact, is nothing more than the absence of *direct* military conflict between the United States and the Soviet Union—which, for practical purposes, reduces to the absence of nuclear war. This shall be termed the "minimalist" meaning of "peaceful coexistence" or "détente".[14] But this is only half the story. It remains to discuss the meaning of "existence" or of "coexistence".

Abstractly considered, the coexistence of two societies involves the spatial delimitation of two qualitatively distinct and politically sovereign entities. No modern society is static: every society is either growing or decaying, its values are enjoyed with either increasing or decreasing intensity. No society is absolutely self-sufficient: every society requires a favorable environment for the survival of its defining characteristics;[15] the environment either facilitates or hinders the achievement of its shared ends or purposes. Furthermore, no modern society is utterly self-contained. This means that the initial definition of coexistence must be qualified. The spatial delimitation of any society is misleading. A society's existence—its political principles and institutions, its military and economic power, its scientific and technological accomplishments, its moral and cultural values—may extend beyond its geographical borders. In the case of the United States, such is the extent of its influence that whether it acts or refrains from acting, it cannot but amplify or attenuate the values or defining characteristics of virtually every nation under the sun. Much the same may be said of the Soviet Union. It thus appears that a nation's existence is coterminous with its power—I mean its intellectual and moral power, no less than its physical power: the power to preserve its own teleological identity against divisive and destructive forces within and without; the power to create and recreate an internal and external environment conducive to—in the case of the United States—liberty and civility.

Because America's existence extends as far as its spatio-temporal influence, its existence cannot but be teleologically diminished when any friend or ally loses its liberty, or when tens of millions of people succumb to communist tyranny. Bearing in mind that there are little more than a score of republics in the world today, as the domain of liberty shrinks, so too does the domain of civility in which nations may resolve their differences by means of persuasion or negotiation rather than by means of force or conquest. Stated another way: as tyranny expands, the greater will be the necessity of employing force to secure justice. Recent events illustrate this convincingly. The communist conquest of Cambodia compelled the United States to use force to rescue the crew of the *Mayagüez*, the American freighter seized in international waters by Cambodian gun-boats.[16] I should emphasize, however, that the use of force in abstraction from its purposes is not in question. Force may either heighten the teleological existence of a regime based on the primacy of persuasion or contribute to the establishment of such a regime in the first place.[17] "The tree of liberty", wrote Jefferson, "must be refreshed from time to time, with the blood of patriots and tyrants." Still, when resort to force, instead of punctuating political life, becomes its virtual *modus operandi*, the tree of liberty can hardly yield the fruit of *homo rationalis et civilis*.[18] But this only means that as the world of Communism expands and the world of freedom contracts, the existence or mode of life of *homo rationalis et civilis* becomes increasingly precarious. To preserve his existence will require larger and larger defense expenditures, hence progressively smaller sums for the cultivation of human excellence or for the pursuit of that fullness of being which is genuine peace. In short, a republic like the United States cannot fully exist as a republic or as a free society in a Soviet or communist dominated environment. To paraphrase Lincoln: This world cannot endure, *permanently* half *slave* and half *free*. Sooner or later it will become *all* one thing, or *all* the other.[19] Therein is the fundamental issue of "peaceful coexistence".

Having analyzed the meaning of "peace" as well as the meaning of "existence", it appears that "peaceful coexistence" between the United States and Russia, so long as the latter remains an imperialistic power, is impossible except in the minimalist sense of the absence of nuclear war.[20] Judging, however, from its ICBM development (on which, more in a moment), it should be evident that the Soviet Union has never deviated from its first-strike nuclear strategy revealed in 1961 by defector Oleg Penkovskiy.[21] More recently, in

112

1971, General I. E. Krupchenko asserted that "The employment of nuclear weapons has greatly increased the role and significance of surprise in combat and has raised the requirements for its attainment". This conforms to the position of Colonel A. A. Sidorenko, one of the Red Army's leading theoreticians, who wrote: "Pre-emption in launching a nuclear strike is expected to be the decisive condition for the attainment of superiority over [the enemy] and the seizure and retention of the initiative".[22] Not that Russia necessarily intends to initiate a nuclear attack upon the United States.[23] For if she acquires a preclusive first-strike capability, many of her objectives can be achieved by nuclear blackmail. From this it follows that "peaceful coexistence", even in the minimalist sense of avoiding nuclear war, is valid only under conditions of nuclear parity. We may therefore conclude that, given the nature of the ideological struggle of which Khrushchev spoke in 1959, *peaceful* coexistence between the Soviet Union and the United States is an utter contradiction in terms.

Now, insofar as "peaceful coexistence", in its minimalist sense, does not preclude non-nuclear military as well as economic and political conflict, the question arises as to where such conflicts are to take place? In what areas of the world is there to be "peaceful coexistence" or ideological struggle between the Soviet Union and the United States? Certainly not in Communist Russia. As Khrushchev said in his speech of June 21, 1963 to the Central Committee of the CPSU:

> If salt is thrown into a mixture of concrete, you will not get any binding material and the concrete will crumble. Peaceful ideological coexistence is a kind of salt.
> Our enemies want to toss this salt into our ideology by appealing for peaceful coexistence in the sphere of ideology. Why? Because ... they think of how they can undermine and weaken the influence of the party among the people—i.e., deprive the masses of their organizing and guiding force. They are powerless to undermine the party from within. ... Now they are doing their best to emasculate the revolutionary soul of the party and to denigrate Marxist-Leninist ideology, to weaken its influence on the ... people.[23]

Furthermore, the Soviet Union will not tolerate ideological coexistence or competition among its satellites. This is manifestly the implication of the Brezhnev Doctrine which merely reiterates the teachings of Lenin.* Intended to justify the Soviet-led invasion of Czechoslovakia in 1968, an invasion predicated on the reasonable assumption that the liberalization of one satellite would lead to that of another—the Brezhnev Doctrine claims a right of the Soviet Union to intervene in the internal affairs of *any* Marxist state which, in the judgment of the Kremlin, deviates from the "common laws of socialist construction".[24] A Soviet imposed orthodoxy is thus to prevail throughout the communist world. That world was described in Khrushchev's Report to the Twentieth Congress of the CPSU in 1956 as the "Zone of Peace", not of "peaceful coexistence". "Peaceful coexistence" applies only to the non-communist world. But inasmuch as "peaceful coexistence" means nothing more than non-nuclear conflict, Soviet leaders look upon the non-communist world as the "Zone of War", a war they have every intention of winning.[25]

This was more or less understood by one of the two principal architects of "détente", Richard Nixon, and before as well as after he became President of the United States. Consider, for example, Mr. Nixon's book *Six Crises*, published in 1962 and republished in 1969 with a new introduction written after his inauguration. In referring to the many briefings he received in preparation for his first trip to Moscow in 1959, Mr. Nixon singles out the advice of John Foster Dulles to whom he had posed the following question: "What above everything else should I try to get across to Khrushchev?"

Mr. Nixon then writes:

Dulles was never a man to give quick answers to important questions. This time he waited longer than usual. Then he replied approximately like this:

"Khrushchev does not need to be convinced of our good intentions. He knows that we are not aggressors and do not threaten the security of the Soviet Union. He understands us. But what he needs to know is that we also understand him. In saying that he is

---

*Thus Lenin in 1918: "No Marxist, without flying in the face of the principles of Marxism and of Socialism generally, can deny that the interests of Socialism are higher than the interests of the right of nations to self-determination." And again in 1922: "[T]he right of self-determination cannot and should not hinder the realization of the right of the working class to its own dictatorship. The former must make room for the latter." Cited in Wladyslaw W. Kulski, *Peaceful Co-Existence: An Analysis of Soviet Foreign Policy.* Chicago: Henry Regnery, 1959, pp. 196, 199: Viewed in this light, the Brezhnev Doctrine (see Appendix 4) would justify Soviet intervention not only in Communist China and Cuba, or in Syria and Mozambique, but in any country drifting toward Marxism, such as Italy or France.

for peaceful competition, he really means competition between his system and ours only in our world, not in his. He says he is for peaceful co-existence. What he means, as he has shown in Hungary, is that while a revolution against a non-Communist government is proper and should be supported, a revolution against a Communist government is invariably wrong and must be suppressed. Thus, the peaceful co-existence which he advocates represents peace for the Communist world and constant strife and conflict for the non-Communist world.

"He must be made to understand that he cannot have it both ways. If we are to have peaceful competition of economic systems and political ideas, it must take place in the Communist world as well as ours. He will deny, of course, that he or his government are connected in any way with Communist activities in other countries—that those activities are simply spontaneous expressions of a people's resentment against capitalist regimes. . . . Show him that we are not taken in at all by the mock innocence of Soviet leaders, that we have concrete proof of the Kremlin's activities around the world. He should be told that until he puts a stop to such activities, his call for reducing of tensions and for peaceful co-existence will have a completely false and hollow ring".[26]

In his talks with Khrushchev, the Vice President heeded the advice of the former Secretary of State—which is not to say Khrushchev was convinced that "we" understood him as well as he understood us.[27] Indeed, given the Kremlin's meticulous scrutiny of the writings and speeches of those who shape public opinion in the United States, the mere fact that Mr. Dulles and Mr. Nixon thought it was of the greatest importance to convince Khrushchev that "we" understood his double-standard conception of "peaceful coexistence" may be construed to mean that a significant number of journalists, academics, and public officials were gullible enough to be taken in by communist duplicity. Whatever the case, no American President has publicly and unambiguously acknowledged the harsh truth that Soviet leaders feel perfectly free to foment and support "constant strife and conflict [in] the non-Communist world" while professing a policy of "peaceful coexistence" with the United States.[27a] To admit this would teach the American people, including some of their opinion-makers, that Russia has ceaselessly been engaged in an indirect but nonetheless real war against the United States and the Free World, a war pursued by means of various clients—such as Cubans in Angola—equipped with Soviet arms and serving, willingly or unwillingly, Soviet strategic objectives. Precisely because this teaching has not been clearly conveyed to the general public, Khrushchev could boast to the Central Committee of the CPSU in 1963 that "During my talks . . . with President Eisenhower [in 1959, following the Nixon trip to Moscow], it was evident that he, like Secretary of State Herter [Dulles' successor], could not pronounce the words 'peaceful coexistence'. However, thanks to our stubborn efforts to strengthen the forces of socialism . . . we have taught them."[28]

Insofar as American statesmen and publicists have failed to expose the duplicity of the Soviet policy of "peaceful coexistence"—showing the wide disparity between the positive and minimalist meanings of the term peace, revealing how it does not even preclude conventional military conflict in the non-communist world—then to the extent that Khrushchev taught them to *pronounce* the words "peaceful coexistence", to that extent the Kremlin has won the psychological war it has relentlessly waged against the mentality of the American people.

This failure of American statesmen and educators—that psychological victory of the Soviet Union—has resulted in the most grotesque and tragic consequences. It is bad enough when public officials, scholars, and journalists reiterate the communist description of externally supported insurrections as "wars of national liberation", albeit between inverted commas. Far worse is it when some use that sophism to compare and confuse the American Revolution with the war between North and South Vietnam.[29] But having been taught to pronounce the words "wars of national liberation", it was inevitable that the inverted commas, inaudible in speech, would become invisible in print, such that upon entering Saigon communist armies were described by some benighted Americans as "liberators". "Peaceful coexistence" has thus borne Orwellian fruit: common sense has been corrupted and political morality turned on its head.

III

Today "peaceful coexistence" is usually called "détente" which literally means the relaxation of tensions. However, as purveyed to the American people by their own leaders and by the mass media, "détente" has come to mean the end of the "cold war" and the beginning of friendly relations between the United States and the Soviet Union. We have seen that "détente" or "peaceful coexistence" means nothing of the kind to the Kremlin. In the same speech which Khrushchev delivered to the Central Committee of the CPSU on June 21, 1963, he went on to say that

> Now a harsher struggle is being waged between the forces of imperialism . . and the forces of socialism, communism. Taras Bulba [who "killed his son Andrey because he went over to the side of the enemies"] waged a national struggle, but we are in a class struggle. The class struggle is harsher, crueller. The class struggle knows no national frontiers. . . .

More recently, in June 1972, only a month after he had signed the "Basic Principles of Relations" defining the policy of "peaceful coexistence" or "détente" between the United States and the Soviet Union, and while the ink was hardly dry on the ABM-SALT Agreement then being debated in Congress, Leonid Brezhnev declared, at a dinner given in honor of Fidel Castro, that "we are aware that success in . . . the struggle for peaceful coexistence in no way implies the possibility of relaxing the ideological struggle. On the contrary, we must be prepared for the struggle to be intensified and [to become] an ever sharper form of confrontation between the systems."[30] And in a collection of speeches published in 1973, Brezhnev went so far as to admit that "all the revolutionary forces . . . [must] be prepared for . . . the use of any forms of struggle—peaceful and non-peaceful, legal and illegal."[31] These statements indicate that the slogan of "détente" is a façade for civil war, a civil war conducted by violent as well as by non-violent means, and on a global scale. "Détente" is indeed intended by the Soviet Union to relax tensions, but only in the West, meaning it is intended to relax Western vigilance. But far from being a post-cold war policy, "détente" is, to say the least, a *pre-war* policy, a policy having deadly consequences, as we shall now see.

Suppose the American people believed that peaceful coexistence with the Soviet Union was not only possible, but that Soviet leaders were sincerely committed to such a policy beyond the minimalist sense of the term. Not that many Americans need believe that there no longer exist important political differences between the two regimes,

117

but merely that such differences could in principle be resolved through "negotiation instead of confrontation." Certain consequences would tend to follow:

(1) More and more people would come to believe that the "cold war" was primarily the result of mutual fear and suspicion engendered by lack of mutual understanding, all of which could largely be overcome by fostering trade and joint scientific and cultural exchange programs.[32]

(2) Accordingly, gestures of good will would follow to assure others of our peaceful intentions. In negotiations with the Soviet Union, gratuitous concessions would be made by the United States to demonstrate our benevolence, and to encourage reciprocity.

(3) Meanwhile, public criticism of Soviet conduct would virtually cease and anti-communist sentiment would diminish to the point where the enemies of republican government would be called our "adversaries" or, more euphemistically, the "other side".[33]

(4) Russian domination of Eastern Europe would not be questioned, and little or nothing would be made of Soviet arms shipments to nations hostile to the United States or to its friends and allies.

(5) To the contrary, reductions in American defense spending and troop deployments would be urged and effectuated—this, in consonance with increasing pacifism on the one hand, and isolationism on the other.[34]

These consequences of "peaceful coexistence" are more than tendencies. They are among the objectives of the Soviet Union. With a candor sometimes lacking in Western media, an editorial in the *Kommunist* (of September 1970) boldly proclaimed that "the policy of peaceful coexistence . . . has facilitated and facilitates the development of class struggle against imperialism inside individual countries as well as on a world scale."[35] Brezhnev was even more candid and revealing when he told a conference of European communist parties in April 1967:

> Experience teaches in particular that the "cold war" and the confrontation of military blocs, the atmosphere of military threats, seriously hampers the activity of revolutionary, democratic forces. In conditions of international tension in bourgeois countries the reactionary elements become active, the military raise their heads, antidemocratic tendencies and anti-Communism are strengthened. And conversely, the past few years have shown quite clearly that in con-

ditions of slackened international tension the pointer of the political barometer moves left.[36]

Whereas in the West in general, and in the United States in particular, periods of international tension strengthen the forces of anti-communism and lead to increased defense expenditures, the relaxation of international tension or "détente" strengthens the forces of anti-anti-communism and leads to a decline in defense expenditures. Here are some of the alarming facts taken largely from 1976 Congressional and military sources.[37]

(1) Not only has Russia surpassed the United States in total military spending, but between 1968 and 1975, the advanced period of "détente", Soviet military expenditures increased 20 percent to 144 billion dollars, while ours decreased some 33 percent to less than 100 billion dollars.* (In 1975, U.S. national defense received its smallest share of the budget since 1940.) But even these figures obscure and minimize the military imbalance. For 53 percent of America's military budget in 1975 was absorbed by military pay and allowances, while another 12 percent consisted in outlays for troop housing, recruiting, human relations and related activities. In other words, only 35 percent of our military budget is in the *force effective* category. The proportion of Soviet force effective spending is more than double this figure.

(2) Again, between 1968 and 1975, in the vital area of military research and development, Soviet spending soared to 9.2 billion dollars while ours declined 30 percent to 7.7 billion. As for expenditures on strategic forces, we are being outstripped 11.8 billion to 7.4 billion dollars.

(3) From 1965 to 1975, American armed forces decreased by 20 percent to 2.1 million men, while the Russians increased theirs by 37 percent to 4.8 million men. Russia has 168 mechanized and armored divisions to our 19, an advantage of better than 8 to 1. In tanks they outnumber us 42,000 to 9,000; in artillery 20,000 to 6,000—and their superiority is in many respects qualitative as well as numerical. And the disparity is increasing at an alarming rate. The Soviets are annually out-producing us 3,000 to 768 in tanks; 928 to 609 in artillery; 1,350

---

*Based on constant (FY 1977) prices. Controversy over how much the Soviet Union is spending on arms often obscures the more decisive issue, namely, which country possesses the more numerous and more powerful strategic and conventional forces.

to 271 in tactical aircraft; and 45 to 9 in underwater and surface naval combatants.*

(4) Since 1967, the United States has maintained a constant number of 1,054 Intercontinental Ballistic Missile (ICBM) launchers, while the Soviets have more than doubled theirs to 1,600. And while they have added four completely new ICBM systems with improved accuracy and greater payload, apart from qualitative improvements, we have not augmented our ICBM arsenal. Two of their systems incorporate new "cold launch" techniques for firing ICBMs after they have first popped out of their silos, enabling rapid refiring. (Our ICBMs are fired in the silo, so that considerable repair is required before reloading.) Finally (and in violation of a U.S. unilateral declaration contained in the SALT I accords), of the four new ICBM systems developed by the Russians, one is a land-mobile ICBM virtually immune to targeting and detection, hence to arms limitation agreements.

(5) In missile throw-weight, the Soviets have an overwhelming advantage of at least 4 to 1. Many experts regard this as the most significant factor in the strategic balance. It indicates not only the size of the warhead that can be delivered, but the potential number of warheads that can be carried by a single Multiple Independently-targetable Reentry Vehicle (MIRV). Although we have 8,500 warheads to their 2,800, given the vastly greater throw-weight of Soviet ICBMs and their newly acquired MIRV capability, they could eventually confront us with 25,000. But the decisive thing is not the number of warheads so much as the number of Russian warheads versus the number of American launchers—and 2,800 is more than enough for the Soviets to initiate a first strike in the not too distant future.

(6) In ballistic missile submarines (nuclear- and diesel-powered), the Russians are ahead of us 73 to 41. And their more advanced Submarine Launched Ballistic Missile (SLBM) has a range of 4,200 miles, more than half again our own.

(7) Once we had the world's most comprehensive continental defense system. In 1974, however, virtually all surface-to-air missile

*These are average annual production rates for 1971-1975. See Secretary of Defense Donald Rumsfeld, *FY 77 U.S. Defense Budget Perspectives*, 8 March 1976 (unpaginated); Statement Submitted to the Congress by General George S. Brown, Chairman of the Joint Chiefs of Staff, *United States Military Posture for FY 1977*, 20 Jan. 1976. pp. 52, 90; "Hearings on Military Posture," House Armed Services Committee (cited below, p. 230, n. 37), Pt. I, pp. 1540-1541.

(SAM) batteries in the United States and Canada were inactivated. In contrast, the Soviets have 12,000, many of which can be fitted with anti-ballistic warheads. And their SAMs are linked up with 5,000 defense radar systems in comparison to the 67 operating in this country. Supporting Russian air defense are 2,600 interceptor aircraft; we have only 249, half in the Air National Guard (hence less than we had at the time of Pearl Harbor). Our meager defense system should be juxtaposed with the fact that Russia has 750 medium-range bombers compared to our 66. With a range of 4,000 miles, they can drop their nuclear bombs on the United States and land in neutral or in friendly territory (such as Cuba). This applies especially to Russia's highly advanced and significantly medium-range Backfire bomber. These facts counterbalance our superiority in long-range heavy bombers, where we have 321 active B-52's to their 140 active Bear and Bison; for the U.S. has scrapped all its medium-range bombers, such as the B-47 and B-58.

(8) Finally, according to the authoritative British source, *Jane's Fighting Ships* (1975-1976), "the Soviet Union has spent 50 percent more than the US in the last ten years and is currently expending one-third more than the United States [on the development of naval forces]." In fact, our active naval ships have declined from 975 in 1968 to 478 in 1976, such that the American navy is presently at its 1939 numerical level. Consequently, whereas Russia now has 240 major warships (cruisers, destroyers, escorts, and carriers), we have only 173, many of which are not as modern or as powerful as their Soviet counterparts. And of profound significance: given the West's dependence on Middle East oil and on open shipping lanes between the Persian Gulf and the industrial centers of the Free World, Russia's 335 attack and cruise missile fleet of submarines (we have only 75) is especially ominous. (It should be noted in this connection that many of the enemy's surface ships, including trawlers, are also armed with cruise missiles.) The only significant advantage the American navy seems to enjoy is in aircraft carriers. (We have of the helicopter variety 12 active carriers, whereas the Soviets have 4, 3 of the helicopter variety.) But in certain areas, like the Mediterranean, carriers ultimately depend on supporting land-based airfields; and a glance at the geopolitical map reveals that Russia's increasing acquisition of air and naval facilities in the Middle East, around Africa, and in the littoral of

the Indian Ocean, greatly reduces the effectiveness of our carrier deployment. Thus, in virtually every major category, the Soviet Union has achieved, or is on the verge of achieving, decisive military superiority over the United States*—and all this during "détente".[38]

With military superiority diplomatic advantages usually follow. Thus, while this country became increasingly preoccupied with domestic concerns, the Soviet Union achieved at Helsinki, on August 1, 1975, what the June 16, 1973 issue of *Izvestia* referred to as "the final recognition of the territorial changes which occurred in Europe as a result of the Second World War."[39] The recognition of Eastern Germany by the United States (preceded by the *Ostpolitik* of the Bonn Republic) had already placed the stamp of legitimacy on Soviet domination of Eastern Europe, the age-old dream of Tsarist Russia. This shift in American foreign policy is but a reflection of "Détente 1933".

While American statesmen have allowed "détente" to render anti-communism unfashionable in the United States,[40] the more cunning leaders of the Kremlin have understood that "détente" could lead to ideological erosion of their own people. It is for this reason that anti-American propaganda has been increased in the Soviet Union. As one Communist explains the problem:

> The climate of international relations necessary for our own offensive in favour of a *détente* may generate trends towards demobilisation inside the country (particularly in the ideological sphere); it may contribute to the emergence of illusions about the possibility of permanent and all-embracing agreements between the two systems, about the disappearance of 'political and social differences' between them. It may make for a 'softening' of attitudes, a weakening of social vigilance *vis-à-vis* imperialism, etc.[41]

Accordingly, the Soviet government has not only increased anti-American propaganda, but it has also intensified and extolled

---

*If it be objected that the U.S. enjoys qualitative superiority, say in the accuracy of its ICBMs, to this it may be replied that (1) we do not really know the accuracy of our ICBMs, having never fired them from their silos (whereas the Russians have); (2) even if our ICBMs are more accurate, their accuracy is substantially offset by the greater throw-weight of Soviet missiles; (3) many of America's most densely populated cities are situated on or near the east and west coasts, rendering them more exposed to nuclear devastation. Finally, unlike the U.S., the Soviets have a first strike or counterforce strategy. Consequently, given a first strike by our enemies, what American President would order the destruction of Russian cities with our surviving missiles, when the Soviets retain countless hundreds more targeted on the defenseless cities of the United States? See Norman Polmar, *Strategic Weapons: An Introduction* (New York: Crane, Russak & Co., Inc., 1976) pp. 65-661.

militarism in the education of Soviet youth. At the same time, both in Russia and among its satellites, a more concentrated effort has been made to suppress dissidents and to stamp out *samizdat*; and even in Yugoslavia, so-called Soviet-American "détente" has witnessed a further diminution of freedom of expression.[42]

The lesson is clear: What we in the West call "détente" is a deadly "zero-sum" game orchestrated by the Soviet Union, a game which, if played by the rules of the Kremlin, can have but one conceivable outcome, the destruction of republican government, of liberty and civility.

Now, before continuing, let us summarize and project some of the consequences of "détente" *as presently conducted by the United States*.

(1) "Détente" cannot but dignify the rulers of the Soviet Union and thereby increase their domestic and international prestige and power.*

(2) "Détente" discourages internal resistance in the Soviet Union, both among intellectuals and among the masses.

(3) "Détente" undermines democratic movements among Soviet satellites.

(4) "Détente" places the stamp of legitimacy on Russian domination of Eastern Europe and thus prolongs the repression of countless millions longing for freedom.

(5) "Détente" enables Moscow to divide or undermine NATO, especially by means of bilateral agreements with individual members of the Western Alliance.

(6) "Détente", insofar as it leads us to treat friends and enemies alike, alienates our friends and thus increases the number or at least the relative strength of our enemies.

(7) "Détente" encourages capital investment in, and facilitates the transfer of technology to, the Soviet Union, the effect of which is to (a) subsidize and modernize Russia's military-industrial complex,† and

---

*See below, p. 136n.

† "In 1972 the Commerce and State Departments gave approval to the Bryant Chucking Grinding Company of Springfield, Vermont, to export to the Soviet Union Centalign B precision grinding machines of the latest generation so sophisticated as to be able to manufacture miniature ball bearings to tolerances of a twenty-fifth millionth of an inch. This means that the Soviet war industry gained 164 of these machines, while the United States reportedly has never owned more that seventy-seven of them. The precision miniature ball bearings are an intricate part of a guidance mechanism for the MIRVs. Consequently, until the Soviets were able to obtain Centalign B machines, they were unable to produce the guidance mechanism essential for

(b) augment Soviet shipment of arms to nations hostile to the United States, as well as arms to terrorist and revolutionary groups seeking to overthrow governments friendly to the United States.

(8) "Détente" facilitates Soviet espionage in the United States, economic as well as military.

(9) "Détente", by silencing criticism of the Russian regime, renders communist propaganda more effective.[43]

(10) "Détente", by discouraging anti-communism, weakens the will to resist communist imperialism.

(11) "Détente" lulls the free world into complacency and thereby leads to reductions in defense expenditures.

(12) "Détente," by eroding the military and political power of the United States, (a) renders this nation more susceptible to economic and nuclear blackmail; (b) encourages communist insurgency or revolutions in the undeveloped areas; (c) fosters neutralism if not a leftward shift toward Moscow on the part of America's former allies; and (d) increases the likelihood of nuclear proliferation among nations seeking to preserve their political independence.[44]

(13) In short, far from being a policy of peace, "détente" is a policy of appeasement which cannot but enfeeble the forces of liberty while strengthening the forces of tyranny, thereby fostering international tension and violence on the one hand, and increasing the likelihood of nuclear war on the other.[45]

All these deadly consequences of "détente" notwithstanding, by no means should the United States engage in a moralistic crusade against the Soviet Union. Civility and magnanimity are perfectly compatible with a firm and determined anti-communist foreign policy, a policy rooted in the urbane principles of the Declaration of Independence and the Farewell Address. Nevertheless, while it will be necessary for the statesman to elucidate those principles, it will be no less necessary for him to enlighten the American people about the true character of the Soviet Union, informing them of (1) its methods of psychological warfare; (2) its training and support for terrorists and assassins;[46] (3) its exploitation of nationalism as a means of fomenting civil war; (4) its offensive and defensive military capabilities, nuclear and conventional; (5) its immediate and long-

---

MIRVing their missile force." See Miles M. Costick, *The Economics of Détente* (Washington, D.C.: Heritage Foundation, 1976), p. 7.

range objectives in Europe, Asia, Africa, and the Middle East—showing *graphically* how those geopolitical objectives threaten the survival and independence of the United States.[47] But let us explore this question of educating the public by way of various illustrations of how *not* to educate the public.

IV

In his prepared statement before the Senate Foreign Relations Committee Hearings on "Détente" (September 19, 1974), Secretary of State Henry Kissinger admitted that there are "deep differences in philosophy and interests between the United States and the Soviet Union", for which reason "we must maintain a strong national defense."[48] Rhetorically, the efficacy of such statements is rendered nugatory when preceded and followed by repeated warnings about the danger of "nuclear holocaust" on the one hand, and by innumerable utterances about "peace" and the "imperative" of "peaceful coexistence" on the other. Similarly, far from enlightening, it can only confuse the public to say "We have profound differences with the Soviet Union—in our values, our methods, our vision of the future", only to conclude immediately thereafter with the exhortation that "it is these very differences which compel any responsible administration to make a major effort to create a more constructive relationship."[49] Such a *non sequitur* merely reinforces the widespread inability to acknowledge and confront, with candor and manliness, the malicious character and designs of our enemies. It is obscurantism to speak of the "profound differences" between the Soviet Union and the United States without once referring to the former as a communist tyranny. Hardly anyone doubts that the "values" and "methods" of that communist regime differ profoundly from those of our own; although a diminishing number of people comprehend the significance of these differences. In fact, if it were understood that the differences involve nothing less than a conflict between a regime whose rulers believe in the *primacy of force*, while those of another believe in the *primacy of persuasion*; or if it were recognized that one nation is governed by the political philosophy of an ant heap, while the other is governed by a political philosophy of free men, then the conclusion, "these very differences . . . which compel any responsible administration to make a major effort to create a more constructive relationship" would be seen in its true light, as an effort to square the circle.

But Dr. Kissinger sees this merely as a paradox. "Paradox", he contends, "confuses our perception of the problem of peaceful coexistence: if peace is pursued to the exclusion of any other goal, other values will be compromised and perhaps lost; but if unconstrained rivalry leads to nuclear conflict, these values, along with everything else, will be destroyed in the resulting holocaust."[50] Let us examine this so-called paradox minutely, for it not only reveals how the American people have been miseducated about American foreign policy, but also the true character of that policy.

The phrase "if peace is pursued to the exclusion of any other goal, other values will be compromised and perhaps lost", manifestly implies the negative if not the minimalist definition of the term peace. Consistently therewith, the phrase "if unconstrained rivalry leads to nuclear conflict, these values, along with everything else, will be destroyed in the resulting holocaust", clearly indicates that "unconstrained rivalry" includes non-nuclear but nonetheless military as well as economic and political conflict. Now, to pursue a policy of "unconstrained rivalry" would require the United States to act belligerently toward, and refuse to negotiate with, the Soviet Union. Such a policy would, as a rule, violate the principles of reason and civility on which the American regime is ultimately based. Such a policy is *not* being advocated here. But it is misleading (and either paternalistic or self-deprecating) for any Western statesman to characterize, as "unconstrained", the rivalry between a communist tyranny, and a liberal democracy—for the former is *intrinsically* unconstrained. Obscured is the fact that that tyranny, the Soviet Union, is an imperialistic and revolutionary power animated by the *unlimited* goal of a communist world, whereas that democracy, the United States, is a status quo power animated by the *limited* (but self-defeating) goal of "peaceful coexistence". Indeed, so long as the United States believes in "détente" as signifying the end of the "cold war", it will lack the moral and psychological stamina even to preserve the status quo. (And during this period of détente" or "peaceful coexistence", have we preserved the status quo in Southeast Asia or in Africa or in the Middle East, to say nothing of Europe?) But again we see that the very notion of *peaceful* coexistence between the United States and the Soviet Union is a contradiction in terms, and precisely because of the "profound differences" and "values" of these two regimes, their fundamentally opposed "visions of the future".

Yet Dr. Kissinger insists on calling it a "paradox", saying, to repeat: "if peace is pursued to the exclusion of any other goal, other values will be compromised and perhaps lost; but if unconstrained rivalry leads to nuclear conflict, these values, along with everything else, will be destroyed in the resulting holocaust." This is not a paradox but an oversimplified statement of the alternatives confronting American foreign policy. If "peace" with the loss of "other values" means anything, it means peace with the loss of this country's defining characteristics, say its freedom or political independence. That is a policy of appeasement, of surrender to the Soviet Union. If *"unconstrained* rivalry" means anything today, it means, as Dr. Kissinger suggests, the policy of "liberation" and "massive retaliation" (which manifestly no one is calling for, now that Russia has achieved at least nuclear parity with the United States).[51] But "détente" is not the only alternative to such extremes, if in fact it constitutes an alternative in the first place. For it is demonstrable that the policy of *containment* avoided the extremes of appeasement and "unconstrained rivalry". Not only did containment refrain from calling for the liberation of the Soviet satellites, but it pursued a course of limited war to resist communist aggression in those areas deemed to be of strategic importance to the United States. Of course, the policy of containment—and as stated in the Introduction, I am proposing a policy of "selective containment"—will no doubt be regarded as a relic of the "cold war". Is it not the case, however, that every statement of the Administration affirming America's commitments to its various allies is an affirmation of the policy of containment? If those commitments mean anything, they mean that the United States will defend its allies against *communist* aggression. What, then, are the differences between the "*cold* war" and "détente" (for both are primarily intended to avoid nuclear war)?[52] The differences have already been anticipated.

—During the "cold war" the United States possessed overall military superiority vis-à-vis the Soviet Union. We have seen that the military balance has been reversed during "détente". During the "cold war" the United States had very little trade with Russia.[53]   Under "détente", or since the presidency of Richard Nixon, there has been a dramatic relaxation of trade restrictions.[54] To mention only a few large-scale projects, American firms are now engaged in:

(1) The development of Russia's petroleum and natural gas resources, including transmission and distribution systems;

(2) The construction of mass production machinery for trucks and cars;

(3) Planning for the construction of huge, sophisticated airplane manufacturing complexes; and, most significantly,

(4) The sale of advanced computers which of course can be used for the design of nuclear weapons and guided missile systems.[55]

These developments are being facilitated by loans granted by the Export-Import Bank. The Eximbank, supported by taxpayer money, provided a loan of $180 million for the production of nitrogen fertilizer alone, a figure equal to more than half the Soviet Union's total exports to this country in 1974.[56] To be sure, Russia encourages the by no means realistic expectation of future shipments of petroleum and natural gas—the only commodities of consequence to the economic and political security of the United States. This is called "trade". It is also called economic "linkage", and is avowedly intended to make political rivals economically interdependent so as to create a "vested interest in mutual restraint".   But how the economic "linkage" just described will make Soviet Russia sufficiently dependent on the United States so as to restrain her imperialistic ambitions—demonstrated by her *offensive* military build up and other ventures to be described in a moment—must be another paradox of the esoteric policy of "détente".[57]* Exoterically, however, it appears very much like a desperate effort on the part of those who shape American foreign policy to buy a generation of peace from the Soviet Union.[58] Even a study uncritical of "détente" itself, a study undertaken by the Congressional Research Service of the Library of Congress, candidly admits that

---

*The belief that interlocking our respective economies will moderate Soviet political conduct is paradoxical. Based on the para-Marxist assumption regarding the primacy of economics over politics (see above, p. 51), it nonetheless betrays an unwillingness to take the Marxist character of Soviet imperialism seriously. Nor is this all. Contrary to the wishful thinking of many liberals and conservatives, interlocking East-West economies could weaken the Free World if the political and defense underpinning of its own economic structure lacks integrity and vigor. Marx-

The process of creating a "vested interest in mutual restraint" is likely to be a very gradual and protracted one. Moreover, future changes in Soviet foreign policy and the motivations of Soviet leaders in their conduct of diplomacy will not be easily discerned. The political benefits to the United States must by their nature be uncertain of fulfillment, especially in the short run. On the other hand, the economic benefits to the Soviet Union from improved commercial relations may be certain and significant, even in the short run. Thus, the risk of unfulfilled expectations appears greater for the United States than for the Soviet Union. More specifically, increased technology transfers to the Soviet Union may show only long-term benefits to the United States in the diplomatic and political area.[59]

The above study bears the date of June 10, 1973. Some four months later, in brazen violation of the "Basic Principles of Relations", the Soviet Union helped to foment the Middle East War of October 6, 1973. Not only did it know about the impending Arab attack on Israel at least four days before the war broke out (yet failed to warn the United States as required by the aforementioned principles), but the Russians (1) called upon all Arab countries to join Egypt and Syria in their war against Israel—this, on October 9 and 10 in messages sent by Brezhnev; (2) transported Moroccan troops into the conflict; (3) alerted its (then) seven airborne divisions for combat on the Egyptian and Syrian fronts (one division was flown to supposedly independent Yugoslavia); (4) dispatched to Egypt two brigades equipped with ground-to-ground Scud missiles reportedly armed with nuclear warheads; and (5) expressed the hope that the war would not interfere with Soviet-American "détente"—this, in a speech delivered in Moscow by Brezhnev on October 8, the day before his call for an Arab crusade against Israel.[60] Not to be outdone by Mr. Brezhnev's ardor for "détente", Secretary Kissinger held a press conference on October 12 in which he apologized, as it were, for Russia's role in the war, saying: "If you compare their conduct in this crisis to their conduct in 1967, one has to say that Soviet behavior has been less provocative, less incendiary, and less geared to military threats, than in the previous crisis."[61] Presumably, this statement is an example of what is called "co-operation" in contradistinction to what is called

---

ist regimes may be better able to sustain such "interdependence", without suffering ideological erosion, than non-Marxist regimes.

"confrontation" between the United States and the Soviet Union. It is, the public has been taught, the only rational alternative to "unconstrained rivalry" with Moscow. Of course, it is nothing but a policy of abject appeasement.

The semantic subversion of American mentality wrought by Soviet propaganda and unwittingly reinforced by American statesmen—Orwell called it "doublethink"—is indicative of the moral disarmament of the United States. When Dr. Kissinger informs the Senate Foreign Relations Committee and the public that "there will be no international stability unless *both* the Soviet Union and the United States conduct themselves with restraint and unless they use their enormous power for the benefit of mankind", he is unwittingly placing a communist tyranny which has enslaved millions of mankind on the same level as a liberal democracy which has liberated millions of mankind.[62] I need hardly add that the Secretary means well, as do countless others who share his views on "détente" and on American-Soviet relations. Nevertheless, while it is necessary to avoid chauvinism, such even-handedness or outward detachment—not uncommon among relativistically inclined political scientists and journalists—appears curious in an American Secretary of State. Not that Dr. Kissinger is a pronounced moral relativist. The question is whether the even-handedness evident in some of his most significant public pronouncements and public deeds is symptomatic of a foreign policy corrosive of conviction. Perhaps the explanation lies in the fact that so many men in public office today are fearful of being labelled moralists or dogmatists.[63] An earlier Kissinger knew better. Thus, in his book *The Necessity for Choice* published in 1961, and one of the finest works on American foreign policy, Professor Kissinger made the following observations:

> Too often the laudable tendency to see the other point of view is carried to the extreme of refusing to make any moral distinctions. In 1948 Henry Wallace professed to be able to discern no difference between the policies of the West and those of the U.S.S.R.—if anything, he was much more charitable towards the latter. And this attitude survives to our day. . . . NATO is equated with the Warsaw Pact; the British landing in Egypt with the Soviet repression of Hungary; our overseas bases with the establishment of a satellite orbit in Eastern Europe. . . .

Some of these reactions express the understandable fear that to admit claims to superior moral values would lead to the demand for a crusade and this to nuclear war—an attitude not dissimilar to that of many serious people towards Hitler in the 1930's. . . .[As] a British Labour leader said in 1937, "Any attempt to separate the sheep from the goats and to have the world divided into two or more camps based on ideological grounds would be absolutely fatal to the future welfare of mankind."[64]

Needless to say, this attempt to de-ideologize international relations, as Professor Kissinger understood in 1961, led directly to the outbreak of the Second World War. But surely the foreign policy suggested by that British Labour leader in 1937 vis-à-vis Nazi Germany is perilously close to that of "détente", the foreign policy of the United States vis-à-vis the Soviet Union.[65] Indeed, to clinch the point, in the sequel to the above passage, Professor Kissinger goes on to say:

After German troops reoccupied the Rhineland in 1936 Arthur Henderson said:

Herr Hitler's statement [offering to negotiate] ought to be taken at face value. Herr Hitler made a statement sinning with one hand but holding out the olive branch with the other, which ought to be taken at face value. They may prove to be the most important gestures yet made. . . . It is idle to say these statements were insincere. . . . The issue is peace and not defense.[66]

Is it not a paradox that Secretary Brezhnev should, during the Middle East War of 1973, call for an Arab jehad against Israel while expressing the hope that the war would not interfere with Soviet-American "détente"?—again "sinning with one hand but holding out the olive branch with the other"![67] And is it not a paradox that Secretary Kissinger should forget or renounce the teachings of Professor Kissinger, that he should close his eyes to the sins of Mr. Brezhnev, preferring to see only that nebulous olive branch called "détente"?

Perhaps the best critic of Secretary Kissinger is Professor Kissinger.* As intimated earlier, the former seems to be reacting

---

*I am fully aware of the fact that a Secretary of State cannot speak with the same candor and independence as a professor of political science, that their "constituencies" differ as does their access to classified materials. The statesman must trim and tack from time to time if he is to promote the principles of his country. But my critique (which also takes account of the changed

against what the latter referred to as "the popular tendency to see complicated political problems in absolute terms of black or white and to identify policy with the amassing of military force." He continues:

> But in attacking such oversimplification, many critics run the risk of reducing all issues to a single shade of gray.
> Self-examination is of the essence in a democracy. But it is impossible to base policy on the deep distrust of the American people revealed by many current expositions. Some critics seem to feel that unless the United States is deprived of all conviction it is likely to prevent a settlement through belligerence or self-righteousness.[69]

Wise as these words are, they fail to indicate with sufficient precision the key problem of statesmanship in any popular form of govenment, the problem emphasized by Washington, that of educating the public. It may be true that the ordinary man tends to see "complicated political problems in absolute terms of black or white".[70] On the one hand, he lacks the sophistication of the better intellectuals, men capable of synthesizing diverse and competing points of view. On the other hand, he is not required to make the decisions of statesmen burdened with the problem of reconciling a welter of conflicting desires and interests. He is not a man of letters or a man of policy. Enough, or rather, it is almost enough, that he be a good judge of character. But now, assuming it to be true that ordinary men (so long as they have not been corrupted by cynicism or relativism), tend to see complex political problems in "absolute terms of black or white", for that very reason it is absolutely essential for the statesman to keep before the eyes of those ordinary men some absolute or unambiguous standards of what is right and honorable. Otherwise, as Washington so passionately warned, the public will be exposed to the divisive and demoralizing influences of internal faction and of external enemies. Lacking such standards, ordinary men—but not only ordinary men—will lose their political bearings. Either they will not support any arduous and long-range foreign policy, or that support will quickly erode.

Professor Kissinger tacitly admits the existence of "black" and "white" (without which he too would lose his political bearings), by taking to task those critics of an earlier American foreign policy who,

---

U.S.-Soviet military balance) places in question Dr. Kissinger's understanding of those principles, hence his capacity to advance America's historic purpose.[68] (See my discussion of the principle of self-determination, pp. 165-166, below, and compare Dr. Kissinger's application of that principle as indicated on p. 166n.

like relativists in general, reduce all issues to "a simple shade of gray". He once recognized that the failure to make moral distinctions can eventuate in the paralysis of a nation's will. And he wisely taught his readers that

> When skepticism becomes an end in itself, it can easily lead to stagnation or resignation. Where nothing is certain, nothing will be strongly maintained. This may make for ease of relations in a stable society. It does not provide the motivation for running risks. And without a willingness to sacrifice, no entrenched system [such as the Soviet Union's?] can possibly be altered. The phrase "give me liberty or give me death" may be trite. But liberty may indeed require a readiness to face death on its behalf.[71]

Skepticism or moral relativism can undermine a nation's freedom and independence. Once a people come to regard violent death as a greater evil than the loss of liberty—which it will do once its nation's foreign policy has become de-ideologized or de-moralized—it will sooner appease than resist its enemies. It was Professor Henry Kissinger who once wrote: ". . . against an opponent known to consider nuclear war as the worst evil, nuclear blackmail is an almost foolproof strategy."[72] All the more reason why Secretary of State Kissinger should not obscure (while acknowledging) the profound moral differences between the United States and the Soviet Union. Nor should he obscure the consequent need for a strong national defence by emphasizing, again and again, the danger and horror of nuclear holocaust. Fear can emasculate as well as moderate a people. It will emasculate them when statesmen fail to reinforce the nation's moral convictions or to strengthen men's sense of right and wrong. Again, "Where nothing is certain, nothing will be strongly maintained." All the more reason, therefore, why Secretary of State Kissinger should not forget the teachings of Professor Kissinger by saying:

> For many Americans, tensions and enmity in international relations are anomalies, the cause of which is attributed either to deliberate malice or misunderstanding. Malice is to be combatted by force, or at least isolation; misunderstanding is to be removed by the strenuous exercise of good will. Communist states on the other hand, regard tensions as inevitable by-products of a struggle between opposing social systems. . . . [73]

I shall return to the sequel in a moment; but to the extent that Dr. Kissinger is here suggesting that neither Americans in general nor Communists have an adequate understanding of the causes of international tensions and enmity, he is comporting himself not as a Secretary of State so much as a detached spectator or political theorist.[74]He is conveying to the American people the impression that to attribute malicious intentions to the Kremlin not only over-simplifies, but perhaps renders more difficult the conduct of foreign policy. Surprisingly, even Professor Kissinger succumbed to such obscurantism in *The Necessity for Choice*. Thus, forgetting that "Where nothing is certain, nothing will be strongly maintained", he writes: "It is not necessary to settle the question of the *real* intentions of the Communist leaders in the abstract."[75] Believing this, statesmen would not (and need not) deem it necessary to educate the public about the "*real* intentions" of the Politburo "in the abstract". But as men draw conclusions, such ideological silence will be construed to mean that the Soviet Union is a more or less conventional regime with which one can enjoy normal relations, a regime harboring no evil designs on the United States. That being the case, the public, and *therefore* the Congress, will wonder why it is necessary to support a strong military defense establishment. Defense against whom? they might well wonder.*

Nevertheless, we are given to believe by both Professor and Secretary of State Kissinger that American statesmen can pursue a rational and realistic foreign policy, concerning either diplomacy, or foreign trade, or military strategy without having or conveying a fairly clear idea about the "*real* intentions" of the Soviet Union. Suppose, then, as many now urge, that nations were to regard each other in morally neutral terms: aside from economics, say in terms of their military capabilities. In that case, allies such as Canada and Australia and, to a lesser extent, non-aligned nations such as Austria and Sweden, would have reason to arm themselves against the United

---

*Some of the questionable activities of the CIA and FBI (such as attempts to discredit individuals and groups opposed to American foreign policy) may be attributed to the failure of statesmen to educate the public about the methods and geopolitical objectives of the Soviet Union. It should nonetheless be understood that the need for covert intelligence operations is magnified by the closed and conspiratorial character of the Soviet system, and by the extremely delicate nature of international relations given the predominance of two nuclear superpowers with worldwide interests. On the other hand, covert intelligence is required the better to inform the people, without compromising sources, of Moscow's own clandestine and subversive activities throughout the world. (This means that the "people's right to know" itself demands a considerable degree of government secrecy. How to balance secrecy and candor is one of the key problems of statesmanship.)

States with the same alacrity as they might against Soviet Russia. Yet it is probably safe to say that these nations, in their most far-fetched contingency plans, do not contemplate any attack upon themselves by this country precisely because they have tacitly or otherwise "settle[d] the question of the *real* intentions of [American] leaders in the abstract", namely as being fundamentally benevolent. To be sure, communist leaders may so regard their own intentions toward the West (which they repeatedly say they will bring to its knees). But when the Soviet Union brutally crushes the Hungarian Revolution in 1956; installs intermediate range ballistic missiles in Cuba in 1962; amasses a Warsaw Pact army of 500,000 men to suppress the modicum of liberalization that had taken place in Czechoslovakia in 1968; systematically violates and abets the violation of the 1970 armistice in the Middle East as well as the 1973 armistice in Vietnam; provides massive military aid and transports Cuban troops in support of communist forces in Angola—in view of all or any part of this, the ordinary man, who admittedly tends to oversimplify political reality, is nonetheless entitled to conclude (*and ought not be discouraged from concluding*) that Soviet leaders harbor something less than benevolent intentions toward any nation seeking freedom or seeking to preserve its political independence. Indeed, because the ordinary man will not have truck with any person who has either harmed or betrayed him, he may even conclude that to disregard the consistent record of Soviet aggression and perfidy is the mark of a soft-headed fool whose end is near. But here again we behold the inability of statesmen to acknowledge the reality and enormity of evil.

Now, in the sequel to the last discussed passage, Secretary of State Kissinger goes on to say that, whereas "Most Americans perceive relations between states as either friendly or hostile, both defined in nearly absolute terms. Soviet foreign policy, by comparison, is conducted in a grey area heavily influenced by the Soviet conception of the balance of forces."[76] This suggests that Russian foreign policy is "relativistic". Bearing in mind, however, the irreconcilable contradiction which Soviet leaders see between Communism and Capitalism, it is clear that Russian foreign policy is relativistic only as concerns means or tactics in contradistinction to ends or strategic objectives. Those tactics, whatever their character, are informed by one clear-cut and absolute goal, world hegemony. Accordingly, Soviet leaders will deliberately relax as well as deliberately create international tensions. They will direct communist parties in other countries to collaborate as well as not to collaborate with bourgeois parties. Indeed, they will not only aid, but they will sacrifice communist parties as they did in pre-war Germany and, more recently, in Egypt, if that will bring them closer to their ultimate objective.[77]

Hence it is dangerous for Secretary of State Kissinger to say that "most Americans perceive relations between states as either friendly or hostile, both defined in absolute terms." Apart from the fact that this statement does little credit to the intelligence of the American people, it can only serve to obscure or trivialize the hostility of the Soviet Union toward the United States and thereby psychologically disarm the public. This done, it ought not surprise us if Dr. Kissinger should fail to win public support for a vigorous foreign policy, say to oppose Soviet expansion in Africa. Is this failure to be attributed to a decline in the will and determination of the American people, or is that decline to be attributed to a failure in American statesmanship?* The question, of course, is rhetorical. It has been answered by Professor Kissinger.

Today, more than ever before, it is crucial—but in an age of relativism incredibly difficult—for American statesmen to educate their countrymen, to affirm publicly and unambiguously, again and again, moral standards of right and wrong, of good and bad, of honorable and dishonorable. This is precisely what Winston Churchill understood to have been lacking in the decade preceding World War II. Yet it was in the present tense that he wrote in *The Gathering Storm* of "how the structure and habits of democratic states . . . lack those elements of persistence *and* conviction which alone can give security to humble masses; how . . . the counsels of prudence and restraint may become the prime agents of mortal dangers; how the middle course adopted from desires for safety and a quiet life lead direct to the bull's-eye of disaster."[78] This is the course of "détente". It is a course rooted in the lack of conviction wrought by relativism or skepticism. That lack of conviction might well be the epitaph of republics throughout history. But there remains another chapter to be written.

---

*It is intellectually and morally questionable for any statesman to say there is no alternative to "détente"—which requires him to collaborate with Communists in Moscow—and, at the same time, to warn non-Communists not to collaborate with Communists in Italy or in France. One cannot dignify a Brezhnev without making a Berlinguer or a Marchais appear more respectable.

CHAPTER 7

PHILOSOPHICAL INTERLUDE

If a great people does not believe that the truth is only to be found in itself alone (in itself alone and in it exclusively); if it does not believe that it alone is fit and destined to raise up and save all the rest by its truth, it would at once sink into being ethnographic material, and not a great people. A really great people can never accept a secondary part in the history of Humanity, nor even one of the first, but will have the first part. A nation which loses this belief ceases to be a nation. But there is only one truth, and therefore only a single one out of the nations can have the true God, even though other nations may have great gods of their own. Only one nation is 'God-bearing', that is the Russian people. . . .

—Dostoevski

May it [the Declaration of Independence] be to the world, what I believe it will be (to some part sooner, to others later, but finally to all), the signal of arousing men to burst the chains . . . [of] ignorance and superstition . . . and to assume the blessings . . . of self-government.

—Thomas Jefferson

It has been frequently remarked that it seems to have been reserved to the people of this country, by their conduct and example, to decide the important question, whether societies of men are really capable or not of establishing good government from reflection and choice, or whether they are forever destined to depend for their political constitutions on accident and force.

—Alexander Hamilton

What this means is that "détente" has itself promoted Marxism in Western Europe by obfuscating the tyranny and treachery of Marxist Russia. In the Spenglerian prognostications of Secretary Kissinger we behold a self-fulfilling prophecy. See below, p. 241, n. 56.

Pascal said that we know too little to be dogmatists and too much to be skeptics. This is why a republic, to survive, requires a "genial orthodoxy". Recurring to my work *On the Silence of the Declaration of Independence*: A genial orthodoxy recognizes that the universe is infinitely more subtle and comprehensive than the deliverances of our intellects. From this we learn modesty and magnanimity. On the other hand, a genial orthodoxy presupposes (as does science itself) that the universe is an intelligible whole—in the words of Whitehead, that "all things great and small are conceivable as exemplifications of general principles which reign throughout the natural order", that "the ultimate natures of things lie together in a harmony which excludes mere arbitrariness".[1] Thus understood, a genial orthodoxy instills a quiet but manly confidence in the power of reason to apprehend truths transcending the vicissitudes and diversities of time and place, truths of abiding and of universal significance. The statesmen of the Declaration of Independence referred to such truths as "Laws of Nature and of Nature's God". These laws are but recurring patterns of behaviors distinguishing things yet relating them to one another. Some of these laws or recurring patterns, it was said, distinguish human behavior from sub-human behavior, for which reason their apprehension is indispensable for a critical as well as constructive approach to the question of how men should live or of how societies should be governed. It is evident, however, that the recurring things never recur in exact detail. Accordingly, what are called laws of nature and, therefore, the question of how men should live, do not seem to admit of final and univocal articulation. Novelty upsets the definitive conclusions of reason. Yet novelty entails contrast, and contrast involves the unavoidable notion of better and worse. The notion of better and worse presupposes some standard, a standard of what is best—an ideal or perfection to be aimed at, but which mankind, fallible as well as mortal, can never fully achieve. These thoughts find exemplification in the seemingly paralogistic phraseology of the Preamble of the Constitution, "to form a more perfect Union".

There may be no final and univocal articulation of how societies should be governed, but it does not follow that all articulations are equally arbitrary, or that the political principles of one society are no more valid than those of another. Unfortunately, relativism emphasizes the diversities existing among mankind, while retreating various uniformities which distinguish the human from the sub-human into an omitted background. But even sheer diversity, which admittedly is as ineluctable as the *principium individuationis*, suggests that the political philosophy of American democracy is preferable to that of Soviet Communism; indeed, that the latter, unlike the former, logically entails a violation of nature, the principle of individuation. Furthermore, the very selective emphasis and self-corrective character of the finite intellect confirms the principle of individuality on the one hand, and suggests the freedom of the intellect on the other, all of which lends support to any liberal society. Finally, the standard for judging the merits of one society over another is implicit in the very notion of selectivity, namely, *comprehensiveness*. By this I mean that that society is the best which brings into mutual coördination and intensification the greatest range of human values, such that freedom dwells with virtue, equality with excellence, solidarity with privacy, wealth with beauty, the here and now with the eternal. Needless to say, American democracy, both in theory and in practice, falls far short of coördinating let alone of fully enjoying all of these values. And yet, it would be neither inaccurate nor immodest to maintain that, both in theory and practice, these values are more in evidence in American democracy than in the world of Communism. Surely the political or deliberative institutions of this country, especially as they may still foster, however feebly, such aristocratic values as civility, deference to merit, respect for custom but more for truth, and, withal, the political and intellectual independence that nurtures men's sense of what is right and honorable—all this contrasts strikingly with what we know to be the brutality, the vaunted egalitarianism, the contempt for custom, and the utter mendaciousness and servility of the Soviet political system.

To this catalogue of differences must be added the rule of law exemplified in the American Constitution. Rooted in the notion of the laws of nature, the rule of law suggests a rational order of things, imbuing mankind with the confidence that the future will resemble the past. (This, incidentally, is the presupposition of inductive logic and of scientific reasoning.) Like the laws of nature, the rule of law precludes sheer arbitrariness. In contradistinction to the "rule of men", the rule of law restrains or imposes limits on what government may or may not do. Hence the provision in the Constitution for independent courts of justice. As Hamilton points out in *Federalist* 78:

> The complete independence of the courts of justice [so lacking in the Soviet Union, I might interject] is peculiarly essential in a limited Constitution. By a limited Constitution, I understand one which contains certain specified exceptions to the legislative authority; such, for instance, as that it shall pass no bills of attainder, no *ex-post-facto* laws, and the like. Limitations of this kind can be preserved in practice no other way than through the medium of courts of justice, whose duty it must be to declare all acts contrary to the manifest tenor of the Constitution void.

But while the rule of law restrains government, it also empowers government, enabling it to fulfill its intended purposes. Thus Madison in *Federalist* 51:

> In framing a government which is to be administered by men over men, the great difficulty lies in this: you must first enable the government to control the governed; and in the next place oblige it to control itself. A dependence on the people is, no doubt, the primary control on the government; but experience has taught mankind the necessity of auxilliary precautions [such as the system of checks and balances, including the independent courts of justice mentioned by Hamilton].

While the rule of law simultaneously restrains and empowers government, it simultaneously restrains and empowers the governed: for the laws embody standards by which to judge and regulate the conduct of men in public as well as in private life. Moreover, because law is, in principle, the result of deliberation, involving the resolution of diverse opinions, passions, and interests (and not only of the living), it tends to be more impartial and more humane than most individuals. The rule of law manifests the quest for comprehensiveness and coherence descriptive of philosophy.

Finally, the rule of law imposes practical restraints on the philosophical intellect, but thereby renders the philosophical intellect *more* rational. In its contemplation of perfections, the philosophical intellect may slight the common experience that the ideal is limited by the real, the future by the past. To be sure, it is of first importance that the philosopher hold before us the vision of what is noble in thought and in conduct, to remind us of human perfection or of human greatness. But the degree to which a people can achieve any perfection will depend on a welter of circumstances: its own intellectual, moral, and material resources; its zest for novelty qualifiied by its customary ways of thinking and doing things. Reason itself, as Whitehead points out, is "the organ of emphasis upon novelty".[2] But the viability of any novel idea in the domain of politics (like the viability of any mutation in the domain of biology), will depend on its capacity to assimilate its environment, which includes the past immanent in the present. The rule of law, which requires that the future shall resemble the past, is not merely a burden imposed upon reason's innovations: it is their salvation. Needless to say, the rule of law (too frequently violated in the United States) is virtually non-existent in the Soviet Union. But so too is the evidence of philosophy.

Having sketched some of the principles of a political philosophy, elements of which will be found in the Declaration of Independence and in the American Constitution, a word is now in order about some of the similarities and differences between Communism and massified monopoly Capitalism, the more or less uncompetitive form of "private" enterprise existing today. First note that Communism and contemporary Capitalism share, in unequal degrees, various vices. Both produce an over-crowded, herdlike technological society destructive of privacy, individuality, and moral responsibility. Both promise to maximize consumption, which can only engender restless pursuit of material gratifications, life without meaning or purpose, and unrelieved boredom. Finally, both ravish nature, obliterating the distinction between town and country as well as the sense of beauty, of awe and solitude essential to any depth of meditation or of character. As for their differences, whereas monopoly Capitalism fosters avarice, the egalitarianism of Communism breeds what is worse, sociological envy. I say worse if only because sociological envy eventuates in *aristocide*, the suppression of genius.[3] And whereas private enterprise *per se* tends toward mutually obstructive diversity, Communism tends toward a stultifying uniformity. Admittedly, the extremes possess the virtue of reminding us of the need for individual freedom and spontaneity on the one hand, and some form of central coördination on the other. However, because there are exceedingly few wise and virtuous men in any society—the best and the brightest very seldom seek, let alone get elected to, political office—for this very reason, the centrifugal and anarchic tendencies of Capitalism are infinitely preferable to the centripetal and tyrannical tendencies of Communism. Lastly, in favor of contemporary Capitalism is this mixed blessing: In a mass society, with so few avenues to positions of architectonic political power, Capitalism provides men of imagination and ambition many opportunities to undertake great industrial and commercial projects having national and even international significance. Notwithstanding their grave abuses and depersonalizing tendencies, large corporations constitute an intermediate tier of power which serves to prevent political tyranny. Furthermore, thanks to the great accumulations of wealth made possible by Capitalism, many private colleges and universities have prospered and have sustained the traditions of intellectual freedom. The task is to develop an American foreign policy capable of preserving those traditions.

CHAPTER 8

BEYOND DETENTE:
TOWARD A POLITICS OF MAGNANIMITY

The American, by nature, is optimistic. He is experimental, an inventor and builder who builds when called upon to build greatly. Arouse his will to believe in himself, give him a great goal to believe in, and he will create the means to reach it. This trait of the American character is our greatest national asset. It is time once more that we rescue it from the sea of fat in which it has been drowning. It is time once more to get on with the business of being true to the work of a Choosing People—a people who voluntarily assume the burden and the glory of advancing mankind's best hopes.

—John F. Kennedy

With malice toward none; with charity for all; with firmness in the right, as God gives us to see the right, let us strive on to finish the work we are in; to bind up the nation's wounds; to care for him who shall have borne the battle, and for his widow, and his orphan—to do all which may achieve and cherish a just, and a lasting peace, among ourselves, and with all nations.

—Abraham Lincoln

I

The time has come to transcend a pseudo-détente, to construct a foreign policy rooted in truth, honor, and courage, a foreign policy that can tap the strengths and rally the loyalties of the American people. No policy can long be effective unless it springs from and gives

143

voice to a nation's originating principles—those great generalities which, even in their vagueness, unite diverse men and render them fellow-countrymen. What also needs to be voiced, however, are the silent presuppositions of the men who first uttered those formative principles; for their silent presuppositions provide the background of meaning which the founding generation took for granted, which history has progressively obscured, and of which the living must be reminded. And so, as Lincoln did more than four score and seven years ago, let us return to those statesmen of '76 who "brought forth on this continent, a new nation, conceived in liberty and dedicated to the proposition that all men are created equal." Never has this nation had greater need to rededicate itself to the principles embodied in the Declaration of Independence. Never has this nation had a more urgent need to recapture the revolutionary spirit of its founders. But what made that revolutionary spirit possible? To answer this question, we must recall and elaborate even further upon themes discussed in earlier chapters.

The Declaration of Independence is a call to arms in a cause fraught with the danger of violent death. Peaceful petitions for a redress of grievances having repeatedly failed, resort to force had become a moral imperative. Still, a "decent respect to the opinions of mankind" required that the statesmen of the Declaration justify what mankind or world opinion then deemed an act of treason, the Americans' refusal to obey the laws of parliament and king. For at that time, most men identified the legal with the just, holding the not unreasonable opinion that to be just is to be law-abiding. Inasmuch, however, as the One or the Few or the Many may pass laws in their own interest rather than in the interest of the common good, there will exist as many notions of justice as there are regimes or distinct forms of government. Mankind would thus be splintered into a multiplicity of distinct species, each with its own morality or way of life, and none would recognize any universal moral standard by which to judge whether one species' way of life was preferable to another's. Under such a relativistic dispensation tyranny would be as legitimate as democracy. Justice would consist in the will of the stronger. Might would make right.

And so, over against the sometimes arbitrary rule of men or the ever-changing and sometimes unequal laws of parliaments and kings, the statesmen of the Declaration appealed to the rational and immutable laws of nature and of nature's God—that universal moral law which constitutes mankind a single species and before which all men are equal in their unalienable rights to life, liberty, and the pursuit of happiness. Those rights are possessed solely by *human* beings. For in the hierarchy of nature, man is the only *meta*-physical animal, the only animal that can transcend the already determined, and this by virtue of his spontaneous yet self-critical power of reason and his self-assertive yet self-restraining sense of dignity. The very resort to revolution—but only after "repeated Petitions ha[d] been answered only by repeated injury"—affirms the moral primacy of reason or persuasion over force and violence. Meanwhile, the sense of dignity suggests the moral primacy of individuality over conformity. A tension thus appears between the particularism of individuality and the universalism of reason, the overcoming of which requires that "decent respect to the opinions of mankind" which springs from civility. It is this virtue that prompts diverse men to resolve their differences through candid discussion and compromise rather than through deception and violence. On the truth of these principles depends the enjoyment of genuine liberty and equality. Only in the wholehearted belief in the truth of those principles could the statesmen of the Declaration proclaim, "we mutually pledge to each other our Lives, our Fortunes and our sacred Honor."

Round that Declaration alone can the American people be rallied in the defense of republican government. From its principles must the statesman fashion an American foreign policy capable of generating the enthusiasm necessary to defend this country against the dedicated disciples of another revolutionary document, the disciples of the *Communist Manifesto*. Recalling, therefore, the discussion of Chapter 4, I shall now set forth, by means of a series of parallel statements, two "philosophical profiles" showing (1) that the leaders of the Soviet Union remain committed to the Marxist-Leninist goal of destroying the traditions of liberty and civility associated with republican government, and (2) that should the leaders of the United States minimize or obscure or fail to recognize and expose that deadly Soviet commitment, then certain principles of the Declaration, though valid in themselves, could render American statesmen sentimentally susceptible to various errors that I freely call, without hyperbole, fatal to Western Civilization. These Philosophical Profiles are primarily intended for the enlightened statesman who will know how to bring philosophy to bear on action, theory on practice.

PHILOSOPHICAL PROFILES

THE UNITED STATES

A. Immutable Laws of Nature:

1. Unity of human nature, meaning, mankind constitutes a single species subject to the same moral law (before which all men are equal in their rights to life, liberty, and the pursuit of happiness).

2. "Our" morality is deduced from that which distinguishes the human from the sub-human, not that which distinguishes one economic class from another.

3. The unity of human nature makes possible the pursuit of a common good (which is but another term for justice or morality) transcending class differences.

4. The purpose of negotiation is to reconcile differences or to reach lasting agreements among nations. Dangers:

(a) American tendency to make gratuitous concessions, sometimes as a gesture of good will.[1]

(b) Tendency to rely on various "agreements in principle" which, because of their generality, may be violated with impunity by adversary.[2]

(c) Tendency to abide by agreements even after violated by adversary.[3]

(d) Tendency to "mirror image", i.e., to believe that one's adversary is similarly motivated or shares similar ends.[4]

"Are we to regard the communist countries as more or less normal states with whom we can have more or less normal relations, or are we to regard them indiscriminately as purveyors of an evil ideology with whom we can never reconcile [sic]?"

—J. William Fulbright[5]

THE SOVIET UNION

A. Dialectical Laws of History:

1. Men's "nature", hence morality, changes in proportion to changes in their economic modes of production (which, because of the penury of nature, entails the division of labor and the oppression of one class by another).

2. "Our morality is deduced from the class struggle of the proletariat. . . . Communist morality is the morality which serves this struggle."

—V.I. Lenin[6]

3. The laws of historical (or economic) development issue in irreconcilable class antagonisms which can only be overcome by the abolition of all class distinctions.

4. "It would be a great mistake to believe that a peaceful agreement about concessions is a peaceful agreement with capitalists. This agreement is equivalent to war."

—V.I. Lenin[7]

"The CPSU has always held, and now holds, that the class struggle between the two systems . . . will continue. That is to be expected since the world outlook and the class aims of socialism and capitalism are opposite and irreconcilable."

—Leonid Brezhnev[8]

"[W]e are aware that success in . . . the struggle for peaceful coexistence in no way implies the possibility of relaxing the ideological struggle. On the contrary, we must be prepared for this struggle to be intensified."

—Leonid Brezhnev[9]

THE UNITED STATES	THE SOVIET UNION

"The Soviets negotiate . . . to separate allies, or to undermine governments with their people, or to win over uncommitted peoples. Or it may be . . . to bring a sense of relaxation, goodwill and security, before some energetic offensive."

—Dean Acheson[10]

B. The Primacy of Reason or Persuasion:

1. Disposed to resolve conflicts peacefully by the methods of international law and diplomacy, employing force only as a last resort. Dangers:

(a) Tendency to overestimate the efficacy of diplomacy—of speech or reason—for the resolution of international conflict. Converse tendency to underestimate the importance of force in the conduct of foreign policy.[11]

(b) Tendency to attribute the causes of international conflict to a lack of mutual understanding among nations which in turn is supposed to beget mutual fear and suspicion.[12]

"Perhaps the single word above all others that expresses America's need is 'empathy', which Webster defines as the 'imaginative projection of one's own consciousness into another being.' "

—J. William Fulbright[13]

2. Disposed to regard reason (or the intellect) as capable of transcending material forces or interests. Dangers:

(a) Tendency to appeal to reason regardless of the character and past behavior of one's adversary.

(b) Tendency to minimize or dismiss as irrelevant those speeches and writings of one's enemies which, by their expression of implacable

B. The Primacy of Force and of "Objective" Material Factors:

1. "The dictatorship of the proletariat means a persistent struggle —bloody and bloodless, violent and peaceful, military and economic, educational and administrative— against the forces and traditions of the old society. The force of habit in millions and tens of millions is a most formidable force."

—V.I. Lenin[14]

"Imperialism will not collapse by itself, automatically. . . . Active and determined action by all the revolutionary forces is needed to overthrow it. . . . [We must] be prepared for . . . the use of any forms of struggle—peaceful and non-peaceful, legal and illegal."

—Leonid Brezhnev[15]

"Not only do we in the GRU [Soviet military intelligence] conduct military, political, economic, and scientific intelligence, but we are engaged in propaganda activities, provocations, blackmailing, terroristic acts, and sabotage."

—Oleg Penkovskiy[16]

2. "During my talks . . . with President Eisenhower, it was evident that he, like Secretary of State Herter, could not pronounce the words 'peaceful coexistence.' However, thanks to our stubborn efforts to strengthen the forces of socialism . . . we have taught them. The U.S. statesmen have begun

hostility toward the United States, appear contrary to reason. (To many men of good will, unrelenting malevolence is incomprehensible.)

"[Statements about Communist aggressiveness and brutality] impute to Soviet leaders a total inhumanity not plausible in nature and out of accord with those humane ideals which we must recognize as lying—together with other elements less admirable in the eyes of some of us—at the origins of European Marxism. I should like, therefore, to end those observations with a plea for something resembling *a new act of faith in the ultimate humanity and sobriety of the people on the other side. . . .*"

—George F. Kennan[17]

"*In addition to* the toll of two world wars, we have lost . . . as a result of internal political and economic 'class' extermination alone—66 (sixty-six) million people!!! . . . [Marxist] ideology bears the entire responsibility for all the blood that has been shed."

—Alexander Solzhenitsyn[18]

C. The Primacy of the Individual:
1. The dignity of the individual resides in the freedom or power of his intellect to apprehend truths transcending the opinions and interests of his class or society. *Abiding by the dictates of those truths, hence truthfulness, is a matter of self-respect or personal honor.* Dangers:

(a) Tendency to rely excessively on personal diplomacy.

(b) Tendency to reveal more than is necessary or prudent when negotiating with adversary.[19]

to pronounce the words 'peaceful coexistence' quite well. What happened? What changed? The words remained the same and so did their meaning. What did change was the balance of power in the international arena. . . ."

—Nikita Khrushchev[20]

"Underlying these changes [which have produced Soviet-American *détente*] are certain stable factors of an objective nature. First, and the most important, . . . is the fact that the relation of the world forces are steadily changing in favor of socialism. . . . The growth of the Soviet Union's military might put an end to any hopes that the United States might reach military supremacy sufficient to allow it to achieve its aims with the use of, or threats of, military force. . . . [*Détente* is merely] a *modus vivendi* between . . . two social systems engaged in a historically inevitable struggle which will and must continue."

—G. Arbatov[21]
Soviet Academy of Sciences (1973)

"They [the Russi.n people] believe in their own national strength, which they demand that other peoples fear, and they are guided by a recognition of the strength of their own regime, of which they themselves are afraid."

—Andrei Amalrik[22]

C. The Primacy of Class or Society:
1. "[Because consciousness is a social product], my standpoint . . . can less than any other make the individual responsible for relations whose creature he socially remains."

—Karl Marx[23]

"Diplomacy . . . [requires that we] study the underlying processes in a particular country . . . including the correlation of forces among various political groups, between struggling classes, etc."

—Valerian A. Zorin[24]

THE UNITED STATES	THE SOVIET UNION

(c) Tendency to err on the side of trust than on the side of suspicion.

"Khrushchev's is a government of adventurers. They are demagogues and liars, covering themselves with the banner of the struggle for peace. Khrushchev . . . is quite prepared to begin a war, if circumstances turn favorably to him."

"I always wonder: Why does the West trust Khrushchev? It is difficult to understand. We in the GRU . . . laugh: What fools, they believed us again!"

—Oleg Penkovskiy[25]

"In these words we find . . . an untruth . . . which has, more than anything else, ruined revolutions . . . a foolish trustfulness . . . a philistine belief in good intentions. . . . This petty-bourgeoise trustfulness is the root of the evil in our revolution."

—V.I. Lenin[26]

"We reject any morality based on extra-human and extra-class concepts."

—V.I. Lenin[27]

"[In] the first postrevolutionary decade . . . people still had their pride, and many of them quite failed to comprehend that morality is a relative thing, having only a class meaning, and they dared to reject the employment offered them [namely, to be informers], and they were all punished without mercy."

—Alexander Solzhenitsyn[28]

"It is hard to tell whether, aside from those purely material criteria [i.e., 'the desire for material well-being . . . and the instinct for self-preservation'], the bulk of our people possess any kind of moral criteria—such as 'honorable' and 'dishonorable', 'good' and 'bad', 'right' and 'wrong', the supposedly eternal principles which function as inhibiting and guiding factors when the mechanism of social constraint begins to fall apart and man is left to his own devices."

—Andrei Amalrik[29]

II

As intimated in previous chapters, the enlightened statesman to whom this work is addressed will have to make greater demands on the intelligence and on the moral qualities of the American people than has ever been made by any President—certainly since Lincoln. He will have to take the American people into his confidence lest they be misinformed, distracted, and divided by the highly selective and fragmented deliverances of the news media (whose ideological bias seems to consist in saying little bad about our enemies and little good about ourselves and about our less-than-perfect allies in Asia and elsewhere). Too long has the character of the American people been insulted by small-souled politicians "who flatter their prejudices to betray their interests". And yet, who are the educators of our politicians? If there has been a decline in statesmanship—I mean in political wisdom—may there not also have been a decline in higher education? Wisdom requires breadth, comprehensiveness. But our universities, with their increasing fragmentation into autonomous departments, have long been preoccupied with the training of specialists, a preoccupation, says Whitehead, which tends to trivialize the teaching profession.[30] Consider the trivialization and degradation of thought and politics that result from the reduction of the complex interdependence and different intensities of men's opinions to "Yeses" and "Noes" on the one hand, and to subrational forces on the other. These insulting (and self-refuting) assaults on the intellect are as much a reflection on higher education as on the ordinary man. If the level of politics has declined, rather than blame the ordinary man, why not examine the self-fulfilling prophecies of behaviorally-oriented social scientists from whom politicians learn how to appeal to men's passions and material interests rather than to their intellects? The truth is, however, that ordinary men cannot be well understood by ordinary behaviorists. No, it takes a rare spirit to sound the depths of any man, whose dreams and silent aspirations are invisible and inaudible to empiricists preoccupied with the "observable". Who, indeed, makes any demands on the ordinary man? Who, then, can honestly say what intellectual and moral demands the ordinary man is capable of responding to, should he be addressed by a statesman possessed of wisdom and courage? What this country desperately needs is a President with magnanimity enough to serve the people at the risk of their displeasure—which may consist in little more than the displeasure of a vocal minority.

Against powerful countervailing forces and tendencies, the statesman will have to restore the moral and political self-confidence of the American people. And he will have to do this without undermining modesty and moderation. Slowly, perhaps painfully slowly, he will have to *inform* the American people's natural aversion to communist dogma, summarizing its basic principles and illustrating them with historical facts revealing the various elements of the Kremlin's octangular strategy of protracted war—but all this while drawing comparisons with the principles of the Declaration of Independence, especially its civility and magnanimity, its sense of what is right and honorable, its manly synthesis of moderation and boldness. Accordingly, he should remind us of the obvious fact of human imperfection existing at all times and in all places. Precisely because no one is perfect or all-wise and wholly virtuous, the Declaration does not proclaim that men have a right to happiness but only to the *pursuit* of happiness.[31] Yet, the mere recognition of human imperfection suggests that we are not entirely ignorant or without any sense of what is base and what is noble. We at least know that we are not mere animals, hence, that it is wrong to act like an animal or to be treated like one. We at least know that what some men understand to be happiness, or how they pursue it, is vile or brutal and rightly arouses contempt or indignation; whereas the understanding of happiness or the way of life of a Socrates or Jesus evokes admiration and reverence. Of course, most people, most of the time, live between moral extremes, and because there are infinite gradations between the good and the bad, we make distinctions between better and worse, preferring to associate with the former than with the latter. Lacking complete self-sufficiency, however, we are sometimes compelled to associate with persons whose character does not command our approval. Needless to say, we prefer these relationships to be as brief, as inconspicuous as possible lest we convey the erroneous and pernicious impression that our association with such persons implies approval of their character or of any of their acts.

And thus it is among governments: there are gradations between the best and the worst.[32] Paraphrasing Churchill, constitutional democracy may not be the best form of government, but looking around the world, there are none better. Today even the worst regimes like to dignify themselves with the appellation of "people's democracy". We know better. The people of such regimes do not enjoy liberty or even genuine equality. Lacking independent courts of justice, the individual can be denied his unalienable rights to life, liberty, and the pursuit of happiness without due process of law, and by men who are not themselves subject to legal restraints and who cannot be made accountable to the people through any truly elective process. As one of many examples of semantic subversion, "people's democracies" are nothing but tyrannies and, from time to time, ought to be publicly described as such lest we degrade the name and meaning of democracy. But just as one democracy is better than other democracies, so one tyranny is worse than other tyrannies. No less than between individuals, so between nations, distinctions of better and worse are indispensable. In the absence of such moral distinctions, we should have to treat all nations alike, friends and foes, governments based on consent and governments based on coercion. But just as necessity may require us to associate for a time with persons we do not wholly approve of, so it is with nations. Lacking omnipotence, a democracy, under extreme circumstances, may have to ally itself temporarily even with a brutal tyranny. Thus, during the Second World War the United States was allied with the Soviet Union against the then more dangerous tyranny of National Socialism, i.e., of Nazi Germany. (It does seem, however, that the U.S. failed to distinguish between a strictly short-run policy of cooperation with Russia against a common foe and everlasting friendship.) And so, by this circuitous route we return to the problem raised in Chapter 5, the problem of diplomatically recognizing a regime utterly opposed to one's own.

At that time it was said that the private citizen, unless otherwise instructed, would tend (and rightly tend) to regard official recognition of any government as an approval of its form. In the case of American recognition of the Soviet Union, two major consequences followed: (1) recogniton dignified and thereby increased the domestic and international prestige of a Marxist regime, and (2) recognition conveyed to the American people the erroneous and, in the long run, the dangerous impression that that regime harbored no hostile intentions toward the United States. The first of these two consequences could not possibly have been wholly avoided if only because the mere act of recognition (following upon, and in contradistinction to, a policy of non-recognition) cannot but render the recognized government as something other than contemptible. Suppose, however, that the recognition decision of 1933 were made under contemporary international circumstances. This being the case, then the second of the two consequences in question could be avoided simply by informing the public of the Marxist or imperialistic objectives of the Soviet Union exemplified in Berlin and Korea under Stalin; in Egypt and Cuba under Khrushchev; and in Vietnam and Africa under Brezhnev. And to forestall various objections, it would be necessary to show that recognition would not only promote either the immediate or the long-range interests of the United States, but also that the good of this country, by virtue of the universal validity of its political principles, embraces the good of mankind. That good, recall from the discussion of the Farewell Address and the Monroe Doctrine, consists in the maintenance of an international environment conducive to the preservation and progress of republican government, an environment in which humanity enjoys more liberty than less liberty, more civility than less civility. If, in the long run, recognition of a tyranny would advance the very principles of the Declaration of Independence, then recognition would be a moral act. But now the statesman will have to be quite specific if his justification for recognizing a tyranny is to carry conviction and be more or less impervious to instant and ill-informed criticism. For the purpose of illustration, let us go back a few years when a President of the United States could have recognized Communist China. Rather than becloud the issue and befuddle the American people by indulging in sweeping homilies about the glories of a repulsive tyranny, a farsighted President could have justified recognition on the grounds that, given China's rivalry with the Soviet Union for international supremacy, diplomatic relations with both regimes could advance the cause of liberty and civility by enabling the United States and its allies to maintain a world system of checks and balances having the following elements and consequences:[33]

(1) Russia would further have to divide its military forces between Eastern Europe and the Sino-Soviet border, relieving pressure on NATO and thereby facilitating some reduction in the defense budgets of the United States and its allies. (Such reductions would probably be reflected in lower taxes and/or increased expenditures for education and social welfare.)

(2) Given increasing Soviet deployments, Communist China, though strengthened by "détente" with the U.S., could not reduce its northern border forces. Sino-American "détente" could thus relieve pressure on such nations as Japan, Taiwan, and India.

(3) The diversion of Soviet forces would make it more rather than less difficult for Russia to fuel tensions in the Middle East.

(4) The foreign policies of various nations would be less rather than more dependent on Moscow and Peking.

Now, the only way the United States can sustain a system of checks and balances between Russia and Communist China is by maintaining sufficient military strength to respond to the USSR on a second front in Europe—something Peking fully appreciates. Suppose, however, that the United States, on pseudo-moralistic grounds, had refused to recognize Communist China? The effect would be to expose Peking to Russian blackmail. Rather than wait for the Soviets to achieve overwhelming military superiority, the Chinese might well seek a limited détente with Moscow. This would involve certain mutual understandings having the following consequences:

(1) Russia could redeploy a good part of its forty-five or so divisions now on the Sino-Soviet border and thereby exert more political and diplomatic pressure on Western Europe. Reluctant to counter this pressure by increasing their military budgets, some members of NATO might seek to appease Russia (a) by extending credits and (b) by pursuing various policies uncoördinated with those of the United States and in conflict with the purpose of the Western Alliance. Indeed, Italy and perhaps even France might succumb to their already powerful communist parties (today, an eventuality that would be accelerated should Spain, following Portugal, shift significantly toward the left). On the other hand, an increasing Soviet threat might lead to an increase in NATO defense budgets, meaning more taxes and less spending for various welfare programs.

(2) Communist China would be more rather than less free to extend its influence throughout Southeast Asia and the South Pacific, including the Philippines which would be more exposed to externally-supported Huk subversion.

(3) Japan would loosen its ties with the United States and, while appeasing Peking, would seek an alliance with the Soviet Union.* (Moscow would not want Japan's industrial capacity and technology to serve Peking's imperialistic ambitions.) Japan's only alternative would be to develop its own nuclear deterrent.

(4) The Soviet Union would now be in a better position to play a commanding role in the Eastern Mediterranean and in the Middle East, the control of which would bring Europe and Japan to their knees.[34]

In short, failing to exploit Sino-Soviet rivalry by refusing to recognize Peking could lead to Soviet domination of two of the three most highly industrialized centers of the world, along with the energy resources of the Persian Gulf. Needless to say, such an outcome

---

*The 1976 Sino-Japanese friendship agreement proves the point.

would not be conducive to the survival of *homo rationalis et civilis*. It would mean the political isolation of the United States and render this country subject to economic and nuclear blackmail masterminded by the Soviet Union. Non-recognition of Red China, far from being a moral act, would doom morality.[35]

Such is the candor required if the statesman would seriously and intelligently seek to consolidate public support for a comprehensive, long-range, and effective foreign policy. But even this degree of candor does not go far enough. To sustain support for a comprehensive and long-range foreign policy, the statesman will have to present the American people with a brief course on geopolitics.

Imagine a President of the United States devoting his Annual State of the World Message to the task of explaining American foreign policy. He might begin as follows:

"The central strategic objective of American foreign policy is and has always been the prevention of a direct attack upon the United States.[36] Thus far in this century America has been most fortunate: We have not been compelled to fight on our own homeland. Instead, we have fought on or close to the territory of our enemies. And since the United States has no territorial ambitions, this means that all our wars have initially been defensive wars. Thus, in World War I and again in World War II, we fought not only to save our allies from oppression, but to prevent Imperial Germany and later Nazi Germany from overrunning Europe and gaining control of the Middle East and North Africa, from whence they could and would have threatened the Western hemisphere. And we fought against Japanese imperialism for related reasons. Again, the Korean war was not simply a war against Communism; it was a war against communist imperialism. To illustrate part of the spectrum of our geopolitical concerns: much as we deplore Communism in Albania, its alliance with China rather. than with Russia renders it strategically isolated, such that Albania is not a serious threat or cause of great concern to us or to our European allies.* In contrast, like the Japanese, we are very much concerned about Communism in

---

*If Albania were a Soviet satellite, Russia could establish naval bases on the Mediterranean, further undermining NATO's southern flank, to say nothing of the Middle East.

North Korea in view of that regime's geopolitical relationship with Moscow and Peking. If the Korean peninsula were united under Communism—and this was Russia's objective in 1950—then Japan would be in the gravest danger, as would the Philippines. Certainly, the United States does not want its last defensive outpost in the Pacific to be our own state of Hawaii.

"But suppose Russia were to achieve political primacy in the Middle East, as she has been attempting to do for more than two decades. The Soviet Union would then have control over Arab oil and over those countries whose economic survival is almost entirely dependent on that source of energy. This means that Moscow would have effective political control over Western Europe's great industrial power as well as Japan's. It means that the United States, whose economy is not only linked with Western Europe and Japan, but increasingly dependent on Arab oil, would be subject to economic blackmail. Sooner or later various countries in Latin America would shift toward or come under the influence of the Soviet Union. The Western hemisphere would thus be exposed to communist imperialism on the one hand, while the United States would be politically isolated on the other. It was precisely to prevent such a disaster from occurring that this country entered into alliances with Western Europe,[37] Japan, South Korea, Taiwan, the Philippines, Australia and New Zealand. All these are defensive alliances intended to prevent communist aggression. Those alliances not only serve the interests of our allies and protect their liberty from communist tyranny, but they enable us to fight against communist imperialism on or close to the enemy's homeland rather than on or close to our own.

"This anti-imperialist policy goes back to the founding of the Republic. In fact, 'American foreign policy after the Revolution was aimed at disengaging European powers from North America, not alone to permit American expansion but to keep the continent from becoming Europe's battlefield.'[38] The very phrase in the Preamble of the American Constitution, 'to form a more perfect Union', reflects the desire of the founding fathers to guard against the imperialistic ambitions of such absolute monarchies as France and Spain. The founders understood that only if the American people were politically united could their government be vigorous

156

enough to prevent those imperialistic regimes from extending their influence in North America, involving us in their rivalries with each other and with Great Britain.[39] The same policy of excluding any imperialistic power from the Western hemisphere is most forcefully stated in the Monroe Doctrine. When President Monroe declared in 1823 'that the American continents, by the free and independent condition which they have assumed and maintained, are henceforth not to be considered as subjects for future colonization of any European powers', he went on to explain by pointing out that 'the political system of [those European] powers is essentially different from that of America', for which reason 'we should consider any attempt on their part to extend their system to any portion of this hemisphere as dangerous to our peace and safety.' The rationale of the Monroe Doctrine (and of American foreign policy) is this: A republic, or any nation seeking to devolop a parliamentary system of government, cannot by itself survive or succeed unless surrounded by other republics, that is, by governments based on the consent of the governed. It was well understood that if any aggressive, imperialistic regime were to gain a foothold in Latin America, the peaceful development of this country would be thwarted. Our wealth and territory would become the object of dynastic greed or of some despot's lust for power. To resist aggression, the United States would have had to become an armed camp. Can government by the consent of the governed survive or succeed with huge standing armies? Could we enjoy freedom of speech and press to the extent we do today if Latin America, including Mexico, had been subject to the imperialistic ambitions of European despotism? Could we enjoy the blessings of liberty if Latin America, including Mexico, were to succumb to communist imperialism?

"Of course, there is no immediately obvious connection between what happens in Africa or in the Middle East or in Asia and the security of the United States. The loss of Indochina does not appear as a clear threat to this country. But every threat will appear remote or ambiguous the further removed it is from our own territory or the earlier we attempt to meet it. It was no comfort to Britain, let alone to Poland, when, in September of 1939, the threat from Nazi Germany was at last unambiguous.[40] How does the loss of Indochina to Communism now appear to the people of the Philippines? How might the fall of the Philippines appear to Americans living in Hawaii? Consider:

> In 1939, Japan, engaged in the conquest of China, occupied the Island of Hainan in the Gulf of Tonkin. . . . Following the surrender of France in June, 1940, Japan forced France to accede to a Japanese share in and administration of Indochina as well as the right to use Saigon as an airbase. In the following year, Japan progressively occupied the remainder of Indochina and began to bring pressure on Thailand. On the 8th of December 1941, from bases at Saigon, Camranh Bay, and Hainan, attacks were launched by sea and air across the Gulf of Siam against the Siamese coast and . . . Malaya. With about 60,000 combat troops, supported by air and naval forces, the Japanese were able to seize Thailand, Malaya, and Singapore within 70 days. By the middle of 1942, the Japanese were in a position to make raids into the Bay of Bengal and to secure their hold on Burma, having conquered the Philippines and the Netherlands East Indies as well.[41]

"Would it be more difficult for Communist China to accomplish what Imperial Japan accomplished by force of arms in the 1940s? and if not China, then Hanoi supported by the Soviet Union? Surely either eventuality would endanger the security of the United States, hence the future of republican government."

*   *   *

Now, using a map of the globe, the President, during his State of the World Message, should show via television how different parts of the world are interrelated—ideologically, economically, and militarily. The geographic relationship of hostile, non-aligned, and friendly powers; the location of major industrial centers, energy sources, sea and air routes; the non-classified disposition of military forces—these and related matters can be made comprehensible to the great majority of the American people. It must and can be graphically shown (1) that America's political and economic security requires that we have alliances throughout the world, especially on both sides of the Eurasian land-mass and in the Western hemisphere; (2) how the loss of one ally, however distant from this country, may encourage enemy encroachments by exposing the flank of another ally (who might then feel compelled to change its political alignment), thereby undermining not the immediate, but the long-range security of the great industrial centers of freedom in Europe, in Japan, and in the United States; (3) that, unlike the Soviet Union, which is nearly self-sufficient in natural resources, the United States—the world's largest "island" nation—has become increasingly dependent on overseas sources of energy and raw materials, for which reason alone we require a most numerous and powerful navy for our political as well as economic survival;[42] (4) why the United States, because of its transcontinental power, must assume and fulfill the responsibility of political leadership of the Free World if Western but also Oriental civilization is to be preserved from the brutal and stultifying uniformity of Communism.

By enlightening the American people more or less in the manner suggested above, the statesman need *not* arouse uncontrollable passions. Again it must be emphasized that political-military vigor and decisiveness are perfectly compatible with moderation and civility, qualities which can be reinforced by appropriate references to the Declaration of Independence and Washington's Farewell Address. True, a little knowledge about geopolitics may be a dangerous thing. But nothing is more dangerous to a republic, especially in this age, than public ignorance. Only by taking the people into his confidence can the statesman win (and deserve) their confidence. Only then can he avoid the easily exploited and demoralizing "credibility gaps" which have long enfeebled American foreign policy.[43] Furthermore, by informing the people as suggested, it will make it infinitely more difficult for the enemy to divide them against their own government.[44] Meanwhile, the mass media would receive a long-needed education.* The intellectual fragmentation and spatio-temporal disconnectedness of news reporting could be significantly mitigated (I do not say entirely overcome given the essence of *news*) by the Annual State of the World Message supplemented by other televised addresses and

---

*Consider, in this connection, Orwell's opinion of the British press in 1944, which, like British intellectuals in general, he deemed "dishonestly uncritical of its [the Soviet Union's] policies"; "Nothing is more important in the world today than Anglo-Russian friendship and co-operation, and that will not be attained without plain speaking. The best way to come to an agreement with a foreign nation is *not* to refrain from criticising its policies. . . . At present, so slavish is the attitude of nearly the whole British press that ordinary people have little idea of what is happening, and may well be committed to policies which they will repudiate in five years' time." (Cited below, p. 224, n. 31.)

periodic press conferences explaining international developments and shifts in American foreign policy.

If it be objected that what I am here proposing will alarm our enemies or make them more belligerent, to this I answer: (1) both the rulers of the Soviet Union and of Communist China would learn nothing from our statesman's lecture on geopolitics that they did not know before; (2) but now, for the first time, the sovereign people of the United States would know what hitherto has, for the most part, been obscured or concealed from them; (3) both Moscow and Peking, realizing that they could no longer divide the American people (or our various alliances), would exercise greater caution and restraint, would be less inclined to foment civil war, indeed, would become more disposed to resolve differences through "negotiation rather than confrontation"; and (4) our enemies respect power, and nothing is more powerful than a free people united and confident in the justice of their cause.

No doubt innocents and enemies alike will or would respond to the geopolitical lecture of our enlightened statesman by crying out that the President is resurrecting the "cold war" and thereby setting in motion a train of events that can only lead to nuclear holocaust. Such hysterical as well as deliberate nonsense can be forestalled simply by being *publicly anticipated*. It can be pointed out that not only do the American people have a *right* to know what their own government understands to be true character and ultimate objectives of the Soviet Union and Communist China, but that the persistent anti-American propaganda of those communist tyrannies has never made this country more bellicose or less disposed to resolve international differences through peaceful negotiations. Besides, I am not proposing that American statesmen should vilify our enemies as our enemies vilify us. Occasional public statements by the President, unambiguously revealing the shifting tactics but undeviating long-range objectives of Moscow and Peking, will suffice. One object of such statements is to reinforce what Americans are for by reminding them of what they are against. One cannot be wholeheartedly for liberty without being wholeheartedly against tyranny. And it is a poor statesman or shallowpate who does not understand that men's negative passions are the allies of their positive passions. The statesmen of the Declaration of Independence understood this very well, which is why no less than half the document is devoted to American grievances against the King.[45] Consider, however, Hamilton's comparison of the American and French Revolutions: "Would to Heaven that we could discern in the Mirror of French affairs, the same humanity, the same decorum, the same gravity, the same order, the same dignity, the same solemnity, which distinguished the course of the American Revolution."[46] Is the American of today less than he was some two hundred years ago? Dare any statesman who would preserve this republic underestimate the character of his contemporaries? Before the unremitting foes of liberty, nothing is more dangerous than public apathy. What is wanting is genuine passion, which can only be sustained, as noted earlier, by ideas—ideas of right and wrong, of the honorable and dishonorable. Nothing is more deadly, therefore, than the soporific of "détente" and its deliberate cover-up of the Kremlin's nakedness.

With presidential lectures on geopolitics embodied in the Annual State of the World Message the American people would learn that their government is engaged in what hitherto has been known as "power-politics". But no longer will it be power-politics in the pejorative sense; for now the use of power will to a large extent be explained to the public and will be explicitly related to just and honorable ends. This is another reason why it is most important to remind the American people of their own War for Independence, when force was employed on behalf of Liberty. Liberty, it must be publicly understood, is not something that can be purchased on credit. It cannot long be enjoyed without sweat, blood, and tears. In this world of imperfect and even vicious men, to desist from using force in defense of liberty is to ensure the victory of the wicked. This is but to say that given human imperfection, coercion is an unavoidable part of political life. Power-politics is a hidden form of coercion. I am arguing not that there is too much power-politics, but that too much of it is hidden, indeed, so much as to poison the wells of liberty. Again, I am not arguing against secrecy *per se*, but rather against the self-defeating secrecy that corrodes public confidence in government, that excessive secrecy which springs from a lack of confidence in the character of the American people. In a profound sense, the character of the American people is all we have. It harbors more than politicians and behaviorists are bold enough to perceive. It has depths and hidden potentialities which elude opinion polls and empirical analysis.

Excessive government secrecy, however well-intentioned, not only disparages the private citizen; it betrays his trust, and so is dishonorable. Also, it represents a paternalistic derogation of the Declaration of Independence. The Declaration, we have seen, affirms the primacy of persuasion and truth over force and deception. By that affirmation the statesmen of the Declaration expressed their confidence in the good sense and sobriety of the American people, which qualities constitute the only justification for government by the consent of the governed. But the government envisioned by the Declaration is representative government, whose very essence involves public debate and discussion—say, rather, speech and speeches, in which men tacitly pledge, as the statesmen of the Declaration expressly pledged, their honor, meaning the truthfulness of what they have publicly a-vowed: and thus it must be if the consent of the governed is to have any rational and moral foundation. In short, political candor must be the rule if statesmen are to abide by the Declaration of Independence. On the other hand, inasmuch as truthfulness is perfectly compatible with thoughtlessness, mere candor, or candor in the absence of wisdom, is hardly sufficient. Indeed, mere candor may be doubly self-destructive: it may undermine confidentiality on the one hand, while forewarning the enemies of republican government on the other. Still, I emphasize that whereas secrecy and mendacity are the methods of tyrannies—for they prefer to manipulate public opinion—candor and veracity are the methods of republics, of regimes which prefer to enlighten public opinion. If, therefore, the United States is to survive as a republic, its statesmen must not embark on a course converging with the Soviet Union, a tyranny whose methods signify a blatant contempt for the ordinary man.

III

Perhaps more than many opinion-makers, the ordinary man is quite capable of understanding the rudiments of foreign policy in general and of power-politics in particular, and with considerably less sentimentalism and self-righteousness. Conflicts between labor and business may lack the complexity of the "cold war", but few workers, and fewer businessmen, were ever so naïve as to believe that their differences could be resolved simply by "mutual understanding". Yet many historically myopic humanists, more precisely, humanitarians, believe that conflicts among nations can be significantly mitigated by various cultural exchange programs. Leaving aside the refutation of this prejudice by the war between France and Germany in 1870, which broke out despite the cultural intimacy of those two nations, is it not obvious that we often dislike various individuals and groups the *more* we understand them and what they stand for? Common experience indicates that mutual understanding may beget mutual hatred as much as anything else—and no less among ordinary humanitarians than among ordinary men! Why should the result differ among nations unqualifiedly opposed to each other on the very question of how societies should be governed and for what ends or purposes?[47] The international euphoria which many decent men expect to issue from mutual understanding among nations would probably consist in the anaesthesia of mutual indifference. The truth is, however, that those who place so much faith in international understanding have very little understanding of the Soviet Union: against all the evidence, they dogmatically refuse to take seriously the enormous ambitions of those who rule the Soviet empire. Of course, wishful thinking springs eternal, especially among sentimentalists who believe that good will without power is sufficient to bring about international concord. The ordinary man knows better. His everyday experiences with his own fellow-citizens teach him a more or less healthy skepticism. At one time or another he has been taken for a "sucker". Hence he avoids doing business with scoundrels when he can, and he is wary of them when he cannot. Why, then, should he be incapable of understanding the rudiments of American foreign policy vis-à-vis the Soviet Union?

The myth has nevertheless been propagated that an avowedly anti-communist foreign policy would eventuate in a "moral" crusade impairing the flexibility required for the conduct of Soviet-American relations. Again the object of concern if not of contempt is the ordinary man who, it will be recalled, was said to see the complex problems of international politics in absolute terms of black and white. Yet the McCarthy-inspired anti-communism of the nineteen-fifties was an insignificant aberration in comparison with the campus-inspired anti-war movement, which is almost to say the anti-anticommunism, of the nineteen-sixties. And certainly that more recent phenomenon has had an infinitely more paralyzing effect on government than its pernicious predecessor and, in part, progenitor. Judging from the political conduct of the average intellectual during the past decade, it is to be doubted whether the average man is more susceptible to "moral" crusades, perhaps because he lacks the intellectual's conceit, ambition, and leisure. Left to himself, the average man will usually mind his own business, while the intellectual, for better and worse, will mind everyone else's. To be sure, if one tendency is not entirely a virtue, the other is not entirely a vice. Once again it appears, therefore, that the elements of foreign policy may more readily be explained in terms of the concrete experiences of the ordinary man than in terms of the abstract pretensions of the ordinary intellectual. Admittedly, the experiences of the ordinary man (not unlike those of many academics) may be narrow, but he is not soft and his vision can be broadened.

If only because ordinary men do not admire softness, the statesman must shun sentimentalism (but not solemnity) if he is to win public support for a principled foreign policy.[48] Accordingly, he must proclaim to the world that the United States is unalterably and wholeheartedly opposed to communist imperialism; that in our dealings with the Soviet Union we shall do nothing to increase its military-industrial power or to prolong its tyrannical grip on the Russian people or on the captive nations of Eastern Europe. This means that:

(1) The United States should not provide any technology, capital investments, or loans which could advance, directly or indirectly, the war-making power of the USSR.

(2) All trade with the Soviet Union should be on a *quid pro quo* basis. But trade must not facilitate Soviet arms shipments to nations hostile to the United States or to our allies. (On the other hand, East-West trade may be linked to agreements requiring mutual reduction of arms shipments to other nations.)

(3) The United States should insist that the size of our embassy and consular staffs in Russia be increased while their Russian counterparts in this country be decreased to the point of approximate

equivalence. (The object here is to reduce Soviet espionage.* As Penkovskiy has warned, "*the majority of the personnel in Soviet embassies abroad are KGB and GRU employees*".)[49]

(4) Soviet propaganda aimed against the United States should be publicly refuted, but not in a defensive manner. (Various proportions of seriousness, sarcasm, and scorn will do nicely.) To prevent semantic subversion, American statesmen should expose the communist use of such terms as "democracy", "socialism"[†], "imperialism", "wars of national liberation", and "self-determination". Such is its importance that the last calls for extended comment. As I have written in my work on the Declaration:

> . . . self-determination is not a principle to be acted upon solely at the establishment of a government and never thereafter. Men never have a right to act irrationally and unjustly. Let the electorate of any country vote unanimously in favor of a communist or fascist tyranny, that act would not only be irrational—for men cannot rationally divest themselves of the power to determine henceforth who shall be their rulers—but it would also be immoral.**

Approaching the problem from another perspective: At the end of World War II, it was reasonable and just to impose on Nazi Germany and Imperial Japan a republican form of government, the only form in which the principle of self-determination is meaningful and continuously operative. By means of freedom of speech and press, together with a multiparty system and periodic elections, the people of those two countries now possess, and have for some time exercised, the power to influence public policy and to change the very men responsible for the formulation and execution of public policy.

---

*According to the 1976 Report of the Senate Intelligence Committee (on American foreign intelligence operations), of the 1,079 Soviet officials on permanent assignment in the United States, 60 per cent are members of the KGB or GRU. Countless other Soviet visitors to the United States are engaged in intelligence work, including students attending American universities. The truth is that Soviet intelligence agents have penetrated the opinion-making organs of this country. See *Human Events*, May 8, 1976, pp. 3-4.

†Concerning socialism, statesmen might point out that Communists have perverted the term by transforming its meaning from the common ownership of the means of production to the centralized control of the means of production. And if it be objected that centralized control is but a means to the achievement of common ownership, it may be replied that six decades of Bolshevism confirm the experience of human history that no oligarchy voluntarily surrenders its power. Thus, far from being a genuinely revolutionary doctrine, Communism has taken on the reactionary character of Fascism.

**Said Lincoln: "[Judge Douglas] contends that whatever community wants slaves has a right to have them. So they have if it is not a wrong. But if it is a wrong, he cannot say any people have a right to do wrong." See Lincoln, *Works*, III, 315.

Such self-determination is not to be found among the peoples of Eastern Europe on whom the Soviet Union imposed Communist dictatorships in violation of the Yalta Agreement. The Soviets have gone even further. In the present era of legal realism and political relativism, where democratic statesmen fail to make lucid and educative distinctions between just and unjust forms of government [concerning which majority rule is not the ultimate standard, lest we abandon our Bill of Rights], Communist propaganda has been most effective in using the language of self-determination to thwart the development of this principle in the Third World. I have especially in mind Communist manipulation of so-called national liberation movements in . . . Asia and Africa. . . . But the same propaganda or obfuscation is employed by the Soviet-supported Palestine Liberation Organization (the PLO), a terrorist group which, in the name of self-determination, would, if permitted, establish a military dictatorship over the Palestinian people comparable to that of Syria.*

---

*When Secretary Kissinger virtually called for the overthrow of the white minority government of Rhodesia, he did so in terms of "majority rule", a principle he evidently deems inapplicable to the white dictatorships of Eastern Europe (see p. 1 above) or to the black dictatorships of Africa. Here, two related questions arise: First, would the elimination of the present regime in Rhodesia result in a government based on the consent of the governed? This is very unlikely, judging from the dictatorial character of the 44 nations included in the Organization of African Unity (the OAU). Second, would a black-ruled Rhodesia be friendly to the Free World? This too is extremely unlikely, considering the voting of the OAU in the United Nations. Such being the case, the overthrow of the existing government of Rhodesia would serve neither the true interests of the Rhodesian people, nor the true interests of the United States. I say it would not serve the interests of the people of Rhodesia because, whatever its faults—and these should not be minimized or left unrectified—the present regime is far more humane, enjoys more liberty and prosperity, and is more conducive to the *further extention* of civil rights, than its neighbor, black-ruled Mozambique. Nevertheless, Dr. Kissinger offered aid to that Marxist tyranny from which, during the first nine months of its existence, over 200,000 people, white and black, fled (and continue to flee), and where untold numbers of others, white, Asian, and mulattoes, have been subjected to police brutality and torture. (In this connection, compare Kissinger's appeal to majority rule for Rhodesia and Stephen Douglas' appeal to majority rule as the very principle on which the white settlers in the territories and the United States should determine whether or not to have slavery. See above, p. 6.) Rigorously applied to regions riven by racial/ethnic differences—think of India, Spain, Quebec, and Northern Ireland—the principle of majority rule promises racial/ethnic wars stretching off into the distant future. There is a paradox here. Majority rule presupposes the intrinsic equality of all men or the intrinsic unity of mankind. However, when applied to regimes rent by racial/ethnic animosity, it tends, no less than minority rule, to eventuate in the practical denial of that equality, hence in the fratricidal fragmentation of mankind. This is but to admit that majorities can be as unjust as minorities, which is the fundamental reason why the founding fathers established a bicameral legislature wherein the Senate, unlike the House, was not, and, in the national perspective, is not based on the principle of majority rule. The founders did not harbor a majoritarian morality, one equivalent to the plebeian and species-splintering morality of Karl Marx. See above, pp. 21, 71-72.

Now, because Dr. Kissinger would like to see black rule in Rhodesia, it does not follow that he regards morality as colored, or that he deems the rule of numerical majorities the ultimate

(I say *military* dictatorship because Islam—the "Army of the Faithful"—has ever had a militaristic ethos. This is why, in Arab societies, military power is equivalent to political legitimacy, and why military leaders have had little difficulty in establishing their authority. Hence, what is called Arab nationalism—and this applies to "wars of national liberation" in Asia and Africa—ought not be confused with the American Revolution. The regimes established as a result of these twentieth-century movements are in almost all instances in fundamental conflict with the principles of the Declaration of Independence. Any attempt, therefore, to justify such movements in terms of the principle of self-determination is philosophically misleading and politically dangerous, if not fatal.)

(5) Soviet violations of international agreements such as the 1969 "International Convention on the Elimination of All Forms of Racial Discrimination" should be exposed and condemned.[50] At one time the proper course would have been to take the issue to the United Nations General Assembly where the Soviet Union could be placed publicly on the defensive. Unfortunately, that body is now dominated by the Soviet-manipulated Afro-Asian bloc which has rendered the United Nations Charter a solemn mockery and the organization itself a positive hindrance to the development of an international environment conducive to liberty and civility.[51] Still, if only to educate public opinion and provide moral leadership, our ambassador to the United Nations should, on appropriate occasions, compare the political acts (and even the forms) of certain UN members—including Marxist Russia—with the principles of the Charter.

(6) In response to any massive and brutal repression of its satellites on the part of the Soviet Union and, *a fortiori*, should Moscow provide arms to any nation engaged in a war with the United States (as we have seen, such an act, according to international law, would render Russia a belligerent), then the President should recall

---

criterion of just government. The truth is that the Secretary is a "power realist" and to a large extent a historicist: Just as he considers Soviet domination of Eastern Europe as irreversible, so he looks upon black domination of all of southern Africa as historically inevitable. As Orwell saw, this is the tendency of intellectuals who worship power, euphemistically called the "forces of history". And so History—some would say the "Laws of Historical Development"—have usurped the place of the "Laws of Nature and of Nature's God." We have come a long way from the statesmen of the Declaration of Independence.

our ambassador and seriously consider severing diplomatic relations.*
(It should be understood that severing *diplomatic* relations with any
country, as did Egypt with the United States and Russia with Israel in
1967, does not preclude all communication between the nations concerned.)

(7) The United States and its allies must develop a flexible and
broad spectrum of military power capable of responding to various
forms and degrees of Soviet-supported aggression. By deliberately
raising the spectre of escalation to nuclear war, Moscow, abetted by
naïve American statesmen, psychologically disarms the United States,
all the while seeking to deter and surpass us on the nuclear level.
Kremlin strategists are probably gambling that a consumer-oriented
society like our own will not stand for the sacrifices required to maintain strategic parity.† Russian nuclear developments since the Cuban
missile crisis of 1962 confirm that the Soviet war plans which Oleg
Penkovskiy photographed and conveyed to British and American intelligence shortly before that crisis, have not changed in the most
decisive respect. But let Colonel Pénkovskiy speak for himself:

> The Soviet leaders know exactly that the Western world and es-
> pecially the Americans do not wish an atomic war. This desire of my
> Western friends for peace is what the Soviet leaders try to use to
> their own advantage. It is they who wish to provoke a new war. This
> would open the road to the subjugation of the entire world. I fear this
> more every day. And my fears confirm my choice to make this invisi-
> ble fight.

---

*In 1975, when the Spanish government executed five terrorists who were actually guilty of
murder, England recalled its ambassador. Yet England is among the first of nations to recognize
genocidal tyrannies.[52]

†Consider the following statement from Russia's main military journal *Communist of the Armed Forces* (December, 1974, No. 23): "In analyzing the economic potential of a state it is
necessary to consider also the characteristics of the country's industrial production. In the USA
the production of such items as objects of luxury, means for advertising, automobiles, household
appliances, etc., which cannot be converted in practice for satisfying military needs or have
limited significance in this area, makes up a significant proportion in total industrial output. . . .
If industrial production currently comprises in the USSR more than 75 percent of the American
level (in 1950 it comprised less than one-third of the USA level), the quantity of production of
means of production [i.e., heavy industry] in the USSR is not less than 90 percent of comparable
production in the USA. It is clear that this has not only tremendous general-economic but also
military-economic significance." Here it should be noted that Kosygin's speech at the 25th
Soviet Party Congress of 1976 revealed that, in 1975, heavy industry production was 72.7 percent
of Russia's total industrial output, and that the new Five Year Plan calls for greater increases in
heavy industry (38-42 percent) than in light and food processing (30-32 percent).

> In Moscow I have lived in a nuclear nightmare. I know the extent of their preparations. I know the poison of the new military doctrine, as outlined in the top-secret "Special Collection"—the plan to strike first, at any costs.[53]

Not only does the Kremlin have a first-strike nuclear strategy, for the strictly military reasons cited in Chapter 6, but it *must and knows it must* have such a strategy if only because Russia's empire could conceivably disintegrate were it to engage in a protracted conventional war (a war which it would not likely win given the industrial capacity and population of the West *united* in defense of liberty). According to Penkovskiy, who perhaps underestimates the staying power of communist regimes, "The Soviet Union is not capable of carrying on a long war. . . . There will be thousands of deserters on the very first day. . . ."[54] The Kremlin certainly remembers how the Ukrainians welcomed the invading armies of Hitler as liberators; and, needless to say, most of the satellites would defect. Thus, quite apart from the obvious advantage of a first-strike, the somewhat precarious nature of the Soviet empire and the ruthlessness of its rulers requires that they should aim for nothing less than overwhelming nuclear superiority over the United States.

(8) As already noted, the Soviet octangular strategy of protracted war employs ambiguity to accomplish its objectives. The most significant example of this is communist exploitation of nationalism in peripheral but nonetheless strategic areas of the globe, that is, in certain former colonial nations. Thus, while providing massive military support to communist forces in Vietnam or, more recently, in Angola, Moscow appeals to such psychologically and politically disarming slogans as "wars of national liberation" and "anti-imperialism" on the one hand, never forgetting, of course, to profess ardent desires for "peace" on the other. Now the point is this. The Soviet strategy of protracted war is designed not only to keep the United States out of the areas in question, but to lure us into long drawn-out conflicts in those areas, as in Vietnam. It was the Vietnam war that enabled Russia to achieve its present military superiority. It was that conflict which so diminished the size of our navy and air force that we can now do little more than defend our own homeland. What must also be understood, however, is that to engage successfully in a protracted war

with the Soviet Union—and we are involved in such a war—the United States, generally, must fight *short*, not *protracted*, wars in peripheral areas of strategic significance. A protracted war on the periphery will tend to consume resources, moral as well as material, with relatively little cost to the real enemy, the Soviet Union. This means we should not ordinarily enter a so-called peripheral conflict unless we are prepared to bring it to a quick and successful conclusion.

As indicated earlier, the United States cannot pursue the policy outlined above without the full cooperation of its allies. Before addressing myself to this problem, however, it will be helpful to set forth certain general rules which ought to govern the United States in its negotiations with the Soviet Union.[55] (Here the reader will recall those errors to which certain American statesmen may be susceptible and which are contained in the Philosophical Profiles appearing earlier in this chapter.)

(1) Avoid major agreements with the Soviet Union without prior and in-process consultation with our allies.

(2) Avoid major agreements made without prior and in-process consultaion with leading members of both parties of Congress.

(3) Avoid summit meetings between heads of state. Greater reliance should be placed on the State Department, on our ambassadors and professional diplomats. On-going diplomacy should be private, but actual agreements public. As Penkovskiy warns: "I think it is necessary to have meetings, secretly conducted. Not summit meetings. These Khrushchev welcomes. He will use the decisions reached at summit meetings to increase his own prestige vis-à-vis the U.S. . . ."[56]

(4) Avoid nuclear weapons agreements whose violation cannot readily be detected. Indeed, because of the long lead-time required in the development of nuclear weapons, the U.S. should enter upon SALT negotiations with the assumption that any agreement will be violated by the USSR.

(5) Avoid agreements which cannot be enforced or whose violation does not entail visibly significant disadvantages to the violator. (So-called agreements in principle are to be shunned. Whereas such agreements can be evaded with impunity by the Soviets, their abrogation by the United States would have to be publicly defended. Also, treaties for keeping the peace or guaranteeing the territorial integrity

of a nation are useless to the guaranteed nation, and worse than useless insofar as they engender a false sense of security.* Such treaties can only benefit nations governed by rulers intending to violate them whenever expedient.)[56]

(6) Do not make gratuitous concessions and fatuous gestures of good will.† (As *Professor* Kissinger wrote: "Anyone succeeding in Communist leadership struggles must be single-minded, unemotional, dedicated, and, above all, motivated by an enormous desire for power. Nothing in the personal experience of Soviet leaders would lead them to accept protestations of good will at face value. Suspiciousness is inherent in their domestic position. It is unlikely that their attitude toward the outside world is more benign than toward their own colleagues. . . .")[57]

(7) Reduce the occasions for personal diplomacy, but also moralistic rigidity. Again consider the teachings of Professor Kissinger in *The Necessity for Choice*: ". . . periods of so-called flexibility have been as barren as those of 'rigidity'. The reluctance to confront the Communists diplomatically had the consequence of eroding the cohesion of the free world and of enabling the Communists to appear as the advocates of peace. But the excursion into a flexibility identified with personal diplomacy ended with American prestige at an unprecedented low and with Soviet negotiators treating their opposite numbers from the West with brutal contempt." And later: ". . . the temptation to conduct personal diplomacy derives from the notion of peace prevalent in both the United States and Great Britain. If peace is the "normal" relation among states, it follows that tensions must be caused by shortsightedness or misunderstanding and that they can be removed by a change of heart of the leading statesmen. . . . If peace ultimately depends on personalities, abstract good will may well seem more important than a concrete program. . . . Is it not possible that the yearning for agreement . . . and the identification of a settlement with good personal relations are themselves obstacles to serious

---

*See following footnote.

†Compare this statement by President Ford (which surely states the position of Secretary Kissinger): "Israel is asked to relinquish territory—a concrete and essentially irreversible step—in return for basically intangible political measures. But it is only in willingness to dare the exchange of the tangible for the intangible that hostility can be ended and peace attained." (*Los Angeles Times*, May 14, 1976, Pt. I, p. 20.) Now substitute Arab for Communist and Soviet in the sequel, and recall the Kissinger-Sonnenfeldt statement cited on p. 1 above.

negotiation?" Professor Kissinger explains the dilemma in ideological terms, saying: "The essence of Marxism-Leninism—and the reason that normal diplomacy with Communist states is so difficult—is the view that 'objective' factors such as the social structure, the economic process, and, above all, the class struggle are more important than the personal convictions of statesmen".[58] What needs to be emphasized, however, is this: (a) personal diplomacy conveys the erroneous impression that Soviet leaders are as much amenable to persuasion and mutual concessions as any other political leaders; (b) because it raises public expectations and hopes for East-West agreements, personal diplomacy exposes Western statesmen to the temptation to make unnecessary concessions in order to gratify or win the favor of various domestic constituencies; (c) because Soviet leaders are not subject to such pressures, they can prolong the negotiating process to their own advantage, relying, in part, on American impatience and concession-oriented pragmatism.

(8) So far as possible, avoid consummating major agreements during presidential election years.[59] (The President of the United States should make special efforts during such electoral periods to educate the public about the realities of international politics. He should try to anticipate aggressive actions by the enemy intended to divide the American people against his administration. Suffice it to recall the military offensives of North Vietnam in 1968 and 1972.) Negotiations should be conducted without the trumpeting that has gone on in recent times, inspired, no doubt, by the desire to win public approval and to strengthen the domestic (partisan) position of this or that President. Magnanimity might not only involve a willingness to incur mass displeasure, but also a willingness to incur no strong reaction at all. Thus conceived, détente on a diplomatic level, carefully limited of course, might have no deleterious effect at home.

(9) Avoid naïve as well as cynical but equally naïve "mirror-imaging". Nothing in the events of the last six decades should lead anyone to believe in the benevolent intentions of the Soviet Union. If only because there are scoundrels in our own society, both in and out of government, it is reasonable to suspect even more ruthless scoundrels among those who wield the publicly unrestrained power of the Kremlin. Finally, because no American in public life today has, or

conveys the impression of having, world-conquering ambitions,[61] it is folly, a no doubt comforting folly, to believe that the ambitions of those who have risen to power in the Kremlin are as modest as our own.

IV

I have been outlining a policy of "selective détente" to be orchestrated by Washington rather than by Moscow. It is, simultaneously, a policy of "selective containment". As noted at the outset of this book, such a policy ever seeks for areas of negotiation and coöperation, but never shirks competition and, when necessary, confrontation. This is why it may be termed a tough-minded policy of magnanimity. The success of this policy will depend on American leadership and closer political ties with our allies. Given, however, the disastrous defeat of the United States in Indochina, how can we possibly overcome the inescapable loss of confidence in American leadership or in the solidity and steadfastness of the American people (to say nothing of American honor)? If the United States could not save South Vietnam from a relatively insignificant power like North Vietnam, why should our friends *and* enemies expect us to defend Japan against the colossus of Red China or against a communist Korea unified with the help of the Soviet Union?[62] And if the United States could succumb to Soviet blackmail and undertake to compel Israel to withdraw toward its pre-1967 borders, thereby facilitating further Russian naval penetration, via the Suez Canal, of the Indian Ocean, hence of the Persian Gulf, why should Turkey or Greece or any European nation whose very survival depends on Arab oil, believe that this country would come to its defense at the risk of nuclear war with the Soviet Union? And will not this demoralized state of the Free World encourage Russia, now that it has virtually achieved nuclear superiority over the United States, to act more aggresively and take even greater risks than Stalin did in Berlin when we had a nuclear monopoly, or as Kruschchev did in Cuba when we had an ICBM advantage of roughly 4 to 1? In the face of these lugubrious considerations, what indeed can the United States do to restore the confidence of our allies and, at the same time, moderate Soviet conduct?

(1) First and foremost the United States must secure its homeland against direct attack from the Soviet Union or from any Soviet client in Latin America. Unless we can adequately defend our own country, we can hardly be expected to defend our allies who, knowing this, will be subject to Russian nuclear blackmail. Unlike Washington, Moscow does not regard nuclear war as unthinkable. Not only does the Politburo have a nuclear war-winning strategy, but Russia is spending 1 billion dollars annually for civil defense (to our 80 million), including dispersal and hardening of industry, cadres for evacuating cities, stockpiling of food and fuel—all the while training Russian youth for nuclear war. Contrary to the McNamara doctrine of 1965, allowing the Soviets to achieve nuclear parity has not produced stability on the strategic level. Only if the United States improves its damage-limiting capabilities are meaningful strategic arms limitation agreements possible.* This country must therefore (a) reverse the present nuclear imbalance by striving for *at least* strategic equivalence with the Soviet Union; (b) improve the survivability of our ICBM and SLBM systems; (c) develop a mobile ballistic missile system virtually immune to Soviet targeting; (d) increase the penetrability and flexibility of our strategic weapons (thereby increasing their deterrent effect); and (e) improve and enlarge our continental air defense system. Meanwhile, and to say the least, we should develop a more numerous and powerful navy capable of controlling our Atlantic and Pacific sea lines of communication, the Caribbean, and the Panama Canal.

(2) NATO's conventional military inferiority to the Warsaw Pact must be overcome.[63] (Recognizing that it has been Soviet policy since the end of World War II to disengage the United States from Europe, it is of the utmost importance *not* to reduce our European-based forces. In the present geostrategic context, the Soviet objective—partly realized at Helsinki by virtue of its military-political ascendency in the Middle East—is to neutralize or Sovietize Europe, isolate the U.S. from its Western allies, then turn to the east to consolidate its Asian empire (which includes, among other things, acquisition of Manchuria

---

*The "action-reaction" hypothesis intended to explain the "arms-race" is refuted by the data presented on pp. 119-121 above. Also, the contention that civil defense programs are provocative is scorned by Moscow. Studies reveal as realistic Soviet claims that its population losses resulting from a U.S. retaliatory attack could be limited to 3 to 4 percent. See Peter Hughes and M.R. Edwards. "Nuclear War in Soviet Military Thinking," *The Journal of Social and Political Affairs*, 1:2 (April 1976), p. 123.

and the elimination of all U.S. influence in the Western Pacific), in short, to achieve the war goals of the Axis powers in World War II.

(3) Excluding at least strategic nuclear weapons, Japan should be encouraged to rearm. In particular, Japanese naval power should be increased to the point where it can make a significant contribution to the defense of the Western Pacific and the sea lines of communication running from the Persian Gulf through the Indian Ocean.

(4) To avoid our own expulsion from the Middle East, the United States should encourage the following kinds of alliances: (a) Iran-Pakistan-Saudi Arabia; (b) Israel-Iran-Ethiopia; (c) Turkey-Iran-Israel-Lebanon (which would require Western support of the Lebanese Christians); and (d) Egypt-Jordan-Saudi Arabia. (Alliances such as these would prevent Soviet domination of the Middle East.) In addition, the United States should try to negotiate a comprehensive Treaty of Friendship and Cooperation with Egypt. In return for the use of Egyptian port and air facilities, we would (i) augment our economic technological assistance, including long-term development programs, and (ii) establish professional schools in business and public administration.* (If Egypt could be somewhat liberalized, she might be persuaded to establish diplomatic relations with Israel.) Meanwhile, the United States, with the active coöperation of our NATO allies, should provide Israel with sufficient arms to deter aggression.

(5) Recalling the Soviet use of economic warfare to advance the cause of Communism (when the Kremlin encouraged the Arab oil embargo of 1973), the United States may in all propriety use its economic power to advance the cause of Republicanism. America's resources being limited, it should be understood that what we give or sell to Russia cannot be given to others in greater need of assistance. Would it not be more consistent with humanity to divert, on appropriate occasions, millions of bushels of grain to the world's suffering in Africa or in Asia than to a tyranny like the Soviet Union, a regime which ex-

---

*Shortly after these words were written, a Soviet-Egyptian trade agreement of almost two-thirds of a billion dollars was concluded. Apparently, the agreement involved payment for Soviet weapons received (but unreported by the Western press) during 1974-76—which places in question the authenticity of the so-called rift between the two countries. See Uri Ra'anan, "The Soviet-Egyptian 'Rift,'" *Commentary*, 61:6 (June 1976), pp.29-35. (Contrary to Kissinger's Mideast policy, it is virtually impossible for the U.S. to supplant the USSR as Egypt's chief arms supplier, if only because Russia's production rate of military hardware far exceeds our own. This means that the leverage we can exert on Egypt by means of economic and technological aid is limited.)

Here it should be noted that the United States cannot readily compete with Russia in supply-

ported grain and flour while three million of its own people were dying of starvation during the famine of 1928-1932? (See below, p. 232, n. 57.) Why indeed should we subsidize the war-making economy of a government which spends more than our own on weapons yet with less than one-half of this country's GNP? Accordingly, as a short- to intermediate-term policy (which of course would have to be coördinated with other elements of the foreign policy proposed in these pages), we should manipulate our agricultural exports to moderate Russia's conduct as well as the politics of various developing nations.[64] There is nothing novel in this proposal, except that a more systematic and sustained effort is required in using America's tremendous feed-grain productivity and food technology to gain diplomatic advantages and for dealing with certain political conflicts where resort to force might otherwise be necessary. For example, withholding grain shipments to the USSR might have helped prevent Moscow's use of Cuban troops to install a communist regime in Angola—the ultimate objective of which is to subvert South Africa. (Here it should be noted that the loss of South Africa's enormous mineral resources, including uranium, iron-ore, gold, copper, platinum, and vanadium, would be disastrous to the West. In addition, communist domination of South Africa would give the Soviets control over one of the world's most important shipping routes, so vital for America, Europe, and the oil producing nations of the Persian Gulf.)

(6) In light of the preceding, the United States (as well as Western Europe and Japan) should seek by every means to become less dependent on Middle East oil so as to reduce Arab influence on American foreign policy. While developing alternative energy sources, the economies (including the commodity markets) of the Free World should be adjusted to minimize waste and the depletion of energy and raw materials. Not only would this help correct the possible undue influence of large domestic corporations and international cartels on foreign policy (see below, p. 222, n.22), it would also tend to (a) lessen the international rivalry resulting from the shipment of arms to Third World areas; (b) discourage the development of militaristic or authoritarian governments in those areas; and (c) promote the international stability and Third World economies required for the growth of republican government.

---

ing conventional military equipment given the radical differences in our respective economies. On the other hand, while we cannot be surpassed in our capacity to provide economic aid, the

(7) The United States, in cooperation with Canada, should under-take a project for diverting the Yukon, the Fraser, the Peace, and other rivers of Alaska and Western Canada[65] in order to (a) irrigate and reclaim the parched plains of the Western United States and Northern Mexico; (b) develop hydroelectric power, granaries, and livestock; and (c) facilitate the growth of small, semi-autonomous cities having rural-urban economies.

(8) In the light of this proposed development, the United States (and Canada) should liberalize immigration policies to admit, over a period of time, several million people from Eastern Europe, reversing in the process the demoralizing tendencies of Helsinki. At the same time, we should insist that the Soviet Union abide by the 1969 "International Convention on the Elimination of All Forms of Racial Discrimination mentioned earlier, which requires Russia "to ... guarantee the right of everyone, without distinction as to race, colour, or national or ethnic origin ... to leave any country, including his own . . . ." (This would have been a fitting response to the Soviet-backed resolution of the United Nations General Assembly condemning Zionism as a form of racism.)

(9) The American government should undertake a world-wide campaign to discredit Marxism and Leninism along lines suggested in the Philosophical Profiles presented in this chapter. (Excluding Western economic and technological assistance—over which we have some control—there are only two things which sustain the tyranny of Communist Russia: *fear* via force, and *fraud* via the cultivation of respect for Marx and Lenin. Revealing *and* relating, in a manner con-sistent with civility, the terrorist and totalitarian character of the Soviet Union on the one hand, and the evils of Marxism and Leninism on the other, would be the most effective way of discrediting the Kremlin and undermining its influence in the world at large.)[66]

(10) Recalling Churchill's warning—that "the structure and habits of democratic states, *unless they are welded into larger organisms*, lack those elements of persistence and conviction which can alone give security to humble masses"—it would be helpful to con-sider what must be done to bring about, during the course of one or two generations, a Commonwealth leading to a United States of Europe. I raise the point only to convey some notion of the magnitude

---

political efficacy of such aid to unstable regimes is quite limited. Hence we should be very selec-tive.

of the task necessary to defend liberty. Nothing less than heroic efforts are demanded; for we face an implacable foe ready to exploit any weakness, any division, any relaxation in and among the forces of freedom. Of course, required above all else is wise and courageous statesmanship. Is the United States incapable of providing such statesmanship? Can it long survive and enjoy the blessings of liberty if such statesmanship is not very soon forthcoming?

EPILOGUE

In War: Resolution
In Defeat: Defiance
In Victory: Magnanimity
In Peace: Good Will

—Winston Churchill

My faithful reader will not have forgotten that this book is primarily intended for the architectonic statesman, the statesman possessed of philosophic insight and practical wisdom. Hence it is not a work of "realism" as the term is generally understood. "Realists" or pragmatists will say that the foreign policy proposed in these pages, even if desirable, is impossible. If so, then to judge from his privately admitted pessimism, Secretary of State Kissinger may very well conceive of himself as presiding over the inevitable decline and fall of the United States of America, just as he portrayed Metternich as having presided over the decline and fall of the Austro-Hungarian Empire.* Admittedly, the moderate policies advocated in this volume may not

---

*See Henry A. Kissinger, *A World Restored, passim.* Publicly, Dr. Kissinger (necessarily) denies the pessimism attributed to him. See "The Politics of Henry Kissinger", transcript of the *Firing Line* program telecast on PBS, Sept. 13, 1975, but on which program Dr. Kissinger admitted to having given President Nixon a copy of Spengler's *Decline of the West*, a charming work, well calculated to hearten the then leader of the Free World in its struggle against Soviet Communism (pp. 1-2). More recently, in Elmo Zumwalt's memoirs, which include notes taken immediately after private conversations with Secretary Kissinger, the retired admiral says of the Secretary that "He states strongly that the President misjudges the people. K feels that U.S. has passed its historic high point like so many other civilizations. He believes U.S. is on downhill and cannot be roused by political challenge. He states that his job is to persuade the Russians to give us the best deal we can get recognizing that the historical forces favor them." *On Watch* (New York: Quadrangle, 1976), p. 319. Now, if Dr. Kissinger is in fact a Spenglerian historicist, then he would be psychologically disinclined to undertake the intellectual and moral efforts required to *reverse* the (allegedly inevitable) decline of the United States. This helps to explain his rhetorical question, "What do those who speak so glibly about one-way streets propose concretely that this country do?" (*National Review*, April 26, 1976, p. 371.) This book is an attempt to answer that question. But the mere fact that Dr. Kissinger could ask such a question indicates that anyone inclined toward historicism is a most dangerous person to have in the position of Secretary of State.

suffice to reverse the decline in American fortunes. I hope they will, and think they might. Of one thing, however, we may be confident: nothing in the founding principles of the American Republic, nothing in the genius of the American people, dooms us to the false dichotomy of surrender or holocaust. These are not the only possible alternatives of free men, of men not tainted by historical determinism or by a fatalistic "realism."

What indeed do "realists" know about the possible? What do they know about the silent, unseen and untapped depths of the American people? It is said by "realists" that Americans are incapable of fighting a protracted war, that they cannot understand a complicated and "incremental" foreign policy. If this is true, it may be less a reflection on the American people than on their educators. But I deny the truth of this unwitting confession of academic failure.* Not only did we fight, but we almost won a protracted war in Vietnam—and this despite the fact that no President ever stood before the nation on television and explained graphically and in geopolitical terms why the defense of South Vietnam was necessary, in the long run, for the defense of the United States.† Why not? Because to have drawn the

---

*Apropos of Vietnam and the campus-centered antiwar movement, consider Orwell's reflections on British public opinion during World War II: "The English intelligentsia, on the whole, were more defeatist than the mass of the people—and some of them went on being defeatist at a time when the war was quite plainly won—partly because they were better able to visualize the dreary years of warfare that lay ahead. Their morale was worse because their imaginations were stronger. The quickest way of ending a war is to lose it, and if one finds the prospect of a long war intolerable, it is natural to disbelieve in the possibility of victory. But there was more to it than that. There was also the disaffection of large numbers of intellectuals, which made it difficult for them not to side with any country hostile to Britain. And deepest of all, there was ad-miration—though only in a very few cases conscious admiration—for the power, energy, and cruelty of the Nazi regime. . . . And if one studied the reactions of the English intelligentsia towards the USSR, there, too, one would find genuinely progressive impulses mixed up with ad-miration for power and cruelty. It would be grossly unfair to suggest that power worship is the only motive for russophile feeling, but it is one motive, and among intellectuals it is probably the strongest one. . . . If one examines the people who . . . are strongly russophile, one finds that, on the whole, they belong to the 'managerial' class . . . not managers in the narrow sense, but scien-tists, technicians, teachers, journalists, broadcasters, bureaucrats, professional politiciams: in general, middling people who feel themselves cramped by a system that is still partly aristocratic, and are hungry for more power and more prestige. These people look towards the USSR and see in it, or think they see, a system which eliminates the upper class, keeps the working class in place, and hands unlimited power to people very similar to themselves." Cited below, p. 223, n. 26.
†See Sir Robert Thompson, "Revolutionary War in Southeast Asia," ORBIS, 19:3 (Fall 1975), pp. 965-968, who points out that the Tet offensives of 1968 "resulted in a crushing military defeat for the North Vietnamese and the Viet Cong, but they gained a striking psychological victory within the United States." And later: "The greatest of the many myths of the Vietnam war was that it was unwinnable. Quite apart from the possibility of different strategies and policies in the

geostrategic connection between the defense of Indochina and the defense of the Western Hemisphere would have required the President to tell the American people the truth about the Soviet Union, about its methods and objectives. It would have been necessary to show how Moscow was arming and using its client, North Vietnam, to disengage the United States from Southeast Asia. In other words, no President of the United States ever told his fellow citizens that we were fighting a defensive war not merely against North Vietnam, but against the Soviet Union, a Marxist regime which has ever been dedicated to the destruction of this country.

Meanwhile, the mass media, whose ideological bias* was never seriously or rather philosophically challenged, let alone refuted, by three administrations, worked feverishly to undermine public support for an unwisely and perhaps ignobly prosecuted, but not, on balance, an unjust war *in view of the consequences now befalling Indochina.* Intimidated by the political obscurantism of the media, and fearful of defending themselves on anti-communist grounds lest they generate anti-communist passions, our political leaders sought to justify a war in terms of the vaguely stated principle of "self-determination", supplemented in due course by even vaguer references to "national secruity". But how can any people fight a war, let alone a protracted war, without engaging their passions against the enemy—to say nothing of imbuing them with a sober concern for their own safety and liberty? How indeed can a people be expected to fight Communism abroad while their political and intellectual leaders were fighting against anti-communism at home?

Never did our leaders inform us that we enjoy the blessing of liberty because we live in a hemisphere relatively free from communist imperialism.† Never did they tell us that if Communism ever achieved a

earlier stages of the war, it could have been won in 1972—i.e., an enforceable settlement could have been obtained which would have ensured the survival of South Vietnam. . . ."

*See Edith Efron, *The News Twisters* (Los Angeles: Nash Publishing Co. 1971), pp. 351, 184-185, 223-225, who methodically analyzed prime-television coverage of the final six weeks of the 1968 presidential campaign. Despite the repeated atrocities of the Viet Cong, the three major networks found nothing to report against the enemy, while one spoke occasionally in favor of the enemy! See also the more recent analysis by Dr. Ernest W. Lefever of the Brookings Institution: *TV and National Defense, An Analysis of CBS News, 1972-1973* (Boston, Virginia: Institute for American Strategy Press, 1974).

†But see Leon Gouré and Morris Rothenberg, *Soviet Penetration of Latin America* (Miami: Center for Advanced International Studies, University of Miami, 1975), *passim.*

solid foothold in this hemisphere the United States, sooner or later, would become an armed camp. Again I ask, could we enjoy freedom of speech and press to the extent we do today if Latin America, including Mexico, were to become a communist sanctuary supported by the missiles of the Soviet Union? Could we again compel the Soviet Union to remove missiles from Cuba or from any other prospective "client" in the Western Hemisphere? Republican government cannot survive without an environment of liberty. There is less liberty in the world now that the United States has been driven out of Indochina: Mr. Thieu's less than fully democratic regime was replaced by an *ideological* dictatorship of enormous proportions, a dictatorship over men's domestic and social lives, their private thoughts and feelings, their religious beliefs and loyalties. Meanwhile, our own world has narrowed, has lost its breadth of vision. The higher, the freedom of the intellect, is being subordinated to the lower, to a levelling equality.*

Unless America understands and comes to grip with the fundamental cause of its defeat in Southeast Asia, it will very soon lose its capacity to survive as a liberal society. In this and in other published works I have argued that the doctrine of moral relativism propagated by our colleges and universities for the better part of this century is in large measure responsible for the present decline of the United States.† To acknowledge the decline but to deny the cause is tacitly to admit the intellectual and moral impotence of the academic profession—for once again, who is it that educates our politicians, our journalists, and those who have made anti-communism unfashionable? Let me not be misunderstood. On any college campus one may expect to find some of the best educators as well as some of the worst—genuine intellectuals as well as pseudo-intellectuals. No statesman, therefore, who wishes to save this divided country from disaster would want to engage in an anti-intellectual crusade. On the contrary, he will seek to correct the anti-intellectual attitudes of too many

*For an example of how an implicit relativism is undermining education at the Naval Academy and the navy's fighting effectiveness, see Admiral Rickover's testimony in *Hearings on Military Posture*, House Armed Services Committee (cited below, p. 230, n. 37), Pt. 4, p. 619.

† Notice the praises various Americans sing of Communist China. This recalls the words of Tocqueville: Americans, he wrote, "have a natural taste for freedom; left to themselves they will seek it, cherish it and view any privation of it with regret. But for equality their passion is ardent, insatiable, invincible; they call for equality in freedom; and if they cannot obtain that, they call for equality in slavery."

Americans. Simultaneously, he will try to overcome the contempt which many intellectuals harbor toward the people, in particular, the middle class. Directly and indirectly, the enlightened statesman will criticize the anti-intellectual dogma which holds that the intellect is incapable of apprehending universally valid standards by which to distinguish the good from the bad—for example, a good educator from a bad educator, or a good regime from a bad regime. Such a statesman will not resort to invective. Rather, he will show "a decent respect to the opinions of mankind", including the opinions of intellectuals. He will be governed not by mean-spiritedness but by magnanimity. And while he gently chides the intellectual, let him not flatter the American people, but rather make greater demands upon them, as Washington did in his Farewell Address. Yet, such is the state of things today that the reflective statesman will have to go even further, will have to be more explicit, if he is to arrest the decline of the United States. He shall have to address the common man with uncommon candor. He shall have to translate the everyday experiences of workingmen into the language of foreign policy. By so doing he will not only enlighten but win the support of the great majority of the American people and, at the same time, guard them against the moral obscurantism of anti-anticommunism. Furthermore, he will thereby attract many intellectuals, liberal and conservative, who have yet to hear a political spokesman with the wisdom and courage to denounce Communism as evil without engendering the evil of McCarthyism.

Let our architectonic statesman only take the American people into his confidence, and let him only make honest and honorable demands on their good sense and sobriety, and they will unite and uphold his cause as their forefathers upheld the cause of those statesmen of '76 who pledged to each other their lives, their fortunes, and their sacred honor.

ALEXANDER SOLZHENITSYN vs THE SPIRIT OF HELSINKI

The Soviet System is so closed that it is almost impossible for you to understand from here. Your theoreticians and scholars write works trying to understand and explain how things occur there. Here are some naïve explanations which are simply funny to Soviet citizens. Some say that the Soviet leaders have now given up their inhumane ideology. Not at all. They haven't given it up one bit.

Some say that in the Kremlin there are some on the left [and] some on the right. And they are fighting with each other, and we've got to behave in such a way as not to interfere with those on the left side. This is all fantasy: . . . There is some sort of a struggle for power, but they all agree on the essentials. . . .

Through the decades of the 20s, the 30s, the 40s, the 50s, the whole Soviet press wrote: Western capitalism—your end is near. But it was as if the capitalists had not heard, could not understand, could not believe this.

Nikita Khrushchev came here and said, "We will bury you!" They didn't believe that either. They took it as a joke.

Now, of course, they have become more clever in our country. Now they don't say "we are going to bury you" any more, now they say "détente".

—Alexander Solzhenitsyn
June 30, 1975

In the speech from which the above remarks are taken,* Nobel Laureate Alexander Solzhenitsyn sought to awaken America to the perilous character of "détente". Speaking from personal experience as well as from long and profound study, he warned that the Helsinki Conference on European Security and Coöperation, far from promoting peace, would mark the "funeral of Eastern Europe" and hasten Soviet ascendency over the West.

The agreements drawn up at the Helsinki Conference were signed by President Ford on August 1, 1975, but only in the face of considerable criticism voiced even by ardent advocates of "détente". Yet no one's criticism was more cogent and more eloquent than Solzhenitsyn's.

---

*Transcript released by the AFL-CIO Department of Public Relations.

Solzhenitsyn spoke from the nation's capital on the eve of Helsinki. With grave irony he revealed to the American people what their own leaders have long obscured, the unrelenting tyranny of the Soviet Union. By exposing the true character of that tyranny, he placed in question the policy of "détente" so fervently pursued by the United States since 1969, the year Dr. Kissinger joined with President Nixon to chart the future course of this country. Solzhenitsyn described in detail the atrocities and treacheries of Russia's leaders from Lenin to Brezhnev. He spoke of the millions of men and women who perished in Soviet concentration or slave-labor camps, and of the millions more who were driven to starvation or massacred. And he pointed out that the concentration camps (described with soul-shattering effect in *The Gulag Archipelago*) were first constructed not by Stalin, but by Lenin, long before Hitler. This Khrushchev conveniently neglected to mention in his "secret speech" of 1956 exposing the crimes of Stalin, crimes to which he himself was a principal accomplice. Yet such concentration camps exist to this very day.

Solzhenitsyn spent eleven years in those diabolical camps. Countless are the people who still remain their silent prisoners. Giving voice to their silence, Solzhenitsyn asked why are the leaders of a free and powerful country shaking the hands of the oppressors of his own? Are they unaware of the blood on those hands? Do they not know about the "psychiatric hospitals" in the Soviet Union, where dissidents—some of Russia's most brilliant men and women—can be heard groaning and dying, having been daily injected with drugs which destroy their brain cells?* This Solzhenitsyn's audience of June 30 might have recalled when Brezhnev, one month later, signed the Helsinki agreements respecting freedom of thought and conscience.

Americans might also have recalled Solzhenitsyn informing them that the secret police maintain electronic spying devices in countless apartments and in almost every institution in Soviet Russia. What are we to say of a people who live under such a tyranny? What are we to say of the smiles of their rulers who came to Helsinki? Surely the people live in fear; and given the government's control of the press, surely most live in darkness. As for the smiles of their rulers, they may be as genuine as "détente". As we have seen from Chapter 6, during the Nixon-Kissinger-Ford period of "détente", while the U.S. reduced defense spending, the USSR embarked on a program of military expansion which can have but one meaning: the Soviets are driving toward global ascendency. Given the facts presented in that chapter, we may well have asked with Solzhenitsyn, who has devoted much of his life to the study of Soviet leaders: "How could one rely on their signatures to documents of détente" such as those signed at Helsinki?

Yet Helsinki, the capital of Finland—a country whose foreign policy is under the control of the Soviet Union, a country whose very name has been adopted by those who fear or foresee the "finlandization" of Europe—is the

---

*See *ibid.* and "Abuse of Psychiatry for Political Repression in the Soviet Union" (cited in the Bibliography, p. 248).

place where, we are told, the "cold war" officially came to an end, where our leaders began a new, constructive era in international relations. Let us examine some of the heralds of this new era.

The most significant declares that "the [thirty-five] participating states regard as inviolable one another's frontiers."* It is this agreement which dignifies and virtually legitimates Soviet domination of Eastern Europe. True, Helsinki only ratified a *de facto* state of affairs. But the Soviet Union has for three decades sought formal Western recognition of that state of affairs, that is, of Russia's World War II conquests, and for reasons commonly overlooked by commentators. First, the Kremlin knows that legal agreements entered into by the West tend to impose on Western governments restraints or inhibitions to which the Soviet Union is relatively immune. Furthermore, the West's formal recognition of Soviet domination of Eastern Europe cannot but demoralize any internal struggle for independence among Russia's satellites.

Another herald of the Helsinki era pledges the signatories "to refrain from direct or indirect assistance to terrorist activities, or to subversive or other activities directed toward the violent overthrow of another participating state." But surely any regime engaged in such activities is not likely to undergo the profound political conversion implicitly required by such a pledge. Are we really to expect the Soviet Union to close down the Patrice Lumumba University as well as other facilities in Odessa, Baku, and Tashkent presently used for training terrorists, saboteurs, and assassins?

Now consider the so-called concessions which the West "exacted" from the Soviet Union, concessions which call for a freer flow of ideas, information, and peoples, as well as respect for fundamental human rights—freedom of thought, freedom of conscience, and freedom of religion.† Hardly any of these conceded rights is not already prescribed by the United Nations Charter. And yet, merely to speak of these as "concessions" is a tacit condemnation of the Soviet regime, suggesting that the Kremlin regards human rights as articles of barter. Admittedly, all nations, our own included, commit injustices from time to time. Among Western democracies, however, injustices are committed in violation of the very principles on which their governments are based—and are moreover condemned in terms of those principles. This is not the case with Russia, whose principles of government are

---

*Incidentally, this agreement favors the Soviet Union against China's vast claims along the Sino-Soviet border.

† In one section the signatories merely promised "to facilitate the improvement of the dissemination, on their territory, of newspapers and printed publications" from other participating states. Another section vaguely says that "the participating states will deal in a positive and humanitarian spirit with the application of persons who wish to be reunited with members of their family." For such reunions to take place, people in West Germany are being compelled to pay ransom-like sums to the East German government. Consider, too, how the Helsinki agreement that all governments "will facilitate wider travel by their citizens" did not prevent Moscow from refusing to grant Andrei Sakharov an exit visa so that he might receive his 1975 Nobel Peace Prize.

themselves engines of injustice. And it is those principles—not simply occasional violations of human rights—that stand silently and ineffectually condemned by the pledges exacted from the Soviet Union at Helsinki. Were the USSR to honor those pledges it would cease to export terror and revolution. It would cease to interfere in the internal affairs of other nations via local communist parties. It would cease to stifle freedom of speech and press which alone would lead to the development of a government that pays a decent respect to the opinions of mankind. Then and then only would there be an end to the "cold war". Then and then only would there be genuine détente.

Moscow is aware of these implications. "No one", said Brezhnev at Helsinki, "should try to dictate to other peoples [sic], on the basis of foreign-policy considerations of one kind or another, the manner in which they ought to manage their internal affairs."* But as any student of international relations knows, the internal affairs and foreign policy of a nation are in decisive respects interwoven and inseparable.† This is perhaps truer of communist regimes in view of their monolithic and doctrinaire character. Not only is Soviet Russia an expansionist or imperialistic power, but the magnitude and universal implications of its imperialism are inconceivable apart from the influence of its Marxist ideology. As Solzhenitsyn emphasized, and as this book has abundantly documented, Marxism still animates the oligarchy in the Kremlin. So long as Russia, with all its military power, remains organized on the universalistic principles of Marxism—principles which entail a one-party state, meaning the destruction of parliamentary government—it will continue to pose a grave threat to the West. The very language of the Helsinki agreements confirms this conclusion, confirming as well the interdependent relationship between the "internal affairs" or domestic structure of the Soviet Union and its foreign policy. *The mere "concessions" exacted from the Soviets represent a concerted effort on the part of the West to moderate the domestic tyranny of the Soviet government, which is but to "interfere" in Russia's internal affairs, and precisely because Russia's internal affairs profoundly affect her policies toward Eastern Europe and the Free World.*** This dilemma was obscured by Dr. Kissinger when he said in 1973: "For half a century we have objected to communist efforts to alter the domestic structures of other countries. For a generation of Cold War we have sought to ease the risks produced by competing ideologies. Are we now to come full circle and *insist* on domestic compatibility [of the Soviet system with Western standards of civility?] as a condition of pro-

---

New York Times, Aug. 2, 1975, p. 8.
†See Henry Kissinger, *American Foreign Policy* pp. 209-210.
**Some time after these words were written, the *New York Times* (of Oct. 22, 1975) published a most perceptive article by Andrei Amalrik in which that courageous man declared: "Whether or not the American leaders recognize it, a fundamental change in the foreign policy of the USSR is impossible without a change in its internal situation [meaning in the very form of its government]" (p. 40).

gress?"* Quite apart from the fact that the pledges of Helsinki will not result in progress unless Russia does in fact alter its domestic structure to the extent of respecting fundamental human rights, Dr. Kissinger here blurs the distinction between *lawful* efforts intended to moderate the unjust practices of the Soviet Union and that regime's *subversive* activities throughout the world.†

Clearly, a fundamental asymmetry exists in the relations between Russia and the West which American statesmen, while they reject "selective détente", seem incapable of facing. For example, when President Ford, in his address to the Helsinki Conference, said that "Military competition must be controlled, political competition must be restrained, [and] crises must not be manipulated or exploited for unilateral advantage", he was not merely reiterating the phraseology of the "Basic Principles of Relations" signed by Brezhnev and Nixon at the conclusion of the SALT I Agreements in 1972, and systematically violated by the Soviet Union in Vietnam and the Middle East in 1973.** He must also have been alluding to Soviet violation of those principles in Portugal during the very meeting he was attending at Helsinki. For even while he and Brezhnev were signing pledges against intervention in the domestic affairs of the participating states, against the continued suppression of human rights, Moscow was supplying funds to the Portuguese Communist Party, enabling that oligarchy to endanger NATO and to impair the rights of the Portuguese people. President Ford nonetheless went on to tell the conferees gathered at Helsinki that "The people of *all* Europe and, I assure you, the people of North America are thoroughly tired of having hopes raised and then shattered by empty words and unfulfilled pledges." Perhaps Mr. Ford had in mind, however, the hopes and unfulfilled pledges associated with the "spirit of Geneva", the "spirit of Camp David", and the "spirit of Glassboro", other heralds of "détente" occuring under the presidencies of Mr. Eisenhower and Mr. Johnson? Whatever the case, when the President went on to conclude by warning the delegates at Helsinki that "we had better say what we mean and mean what we say, or we will have the anger of our citizens to answer",†† surely he was not addressing the Soviet Union or Mr. Brezhnev who, unlike Mr. Ford, needs not feel too concerned about incurring the wrath of his people. Notice, however, that Mr. Ford, not unlike Dr. Kissinger, succumbed to the profound tendency of this Orwellian age to obscure, at least verbally, the differences between democratic regimes and the Soviet political system.*** Perhaps this is why Solzhenitsyn reminded his American audience of the true character of that system "where for forty years", he said, "there haven't been genuine elections but simply a comedy,

---

*Address delivered to the Pacem in Terris III Conference, Washington, D.C., Oct. 8, 1973, in Kissinger, *American Foreign Policy*, p. 264.
†See below, p. 223, n. 24.
**See *New York Times*, Aug. 2, 1975, p. 9, and Appendix 5.
††New York Times, Aug. 2, 1975, p. 9.
***See above, p. 96, *in re* Franklin Roosevelt's toast to Stalin at Teheran.

a farce." It is a system, he went on to say, "which has no legislative organs", a system "without an independent press; a system without an independent judiciary; where the people have no influence either on external or internal policy; where any thought which is different from what the state thinks is crushed." Accordingly, the rulers of Russia need have no fear that their repeated violations of agreements equivalent to those of Helsinki will arouse the anger of their own people. Nor, it seems, need they greatly fear that such violations will arouse the anger of the West. Indeed, given all the "empty words and unfulfilled pledges" complained of by President Ford on the one hand, and the retreats and concessions of the West on the other, the question arises: Are Western statesmen any longer capable of anger?

Anger, as Plato understood, is the passion of justice. It is also a passion closely linked to the sense of honor. It is a dangerous passion unless under the governance of reason. Is it possible, however, that without a profound sense of honor reason falters and is blind?*

---

*So Hamilton thought of Aaron Burr. See above, p. 100. For a discussion of the relationship between honor and statesmanship, see my *On the Silence of the Declaration of Independence*, pp. 21-26.

THE FAREWELL ADDRESS OF GEORGE WASHINGTON
September 19, 1796*

Friends, and Fellow-Citizens: The period for a new election of a Citizen, to Administer the Executive government of the United States, being not far distant, and the time actually arrived, when your thoughts must be cloathed with that important trust, it appears to me proper, especially as it may conduce to a more distinct expression of the public voice, that I should now apprise you of the resolution I have formed, to decline being considered among the number of those, out of whom a choice is to be made.

I beg you, at the same time, to do me the justice to be assured, that this resolution has not been taken without a strict regard to all the considerations appertaining to the relation, which binds a dutiful citizen to his country, and that, in withdrawing the tender of service which silence in my situation might imply, I am influenced by no diminution of zeal for your future interest, no deficiency of grateful respect for your past kindness; but am supported by a full conviction that the step is compatible with both.

The acceptance of, and continuance hitherto in, the office to which your Suffrages have twice called me, have been a uniform sacrifice of inclination to the opinion of duty, and to a deference for what appeared to be your desire. I constantly hoped, that it would have been much earlier in my power, consistently with motives, which I was not at liberty to disregard, to return to that retirement, from which I had been reluctantly drawn. The strength of my inclination to do this, previous to the last Election, had even led to the preparation of an address to declare it to you; but mature reflection on the then perplexed and critical posture of our Affairs with foreign Nations, and the unanimous advice of persons entitled to my confidence, impelled me to abandon the idea.

I rejoice, that the state of your concerns, external as well as internal, no longer renders the pursuit of inclination incompatible with the sentiment of

**The Writings of George Washington*, pp. 214-238 (cited below, p. 213, n. 1).

duty, or propriety; and am persuaded whatever partiality may be retained for my services, that in the present circumstances of our country, you will not disapprove my determination to retire.

The impressions, with which I first undertook the arduous trust, were explained on the proper occasion. In the discharge of this trust, I will only say, that I have, with good intentions, contributed towards the Organization and Administration of the government, the best exertions of which a very fallible judgment was capable. Not unconscious, in the outset, of the inferiority of my qualifications, experience in my own eyes, perhaps still more in the eyes of others, has strengthned the motives to diffidence of myself; and every day the encreasing weight of years admonishes me more and more, that the shade of retirement is as necessary to me as it will be welcome. Satisfied that if any circumstances have given peculiar value to my services, they were temporary, I have the consolation to believe, that while choice and prudence invite me to quit the political scene, patriotism does not forbid it.

In looking forward to the moment, which is intended to terminate the career of my public life, my feelings do not permit me to suspend the deep acknowledgment of that debt of gratitude which I owe to my beloved country, for the many honors it has conferred upon me; still more for the stedfast confidence with which it has supported me; and for the opportunities I have thence enjoyed of manifesting my inviolable attachment, by services faithful and persevering, though in usefulness unequal to my zeal. If benefits have resulted to our country from these services, let it always be remembered to your praise, and as an instructive example in our annals, that, under circumstances in which the Passions agitated in every direction were liable to mislead, amidst appearances sometimes dubious, viscissitudes of fortune often discouraging, in situations in which not unfrequently want of Success has countenanced the spirit of criticism, the constancy of your support was the essential prop of the efforts, and a guarantee of the plans by which they were effected. Profoundly penetrated with this idea, I shall carry it with me to my grave, as a strong incitement to unceasing vows that Heaven may continue to you the choicest tokens of its beneficence; that your Union and brotherly affection may be perpetual; that the free Constitution, which is the work of your hands, may be sacredly maintained; that its Administration in every department may be stamped with wisdom and Virtue; that, in fine, the happiness of the people of these States, under the auspices of liberty, may be made complete, by so careful a preservation and so prudent a use of this blessing as will acquire to them the glory of recommending it to the applause, the affection, and adoption of every nation which is yet a stranger to it.

Here, perhaps, I ought to stop. But a solicitude for your welfare, which cannot end but with my life, and the apprehension of danger, natural to that solicitude, urge me on an occasion like the present, to offer to your solemn contemplation, and to recommend to your frequent review, some sentiments; which are the result of much reflection, of no inconsiderable observation, and which appear to me all important to the permanency of your felicity as a People. These will be offered to you with the more freedom, as you can only see in them the disinterested warnings of a parting friend, who can possibly have no personal motive to bias his counsel. Nor can I forget, as an encouragement to it, your indulgent reception of my sentiments on a former and not dissimilar occasion.

Interwoven as is the love of liberty with every ligament of your hearts, no recommendation of mine is necessary to fortify or confirm the attachment.

The Unity of Government which constitutes you one people is also now dear to you. It is justly so; for it is a main Pillar in the Edifice of your real independence, the support of your tranquility at home; your peace abroad; of your safety; of your prosperity; of that very Liberty which you so highly prize. But as it is easy to foresee, that from different causes and from different quarters, much pains will be taken, many artifices employed, to weaken in your minds the conviction of this truth; as this is the point in your political fortress against which the batteries of internal and external enemies will be most constantly and actively (though often covertly and insidiously) directed, it is of infinite moment, that you should properly estimate the immense value of your national Union to your collective and individual happiness; that you should cherish a cordial, habitual and immoveable attachment to it; accustoming yourselves to think and speak of it as the Palladium of your political safety and prosperity; watching for its preservation with jealous anxiety; discountenancing whatever may suggest even a suspicion that it can in any event be abandoned, and indignantly frowning upon the first dawning of every attempt to alienate any portion of our Country from the rest, or to enfeeble the sacred ties which now link together the various parts.

For this you have every inducement of sympathy and interest. Citizens by birth or choice, of a common country, that country has a right to concentrate your affections. The name of AMERICAN, which belongs to you, in your national capacity, must always exalt the just pride of Patriotism, more than any appellation derived from local discriminations. With slight shades of difference, you have the same Religion, Manners, Habits and political Principles. You have in a common cause fought and triumphed together. The independence and liberty you possess are the work of joint councils, and joint efforts; of common dangers, sufferings and successes.

But these considerations, however powerfully they address themselves to your sensibility are greatly outweighted by those which apply more immediately to your Interest. Here every portion of our country finds the most commanding motives for carefully guarding and preserving the Union of the whole.

The *North*, in an unrestrained intercourse with the *South*, protected by the equal Laws of a common government, finds in the productions of the latter, great additional resources of Maritime and commercial enterprise and precious materials of manufacturing industry. The *South* in the same intercourse, benefitting by the Agency of the *North*, sees its agriculture grow and its commerce expand. Turning partly into its own channels the seamen of the

North, it finds its particular navigation envigorated; and while it contributes, in different ways, to nourish and increase the general mass of the National navigation, it looks forward to the protection of a Maritime strength, to which itself is unequally adapted. The *East*, in a like intercourse with the *West*, already finds, and in the progressive improvement of interior communications, by land and water, will more and more find a valuable vent for the commodities which it brings from abroad, or manufactures at home. The *West* derives from the *East* supplies requisite to its growth and comfort, and what is perhaps of still greater consequence, it must of necessity owe the *secure* enjoyment of indispensable *outlets* for its own productions to the weight, influence, and the future Maritime strength of the Atlantic side of the Union, directed by an indissoluble community of Interest as *one Nation*. Any other tenure by which the *West* can hold this essential advantage, whether derived from its own separate strength, or from an apostate and unnatural connection with any foreign Power, must be intrinsically precarious.

While then every part of our country thus feels an immediate and particular Interest in Union, all the parts combined cannot fail to find in the united mass of means and efforts greater strength, greater resource, proportionably greater security from external danger, a less frequent interruption of their Peace by foreign Nations; and, what is of inestimable value! they must derive from Union an exemption from those broils and Wars between themselves, which so frequently afflict neighbouring countries, not tied together by the same government; which their own rivalships alone would be sufficient to produce, but which opposite foreign alliances, attachments and intrigues would stimulate and embitter. Hence likewise they will avoid the necessity of those overgrown Military establishments, which under any form of Government are inauspicious to liberty, and which are to be regarded as particularly hostile to Republican Liberty: In this sense it is, that your Union ought to be considered as a main prop of your liberty, and that the love of the one ought to endear to you the preservation of the other.

These considerations speak a persuasive language to every reflecting and virtuous mind, and exhibit the continuance of the UNION as a primary object of Patriotic desire. Is there a doubt, whether a common government can embrace so large a sphere? Let experience solve it. To listen to mere speculation in such a case were criminal. We are authorized to hope that a proper organization of the whole, with the auxiliary agency of government for the respective subdivisions, will afford a happy issue to the experiment. 'Tis well worth a fair and full experiment. With such powerful and obvious motives to Union, affecting all parts of our country, while experience shall not have demonstrated its impracticability, there will always be reason, to distrust the patriotism of those, who in any quarter may endeavor to weaken its bands.

In contemplating the causes which may disturb our Union, it occurs as matter of serious concern, that any ground should have been furnished for characterizing parties by *Geographical* discriminations: *Northern* and

Southern; *Atlantic* and *Western*; whence designing men may endeavour to excite a belief that there is a real difference of local interests and views. One of the expedients of Party to acquire influence, within particular districts, is to misrepresent the opinions and aims of other Districts. You cannot shield yourselves too much against the jealousies and heart burnings which spring from these misrepresentations. They tend to render Alien to each other those who ought to be bound together by fraternal affection. The Inhabitants of our Western country have lately had a useful lesson on this head. They have seen, in the Negotiation by the Executive, and in the unanimous ratification by the Senate, of the Treaty with Spain, and in the universal satisfaction at that event, throughout the United States, a decisive proof how unfounded were the suspicions propagated among them of a policy in the General Government and in the Atlantic States unfriendly to their Interests in regard to the MISSISSIPPI. They have been witnesses to the formation of two Treaties, that with Great Britain and that with Spain, which secure to them every thing they could desire, in respect to our Foreign relations, towards confirming their prosperity. Will it not be their wisdom to rely for the preservation of these advantages on the UNION by which they were procured? Will they not henceforth be deaf to those advisers, if such there are, who would sever them from their Brethren and connect them with Aliens?

To the efficacy and permanency of Your Union, a Government for the whole is indispensable. No Alliances however strict between the parts can be an adequate substitute. They must inevitably experience the infractions and interruptions which all Alliances in all times have experienced. Sensible of this momentous truth, you have improved upon your first essay, by the adoption of a Constitution of Government, better calculated than your former for an intimate Union, and for the efficacious management of your common concerns. This government, the offspring of our own choice uninfluenced and unawed, adopted upon full investigation and mature deliberation, completely free in its principles, in the distribution of its powers, uniting security with energy, and containing within itself a provision for its own amendment, has a just claim to your confidence and your support. Respect for its authority, compliance with its Laws, acquiescence in its measures, are duties enjoined by the fundamental maxims of true Liberty. The basis of our political systems is the right of the people to make and to alter their Constitutions of Government. But the Constitution which at any time exists, 'till changed by an explicit and authentic act of the whole People, is sacredly obligatory upon all. The very idea of the power and the right of the People to establish Government presupposes the duty of every Individual to obey the established Government.

All obstructions to the execution of the Laws, all combinations and Associations, under whatever plausible character, with the real design to direct, control, counteract, or awe the regular deliberation and action of the Constituted authorities are distructive of this fundamental principle and of fatal tendency. They serve to organize faction, to give it an artificial and ex-traordinary force; to put in the place of the delegated will of the Nation, the will of a party; often a small but artful and enterprizing minority of the Com-munity; and, according to the alternate triumphs of different parties, to make the public administration the Mirror of the ill concerted and incongruous project of faction, rather than the organ of consistent and wholesome plans digested by common councils and modified by mutual interests. However combinations or Associations of the above description may now and then answer popular ends, they are likely, in the course of time and things, to become potent engines, by which cunning, ambitious and unprincipled men will be enabled to subvert the Power of the People, and to usurp for themselves the reins of Government; destroying afterwards the very engines which have lifted them to unjust dominion.

Towards the preservation of your Government and the permanency of your present happy state, it is requisite, not only that you steadily dis-countenance irregular oppositions to its acknowledged authority, but also that you resist with care the spirit of innovation upon its principles however specious the pretexts. One method of assault may be to effect, in the forms of the Constitution, alterations which will impair the energy of the system, and thus to undermine what cannot be directly overthrown. In all the changes to which you may be invited, remember that time and habit are at least as necessary to fix the true character of Governments, as of other human in-stitutions; that experience is the surest standard, by which to test the real tendency of the existing Constitution of a country; that facility in changes upon the credit of mere hypotheses and opinion exposes to perpetual change, from the endless variety of hypotheses and opinion. And remember, especial-ly, that for the efficient management of your common interests, in a country so extensive as ours, a Government of as much vigor as is consistent with the perfect security of Liberty is indispensable. Liberty itself will find in such a Government, with powers properly distributed and adjusted, its surest Guardian. It is indeed little else than a name, where the Government is too feeble to withstand the enterprises of faction, to confine each member of the Society within the limits prescribed by the laws and to maintain all in the secure and tranquil enjoyment of the rights of person and property.

I have already intimated to you the danger of Parties in the State, with particular reference to the founding them on Geographical discriminations. Let me now take a more comprehensive view, and warn you in the most solemn manner against the baneful effects of the Spirit of Party, generally.

This spirit, unfortunately, is inseperable from our nature, having its root in the strongest passions of the human Mind. It exists under different shapes in all Governments, more or less stifled, controlled, or repressed; but, in those of the popular form it is seen in its greatest rankness and is truly their worst enemy.

The alternate domination of one faction over another, sharpened by the spirit of revenge natural to party dissention, which in different ages and countries has perpetrated the most horrid enormities, is itself a frightful despotism. But this leads at length to a more formal and permanent despotism. The disorders and miseries, which result, gradually incline the minds of men to seek security and repose in the absolute power of an Individual: and sooner or later the chief of some prevailing faction more able or more fortunate than his competitors, turns this disposition to the purposes of his own elevation, on the ruins of Public Liberty.

Without looking forward to an extremity of this kind (which nevertheless ought not to be entirely out of sight) the common and continual mischiefs of the spirit of Party are sufficient to make it the interest and the duty of a Wise People to discourage and restrain it.

It serves always to distract the Public Councils and enfeeble the Public administration. It agitates the Community with ill founded jealousies and false alarms, kindles the animosity of one part against another, foments occasionally riot and insurrection. It opens the door to foreign influence and corruption, which find a facilitated access to the government itself through the channels of party passions. Thus the policy and the will of one country, are subjected to the policy and will of another.

There is an opinion that parties in free countries are useful checks upon the Administration of the Government and serve to keep alive the spirit of Liberty. This within certain limits is probably true, and in Governments of a Monarchical cast Patriotism may look with endulgence, if not with favour, upon the spirit of party. But in those of the popular character, in Governments purely elective, it is a spirit not to be encouraged. From their natural tendency, it is certain there will always be enough of that spirit for every salutary purpose. And there being constant danger of excess, the effort ought to be, by force of public opinion, to mitigate and assuage it. A fire not to be quenched; it demands a uniform vigilance to prevent its bursting into a flame, lest instead of warming it should consume.

It is important, likewise, that the habits of thinking in a free Country should inspire caution in those entrusted with its administration, to confine themselves within their respective Constitutional spheres; avoiding in the exercise of the Powers of one department to encroach upon another. The spirit of encroachment tends to consolidate the powers of all the departments in one, and thus to create whatever the form of government, a real despotism. A just estimate of that love of power, and proneness to abuse it, which predominates in the human heart is sufficient to satisfy us of the truth of this position. The necessity of reciprocal checks in the exercise of political power; by dividing and distributing it into different depositories, and constituting each the Guardian of the Public Weal against invasions by the others, has been evinced by experiments ancient and modern; some of them in our country and under our own eyes. To preserve them must be as necessary as to institute them. If in the opinion of the People, the distribution or modification of the Constitutional powers be in any particular wrong, let it be corrected by an amendment in the way which the Constitution designates. But let there be no change by usurpation; for though this, in one instance, may be the instrument of good, it is the customary weapon by which free governments are destroyed. The precedent must always greatly overbalance in permanent evil any partial or transient benefit which the use can at any time yield.

Of all the dispositions and habits which lead to political prosperity, Religion and morality are indispensable supports. In vain would that man claim the tribute of Patriotism, who should labour to subvert these great Pillars of human happiness, these firmest props of the duties of Men and citizens. The mere Politician, equally with the pious man ought to respect and to cherish them. A volume could not trace all their connections with private and public felicity. Let it simply be asked where is the security for property, for reputation, for life, if the sense of religious obligation *desert* the oaths, which are the instruments of investigation in Courts of Justice? And let us with caution indulge the supposition, that morality can be maintained without religion. Whatever may be conceded to the influence of refined education on minds of peculiar structure, reason and experience both forbid us to expect that National morality can prevail in exclusion of religious principle.

'Tis substantially true, that virtue or morality is a necessary spring of popular government. The rule indeed extends with more or less force to every species of free Government. Who that is a sincere friend to it, can look with indifference upon attempts to shake the foundation of the fabric?

Promote then as an object of primary importance, Institutions for the general diffusion of knowledge. In proportion as the structure of a government gives force to public opinion, it is essential that public opinion should be enlightened.

As a very important source of strength and security, cherish public credit. One method of preserving it is to use it as sparingly as possible: avoiding occasions of expense by cultivating peace, but remembering also that timely disbursements to prepare for danger frequently prevent much greater disbursements to repel it; avoiding likewise the accumulation of debt, not only by shunning occasions of expense, but by vigorous exertions in time of Peace to discharge the Debts which unavoidable wars may have occasioned, not ungenerously throwing upon posterity the burden which we ourselves ought to bear. The execution of these maxims belongs to your Representatives, but it is necessary that public opinion should cooperate. To facilitate to them the performance of their duty, it is essential that you should practically bear in mind, that towards the payment of debts there must be Revenue; that to have Revenue there must be taxes; that no taxes can be devised which are not more or less inconvenient and unpleasant; that the intrinsic embarrassment inseparable from the selection of the proper objects (which is always a choice of difficulties) ought to be a decisive motive for a candid construction of the Conduct of the Government in making it, and for a spirit of acquiescence in the measures for obtaining Revenue which the public exigencies may at any time dictate.

Observe good faith and justice towards all Nations. Cultivate peace and harmony with all. Religion and morality enjoin this conduct; and can it be that good policy does not equally enjoin it? It will be worthy of a free, enlightened, and, at no distant period, a great Nation, to give to mankind the magnanimous and too novel example of a People always guided by an exalted justice and benevolence. Who can doubt that in the course of time and things the fruits of such a plan would richly repay any temporary advantages which might be lost by a steady adherence to it? Can it be, that Providence has not connected the permanent felicity of a Nation with its virtue? The experiment, at least, is recommended by every sentiment which ennobles human nature. Alas! is it rendered impossible by its vices?

In the execution of such a plan nothing is more essential than that permanent, inveterate antipathies against particular Nations and passionate attachments for others should be excluded; and that in place of them just and amicable feelings towards all should be cultivated. The Nation, which indulges towards another an habitual hatred, or an habitual fondness, is in some degree a slave. It is a slave to its animosity or to its affection, either of which is sufficient to lead it astray from its duty and its interest. Antipathy in one Nation against another, disposes each more readily to offer insult and injury, to lay hold of slight causes of umbrage, and to be haughty and intractable, when accidental or trifling occasions of dispute occur. Hence frequent collisions, obstinate, envenomed and bloody contests. The Nation, prompted by ill will and resentment sometimes impels to War the Government, contrary to the best calculations of policy. The Government sometimes participates in the national propensity, and adopts through passion what reason would reject; at other times, it makes the animosity of the Nation subservient to projects of hostility instigated by pride, ambition and other sinister and pernicious motives. The peace often, sometimes perhaps the Liberty, of Nations has been the victim.

So likewise, a passionate attachment of one Nation for another produces a variety of evils. Sympathy for the favourite nation, facilitating the illusion of an imaginary common interest, in cases where no real common interest exists, and infusing into one the enmities of the other, betrays the former into a participation in the quarrels and Wars of the latter, without adequate inducement or justification: It leads also to concessions to the favourite Nation of privileges denied to others, which is apt doubly to injure the Nation making the concessions; by unnecessarily parting with what ought to have been retained; and by exciting jealously, ill will, and a disposition to retaliate, in the parties from whom equal privileges are withheld: And it gives to ambitious, corrupted, or deluded citizens (who devote themselves to the favourite Nation) facility to betray, or sacrifice the interests of their own country, without odium, sometimes even with popularity; gilding with the appearances of a virtuous sense of obligation a commendable deference for public opinion, or a laudable zeal for public good, the base or foolish compliances of ambition, corruption or infatuation.

As avenues to foreign influence in innumerable ways, such attachments are particularly alarming to the truly enlightened and independent Patriot. How many opportunities do they afford to tamper with domestic factions, to practice the arts of seduction, to mislead public opinion, to influence or awe the public Councils! Such an attachment of a small or weak, towards a great and powerful Nation, dooms the former to be the satellite of the latter.

Against the insidious wiles of foreign influence, (I conjure you to believe me fellow citizens) the jealousy of a free people ought to be *constantly* awake; since history and experience prove that foreign influence is one of the most baneful foes of Republican Government. But that jealousy to be useful must be impartial; else it becomes the instrument of the very influence to be avoided, instead of a defence against it. Excessive partiality for one foreign nation and excessive dislike of another, cause those whom they actuate to see danger only on one side, and serve to veil and even second the arts of influence on the other. Real Patriots, who may resist the intrigues of the favourite, are liable to become suspected and odious; while its tools and dupes usurp the applause and confidence of the people, to surrender their interests.

The Great rule of conduct for us, in regard to foreign Nations is in extending our commercial relations to have with them as little *political* connection as possible. So far as we have already formed engagements let them be fulfilled, with perfect good faith. Here let us stop.

Europe has a set of primary interests, which to us have none, or a very remote relation. Hence she must be engaged in frequent controversies, the causes of which are essentially foreign to our concerns. Hence therefore it must be unwise in us to implicate ourselves, by artificial ties, in the ordinary vicissitudes of her politics, or the ordinary combinations and collisions of her friendships, or enmities.

Our detached and distant situation invites and enables us to pursue a different course. If we remain one People, under an efficient government, the period is not far off, when we may defy material injury from external annoyance; when we may take such an attitude as will cause the neutrality we may at any time resolve upon to be scrupulously respected; when belligerent nations, under the impossibility of making acquisitions upon us, will not lightly hazard the giving us provocation; when we may choose peace or war, as our interest guided by our justice shall Counsel.

Why forego the advantages of so peculiar a situation? Why quit our own to stand upon foreign ground? Why, by interweaving our destiny with that of any part of Europe, entangle our peace and prosperity in the toils of European Ambition, Rivalship, Interest, Humour or Caprice?

'Tis our true policy to steer clear of permanent Alliances, with any portion of the foreign world. So far, I mean, as we are now at liberty to do it, for let me not be understood as capable of patronising infidelity to existing engagements (I hold the maxim no less applicable to public than to private affairs, that honesty is always the best policy). I repeat it therefore, let those engagements be observed in their genuine sense. But in my opinion, it is unnecessary and would be unwise to extend them.

Taking care always to keep ourselves, by suitable establishments, on a respectably defensive posture, we may safely trust to temporary alliances for extraordinary emergencies.

Harmony, liberal intercourse with all Nations, are recommended by policy, humanity and interest. But even our Commercial policy should hold an equal and impartial hand: neither seeking nor granting exclusive favours or preferences; consulting the natural course of things; diffusing and diversifying by gentle means the streams of Commerce, but forcing nothing; establishing with Powers so disposed; in order to give to trade a stable course, to define the rights of our Merchants, and to enable the Government to support them; conventional rules of intercourse, the best that present circumstances and mutual opinion will permit, but temporary, and liable to be from time to time abandoned or varied, as experience and circumstances shall dictate, constantly keeping in view, that 'tis folly in one Nation to look for disinterested favours from another; that it must pay with a portion of its Independence for whatever it may accept under that character; that by such acceptance, it may place itself in the condition of having given equivalents for nominal favours and yet of being reproached with ingratitude for not giving more. There can be no greater error than to expect, or calculate upon real favours from Nation to Nation. 'Tis an illusion which experience must cure, which a just pride ought to discard.

In offering to you, my Countrymen these counsels of an old and affectionate friend, I dare not hope they will make the strong and lasting impression, I could wish; that they will control the usual current of the passions, or prevent our Nation from running the course which has hitherto marked the Destiny of Nations: But if I may even flatter myself, that they may be productive of some partial benefit, some occasional good; that they may now and then recur to moderate the fury of party spirit, to warn against the mischiefs of foreign Intrigue, to guard against the Impostures of pretended patriotism; this hope will be a full recompense for the solicitude for your welfare, by which they have been dictated.

How far in the discharge of my Official duties, I have been guided by the principles which have been delineated, the public Records and other evidences of my conduct must Witness to You and to the world. To myself, the assurance of my own conscience is, that I have at least believed myself to be guided by them.

In relation to the still subsisting War in Europe, my Proclamation of the 22d. of April 1793 is the index to my Plan. Sanctioned by your approving voice and by that of Your Representatives in both Houses of Congress, the spirit of that measure has continually governed me; uninfluenced by any attempts to deter or divert me from it.

After deliberate examination with the aid of the best lights I could obtain I was well satisfied that our Country, under all the circumstances of the case, had a right to take, and was bound in duty and interest, to take a neutral position. Having taken it, I determined, as far as should depend upon me, to maintain it, with moderation, perserverence and firmness.

The considerations, which respect the right to hold this conduct, it is not necessary on this occasion to detail. I will only observe, that according to my understanding of the matter, that right, so far from being denied by any of the Belligerent Powers has been virtually admitted by all.

The duty of holding a Neutral conduct may be inferred, without any thing more, from the obligation which justice and humanity impose on every Nation, in cases in which it is free to act, to maintain inviolate the relations of Peace and amity towards other Nations.

The inducements of interest for observing that conduct will best be referred to your own reflections and experience. With me, a predominant motive has been to endeavour to gain time to our country to settle and mature its yet recent institutions, and to progress without interruption, to that degree of strength and consistency, which is necessary to give it, humanly speaking, the command of its own fortunes.

Though in reviewing the incidents of my Administration, I am unconscious of intentional error, I am nevertheless too sensible of my defects not to think it probable that I may have committed many errors. Whatever they may be I fervently beseech the Almighty to avert or mitigate the evils to which they may tend. I shall also carry with me the hope that my Country will never cease to view them with indulgence; and that after forty-five years of my life dedicated to its Service, with an upright zeal, the faults of incompetent abilities will be consigned to oblivion, as myself must soon be to the Mansions of rest.

Relying on its kindness in this as in other things, and actuated by that fervent love towards it, which is so natural to a Man, who views in it the native soil of himself and his progenitors for several Generations; I anticipate with pleasing expectation that retreat, in which I promise myself to realize, without alloy, the sweet enjoyment of partaking, in the midst of my fellow Citizens, the benign influence of good Laws under a free Government, the ever favourite object of my heart, and the happy reward, as I trust, of our mutual cares, labours and dangers.

THE MONROE DOCTRINE
Seventh Annual Message
December 2, 1823*

At the proposal of the Russian Imperial Government, made through the minister of the Emperor residing here, a full power and instructions have been transmitted to the minister of the United States at St. Petersburg to arrange by amicable negotiation the respective rights and interests of the two nations on the northwest coast of this continent. A similar proposal had been made by His Imperial Majesty to the Government of Great Britian, which has likewise been acceded to. The Government of the United States has been desirous by this friendly proceeding of manifesting the great value which they have invariably attached to the friendship of the Emperor and their solicitude to cultivate the best understanding with his Government. In the discussions to which this interest has given rise and in the arrangements by which they may terminate the occasion has been judged proper for asserting, as a principle in which the rights and interests of the United States are involved, that the American continents, by the free and independent condition which they have assumed and maintain, are henceforth not to be considered as subjects for future colonization by any European powers. . . . Of events in [Europe] . . . with which we have so much intercourse and from which we derive our origin, we have always been anxious and interested spectators. The citizens of the United States cherish sentiments the most friendly in favor of the liberty and happiness of their fellow-men on that side of the Atlantic. In the wars of the European powers in matters relating to themselves we have never taken any part, nor does it comport with our policy so to do. It is only when our rights are invaded or seriously menaced that we resent injuries or make preparation for our defense. With the movements in this hemisphere we are of necessity more immediately connected, and by causes which must be obvious to all enlightened and impartial observers. The political system of the allied powers is essentially different in this respect from that of America. This difference

*Messages and Papers of the Presidents 1789-1902 (11 vols.; Washington, D.C.: Bureau of National Literature and Art, 1907), II, 209, 218, 219.

proceeds from that which exists in their respective Governments; and to the defense of our own, which has been achieved by the loss of so much blood and treasure, and matured by the wisdom of their most enlightened citizens, and under which we have enjoyed unexampled felicity, this whole nation is devoted. We owe it, therefore, to candor and to the amicable relations existing between the United States and those powers to declare that we should consider any attempt on their part to extend their system to any portion of this hemisphere as dangerous to our peace and safety. With the existing colonies or dependencies of any European power we have not interfered and shall not interfere. But with the Governments who have declared their independence and maintained it, andwhose independence we have, on great consideration and on just principles, acknowledged, we could not view any interposition for the purpose of oppressing them, or controlling in any other manner their destiny, by an European power in any other light than as the manifestation of an unfriendly disposition toward the United States. . . .

The late events in Spain and Portugal show that Europe is still unsettled. Of this important fact no stronger proof can be adduced than that the allied powers should have thought it proper, on any principle satisfactory to themselves, to have interposed by force in the internal concerns of Spain. To what extent such interposition may be carried, on the same principle, is a question in which all independent powers whose governments differ from theirs are interested, even those most remote, and surely none more so than the United States. Our policy in regard to Europe, which was adopted at an early stage of the wars which have so long agitated that quarter of the globe, nevertheless remains the same, which is, not to interfere in the internal concerns of any of its powers; to consider the government *de facto* as the legitimate government for us; to cultivate friendly relations with it, and to preserve those relations by a frank, firm, and manly policy, meeting in all instances the just claims of every power, submitting to injuries from none. But in regard to those continents circumstances are eminently and conspicuously different. It is impossible that the allied powers should extend their political system to any portion of either continent without endangering our peace and happiness; nor can anyone believe that our southern brethren, if left to themselves, would adopt it of their own accord. It is equally impossible, therefore, that we should behold such interposition in any form with indifference.

THE BREZHNEV DOCTRINE

Speech by Leonid Brezhnev, General Secretary of the Soviet Communist Party, at the Fifth Congress of the Polish United Workers' Party, Warsaw, November 12, 1968 *

. . . . The socialist states stand for strict respect for the sovereignty of all countries. We emphatically oppose interference into the affairs of any states, violations of their sovereignty.

At the same time the establishment and defense of the sovereignty of states which have embarked upon the road of building socialism, is of particular significance for us Communists. The forces of imperialism and reaction seek to deprive the people now of this, now of that, socialist country, of their sovereign right they have gained to insure the prosperity of their country, the well-being and happiness of the broad mass of the working people through building of a society, free from any oppression and exploitation. And when encroachments of this right encounter a harmonious rebuff by the socialist camp, bourgeois propagandists raise a clamor around "defense of sovereignty" and "non-intervention". It is clear that this is utter fraud and demagogy on their part. In reality these shouters do not care for the maintenance of socialist sovereignty but for its destruction.

It is common knowledge that the Soviet has done much for the real strengthening of the sovereignty and independence of the socialist countries. The CPSU has always advocated that each socialist country determine the specific forms of its development along the road of socialism with consideration for its specific national conditions.

However, it is known, comrades, that there also are common laws governing socialist construction, a deviation from which might lead to a deviation from socialism as such. And when the internal and external forces hostile to socialism seek to revert the development of any socialist country toward the

---

*"Czechoslovakia and the Brezhnev Doctrine," Prepared by the *Subcommittee on National Security and International Operations of the Committee on Government Operations*, U.S. Senate (Washington, D.C. :U.S.Government Printing Office, 1969). pp. 22-23.

restoration of the capitalist order, when a threat to the cause of socialism in that country, a threat to the security of the socialist community as a whole, emerges, this is no longer only a problem of the people of that country but also a common problem, concern, for all socialist states.

It goes without saying that such an action as military aid to a fraternal country to cut short the threat to the socialist order is an extraordinary enforced step; it can be sparked off only by direct actions of the enemies of socialism inside the country and beyond its boundaries, actions creating a threat to the common interests of the camp of socialism.

Experience shows that in present conditions the victory of the socialist order in this or that country can be regarded as final and the restoration of capitalism can be regarded as excluded only if the Communist Party, as the guiding force of society, firmly carries through a Marxist-Leninist policy in the development of all spheres of public life; only if the party indefatigably strengthens the defense of the country, the defense of its revolutionary gains, if it maintains itself and propagates amidst the people vigilance with regard to the class enemy, irreconcilability to bourgeois ideology; only if the principle of socialist internationalism is being sacredly observed, the unity and fraternal solidarity with other socialist countries is being strengthened. . . .

BASIC PRINCIPLES OF RELATIONS BETWEEN THE UNITED STATES OF AMERICA AND THE UNION OF SOVIET SOCIALIST REPUBLICS

Moscow, May 29, 1972*

The United States of America and the Union of Soviet Socialist Republics,

Guided by their obligations under the Charter of the United Nations and by a desire to strengthen peaceful relations with each other and to place these relations on the firmest possible basis,

Aware of the need to make every effort to remove the threat of war and to create conditions which promote the reduction of tensions in the world and the strengtheing of universal security and international cooperation,

Believing that the improvement of US-Soviet relations and their mutually advantageous development in such areas as economics, science and culture, will meet these objectives and contribute to better mutual understanding and business-like cooperation, without in any way prejudicing the interests of third countries,

Conscious that these objectives reflect the interests of the peoples of both countries,

Have agreed as follows:

First. They will proceed from the common determination that in the nuclear age there is no alternative to conducting their mutual relations on the basis of peaceful coexistence. Differences in ideology and in the social systems of the USA and the USSR are not obstacles to the bilateral development of normal relations based on the principles of sovereignty, equality, non-interference in internal affairs and mutual advantage.

Second. The USA and the USSR attach major importance to preventing the development of situations capable of causing a dangerous exacerbation of their relations. Therefore, they will do their utmost to avoid military confrontations and to prevent the outbreak of nuclear war. They will always exercise restraint in their mutual relations, and will be prepared to negotiate and settle differences by peaceful means. Discussions and negotiations on outstanding issues will be conducted in a spirit of reciprocity, mutual accommodation and mutual benefit.

---

*"U.S.-Soviet Commercial Relations: The Interplay of Economics, Technology Transfer, and Diplomacy," Prepared for the *Subcommittee on National Security Policy and Scientific Developments of the Committee on Foreign Affairs*, U.S. House of Representatives (Washington, D.C.: U.S. Government Printing Office, 1973), pp. 81-83.

Both sides recognize that efforts to obtain unilateral advantage at the expense of the other, directly or indirectly, are inconsistent with these objectives. The prerequisites for maintaining and strengthening peaceful relations between the USA and the USSR are the recognition of the security interests of the Parties based on the principle of equality and the renunciation of the use or threat of force.

Third. The USA and the USSR have a special responsibility, as do other countries which are permament members of the United Nations Security Council, to do everything in their power so that conflicts or situations will not arise which would serve to increase international tensions. Accordingly, they will seek to promote conditions in which all countries will live in peace and security and will not be subject to outside interference in their internal affairs.

Fourth. The USA and the USSR intend to widen the juridical basis of their mutual relations and to exert the necessary efforts so that bilateral agreements to which they are jointly parties are faithfully implemented.

Fifth. The USA and the USSR reaffirm their readiness to continue the practice of exchanging views on problems of mutual interest and, when necessary, to conduct such exchanges at the highest level, including meetings between leaders of the two countries.

The two governments welcome and will facilitate an increase in productive contacts between representatives of the legislative bodies of the two countries.

Sixth. The Parties will continue their efforts to limit armaments on a bilateral as well as on a multilateral basis. They will continue to make special efforts to limit strategic armaments. Whenever possible, they will conclude concrete agreements aimed at achieving these purposes.

The USA and the USSR regard as the ultimate objective of their efforts the achievement of general and complete disarmament and the establishment of an effective system of international security in accordance with the purposes and principles of the United Nations.

Seventh. The USA and the USSR regard commercial and economic ties as an important and necessary element in the strengthening of their bilateral relations and thus will actively promote the growth of such ties. They will facilitate cooperation between the relevant organizations and enterprises of the two countries and the conclusion of appropriate agreements and contracts, including long-term ones.

The two countries will contribute to the improvement of maritime and air communications between them.

Eighth. The two sides consider it timely and useful to develop mutual contacts and cooperation in the fields of science and technology. Where suitable, the USA and the USSR will conclude appropriate agreements dealing with concrete cooperation in these fields.

Ninth. The two sides reaffirm their intention to deepen cultural ties with one another and to encourage fuller familiarization with each other's cultural values. They will promote improved conditions for cultural exchanges and tourism.

Tenth. The USA and the USSR will seek to ensure that their ties and cooperation in all the above-mentioned fields and in any others in their mutual interest are built on a firm and long-term basis. To give a permanent character to these efforts, they will establish in all fields where this is feasible joint commissions or other joint bodies.

Eleventh. The USA and the USSR make no claim for themselves and would not recognize the claims of anyone else to any special rights or advantages in world affairs. They recognize the sovereign equality of all states.

The development of U.S.-Soviet relations is not directed against third countries and their interests.

Twelfth. The basic principles set forth in this document do not affect any obligations with respect to other countries earlier assumed by the USA and the USSR.

For the United States of America
Richard Nixon
President of the United States of America
For the Union of Soviet Socialist Republics
Leonid I. Brezhnev
General Secretary of the Central Committee, CPSU

NOTES

PREFACE

1. *A Discourse on Statesmanship: The Design and Transformation of the American Polity* (Urbana, Ill.: University of Illinois Press, 1974).

2. *The Philosophy of the American Constitution: A Reinterpretation of the Intentions of the Founding Fathers* (New York: Free Press, 1968), and *On the Silence of the Declaration of Independence* (Amherst: University of Massachusetts Press, 1976).

3. Jefferson, as Rector of the University of Virginia, recommended the inclusion of the Farewell Address, along with *The Federalist* and other writings, in a required textbook for the university's law school (which Madison called the "school of politics").

4. In his *Letter to the Soviet Leaders* (New York: Harper & Row, 1974), from which the epigraph of this Preface is taken, Alexander Solzhenitsyn writes: ". . . witness how mighty America lost to tiny North Vietnam, how easily the nerves of American society and American youth gave way, precisely because the United States has a weak and undeveloped national consciousness" (p. 46).

CHAPTER 1

1. See Georges Clemenceau, *Grandeur and Misery of Victory* (New York: Harcourt, Brace & Co., 1930), p. 272. I am indebted to William Morrisey for bringing this statement to my attention.

2. Henry A. Kissinger (ed.), *Problems of National Security* (New York: Praeger Publications, 1965), p. 477.

3. Although Secretary Kissinger might agree with the principles about to be enunciated, we already have seen, and will see more fully in Chapter 6, that he is not always consistent in his statement of these principles, and that his actions, in the main, are not conducive to their fulfilment.

4. I have in mind two kinds of moralists, one on the "right", the other on the "left", meaning, respectively, *fanatical* anti-communists, and anti-anticommunists. The latter are the principal concern of this discussion in view of their predominance. But rather than use distracting and invidious quotation marks or other designations to distinguish these two species of moralists, I shall rely on the reader to judge from the context whether one or the other or both are intended.

5. *The Necessity for Choice* (New York: Harper & Row, 1961), p.289, which constitutes an implicit critique of J. William Fulbright, *Old Myths and New Realities* (New York: Vintage Books, 1964), p. 77. Although Fulbright is primarily a pragmatist, moralistic elements are not absent from his thought, as may be seen in his *Arrogance of Power* (New York: Vintage Books, 1966), pp.7, 250, 254-255. The truth is that very few people are consistent pragmatists or, for that matter, consistent moralists. Dr. Kissinger, of course, is not a moralist and does not, or once did not, commit the error of "confusing dogmatism with morality", to quote from *The Necessity for Choice*, p. 352. Unfortunately, he has never made it clear to the public just what is the nature of morality. And though he has publicly denied that morality and pragmatism are antithetical, he seems in fact to have shifted toward the pragmatism of Fulbright.

6. Obviously this does not apply to moralists of the "right" associated with the policy of "liberation", a policy which can hardly be contemplated now that the Soviet Union, in addition to its conventional military superiority, has achieved at least nuclear parity with the United States. Here I should make it perfectly clear that this book is not the work of a "cold warrior", any appearances to the contrary notwithstanding. Although I abhor Communism, I am well aware that the moralistic or fanatical anti-communism of the "right" is sterile, to say the least.

7. Henry A. Kissinger, *A World Restored: Metternich, Castlereagh and the Problems of Peace 1812-1822* (Boston: Houghton Mifflin Co., 1973), p. 1. See also the same position taken in *The Necessity for Choice*, pp. 86, 89, 97, 184.

8. As Professor Kissinger has wisely written: "We will finally be judged not so much by the cleverness of our arguments as by the purposefulness and conviction, indeed by the majesty, of our conduct." See *ibid.*, p. 339.

9. In his press conference of Dec. 27, 1973, Secretary Kissinger explicitly rejected a policy of "selective détente", saying: ". . . it is obvious that it is not possible for a country to exacerbate tensions in one area and to seek relaxation in another. This Administration has consistently opposed the notion of selective détente, in which one area would be pacified while there would be very active conflict in another." Cited in Foy D. Kohler *et al, The Soviet Union and the October 1973 Middle East War: Implications for Détente* (Miami: Center for Advanced International Studies, University of Miami, 1974), p. 4 (hereafter cited as Kohler, *Middle East War*). This publicly professed either/or foreign policy is hardly consistent with Dr. Kissinger's apparent abhorrence of black and white distinctions or with his predilection for "nuance". But see above, pp. 127, 130-133, 136, for related and contradictory policy statements. More recently, in his press conference of December 23, 1975 on Angola, Secretary Kissinger declared: "The issue is not whether a pro-Soviet faction is becoming dominant in Angola. . . . We accepted in Mozambique [but not in Chile, Dr. Kissinger]. . . a pro-Marxist faction that came to power by indigenous means . . . [T]he issue is whether the Soviet Union, backed by a Cuban expeditionary force, can impose on two-thirds of the population its own brand of government." *New York Times*, Dec. 24, 1975, p. 7. This publicly confusing position can hardly stand the test of geopolitical analysis.

10. For one of the finest works on Lincoln's statesmanship, see Harry V. Jaffa, *Crisis of the House Divided* (New York: Doubleday & Co., 1959), republished by the University of Washington Press in 1973. As the reader will see, I shall apply Lincoln's statesmanship on a domestic issue, that of slavery in the territories, to foreign affairs. Since the territories were not sovereign states, the analogy is not in all respects

applicable. Nevertheless, in the main, the value and validity of the analogy will soon be apparent.

11. Needless to say, I am speaking of the abolitionists who, with regard to slavery, have much in common with anti-communist "liberationists". Disconcerting as it will no doubt be, contemporary anti-anti-communists stand on the same moral grounds as Stephen Douglas (of whom, more in a moment). Unfortunately, it is beyond the scope of this work to develop the curious similarities and differences between the various species of moralists and pragmatists on the issues of slavery and Communism.

12. *The Collected Works of Abraham Lincoln* (9 vols.; New Brunswick, N. J.: Rutgers University Press, 1953-55), II, 461-462 (cited hereafter as *Works*).

13. *Ibid.*, III, 254-255.

14. *Ibid.*, III, 254.

15. See *ibid.*, II, 465, where Lincoln says that the purpose and effect of the Nebraska doctrine and Dred Scott "is to *educate* and *mould* public opinion, at least *Northern* public opinion, to not *care* whether slavery is voted *down* or voted *up*." Is it unjust to say that this comes very close to the attitude of anti-anti-communism?

16. Consider Communist Russia's dependence on Western capital and technology (of which, more later). Consider too its dependence on the granaries of the West to feed its own people.

17. See above, pp. 176-177.

CHAPTER 2

1. All references to the Farewell Address are taken from George Washington, *The Writings of George Washington* (39 vols; Washington, D.C.: U. S. Government Printing Office, 1931-44), XXXV, p. 217, reprinted in its entirety as Appendix 2 above.

2. Alexander Hamilton, John Jay, and James Madison, *The Federalist* (New York: Modern Library, 1938), Edward Meade Earle, ed., p. 55. All further references to *The Federalist* will be to this edition.

3. James Madison, *The Writings of James Madison* (9 vols.; New York: G. P. Putnam's Sons, 1900-10), Gaillard Hunt, ed., V, 29.

4. See Paul Eidelberg, *Discourse on Statesmanship*, p. 36.

5. Alfred North Whitehead, *Adventures of Ideas* (New York: Macmillan Co., 1933), p. 65.

6. See Paul Eidelberg, *The Philosophy of the American Constitution*, pp. 133-134.

7. Paul Eidelberg, *On the Silence of the Declaration of Independence*, p. 9.

8. In *Federalist* 6, however, Hamilton suggests that the form of government is not a principal cause of international conflict. But before resting with this conclusion, one must reflect upon Hamilton's rhetorical objective in that number. Be this as it may, there can be no doubt that Hamilton, like Madison, traces the ultimate cause of war to human nature.

9. For a further discussion of the Madisonian solution to the problem of faction, see my *Discourse on Statesmanship*, under Index.

10. As a matter of fact, consistent with British practice and terminology, it was not uncommon in those days (and this is certainly true of Hamilton) to identify the executive branch as the "government".

11. For a further discussion of this passage, see *ibid.*, pp. 302-304. See, also, *Federalist* 37 (cited above, p. 31).

12. Here I wish to acknowledge Professor Herbert Storing of the University of Chicago for this insight.

13. For an elaboration of this point, see my *Discourse on Statesmanship*, p. 52.

14. Abraham Lincoln, *Works*, IV, 267-268. See, also, Linclon's "Address Before the Young Men's Lyceum of Springfield", *ibid.*, I, 112-113, for a qualification of the preceding.

15. Harry V. Jaffa, *Crisis of the House Divided*, p. 195. See, also, my *Discourse on Statesmanship*, pp. 437-440, for a discussion of the rule of law versus the rule of reason.

16. See *Federalist* 78, p. 503.

17. See *Federalist* 73, p. 478, *Federalist* 49, pp. 328-329, and *Federalist* 62, pp. 405, 407.

18. See *Federalist* 70, p. 455.

19. 1 *Cranch* 137, 165-166 (1803). Notice that Marshall is careful to make a distinction between the discretionary powers of the President and the rights of individuals. He knew that the courts are not designed to decide cases involving political matters such as national security. Rather, they are designed to decide cases concerning individual rights. Unfortunately, these two subjects sometimes overlap. This means that the legitimate exercise of executive discretion may sometimes implicate the rights of some individual. For example, the executive may possess certain confidential documents relevant to the case of an individual accused of some criminal offense, but the disclosure of which documents might undermine national security. Recognizing this, the Congress, in 1957, provided by law (the Jencks Act) that the government may refuse to disclose such documents even though, in some instances, this could lead to a mistrial or to the termination of a prosecution. By so doing, Congress was merely recognizing that there are circumstances in which legitimate national interests outweigh the interest in punishing a particular individual.

20. John Stuart Mill, *Representative Government* in *Utilitarianism, Liberty, and Representative Government*, (New York: E. P. Dutton & Co., 1951, pp. 240-241.

21. See the author's *Discourse on Statesmanship*, pp. 86, 200-201, 321.

22. See *ibid.*, pp. 211-212, 239.

23. *The Writings of George Washington*, XXXV, 316-317 (Dec. 7, 1796). For a discussion of this proposal, see my *Discourse on Statesmanship*, pp. 220-224.

24. See *ibid.*, p. 214.

CHAPTER 3

1. Man is the only creature endowed with the freedom to violate his own nature, the only creature, therefore, with a sense of shame. Thus Nietzsche could say man is the beast with red cheeks.

2. Edward Dumbauld (ed.), *The Political Writings of Thomas Jefferson* (New York: Liberal Arts Press, 1955), p. 91.

3. See my *Discourse on Statesmanship*, pp. 23, 180-190.

4. See my *Philosophy of the American Constitution*, p. 219.

5. As we shall see in Chapter 8, however, this intended quality of American foreign policy can lead to unintended and pernicious consequences.

6. By no means do I wish to dignify Senator Fulbright's characterization of American foreign policy of the 1960's as arrogant. A criticism of Senator Fulbright's thoughts on foreign policy will be found in my essay *On the Silence of the Declaration of Independence*, pp. 36-42.

7. This departure from the Platonic and Aristotelian emphasis on internal perfection as opposed to external glory ought not be evaluated simply according to classical criteria; or rather, the adequacy of classical standards ought not be taken for granted. It can be argued that the goals of the United States, as conceived in the Farewell Address, are more magnificient than those of classical regimes.

8. See below, p. 216, n. 19.

9. So too, of course, is justice understood as a system of rewarding each according to his merit.

10. A policy of indiscriminate as opposed to selective détente may thus be regarded as a manifestation of a hedonistic and permissive society.

11. *The Book of Morals and Conduct*, cited in Bernard Lewis, "Friends and Enemies", *Encounter* (Feb. 1968), p. 3.

12. It may sometimes be necessary for a republic to befriend a tyranny in order to defend itself against a still worse tyranny. See above, pp. 152-153.

13. A foreign policy based on moral relativism is not to be confused with a policy of neutrality or of non-belligerancy, such as that proclaimed by the Washington Administration vis-à-vis France and England. In this connection, see Hamilton's *Pacificus* papers in *The Works of Alexander Hamilton* (12 vols.; New York: G. P. Putnam's Sons, 1904), Henry Cabot Lodge, ed., IV, 432-489.

14. A twelve-year study using computers to prove the obvious was recently announced in the *Honolulu Star Bulletin*, Jan. 27, 1975, p. A-16. The director of the study, Professor R. J. Rummel, reports that he and his colleagues, after analyzing millions of bits of information on international relations, focusing especially on the United States, the Soviet Union, and Communist China, find that "Nations that . . . trade a lot, that have much communication and contact, have as much conflict as nations that ignore each other. . . . Peace is not to be bought by trade, nor apparently by any other kind of coöperation." The study is to be published in a book entitled *National Attributes and Behavior: Data, Dimensions and Linkages*.

The subject of American-Soviet trade will be discussed in Chapters 4 and 5. See above, esp. pp. 87-90, 97-98, 128-129.

15. See Robert Conquest *et al*, "Détente: An Evaluation", reprinted from the *International Review*, No. 1, Spring 1974, for the Subcommittee on Arms Control of the Committee on Armed Services, U. S. Senate (Washington, D.C.: U. S. Government Printing Office, 1974), p. 11.

16. See "Negotiation and Statecraft", *Hearings Before the Permanent Subcommittee on Investigations of the Committee on Government Operations*, U.S. Senate, 93rd Cong., 1st sess. (Washington, D.C.: U.S. Government Printing Office, 1973), Part II with Leopold Labedz, pp. 106-107 (cited hereafter as *Labedz*), and Part I with Walter Laqueur, pp. 15-17 (cited hereafter as *Laqueur*).

17. See below, p. 241, n. 52, for Secretary Kissinger's views on this subject.

18. Rhetorically, of course, it would have been imprudent for the Declaration to have implied that monarchies in general are unjust regimes, for this would have won

enmity rather than support from monarchical Europe. Incidentally, Tsarist Russia did not recognize the United States until 1809.

19. Consider in this connection the criticism once directed against the "authoritarian" government of our former ally, South Vietnam. The same criticism is now being levelled against the governemnt of South Korea which, in consequence of the defeat of the United States in Indochina as well as in response to threats from the North, has placed stringent restricitons on freedom of speech and press. On the other hand, note how many of the same critics are anxious for the United States to extend diplomatic relations with Cuba, a regime in which freedom of speech and press is utterly non-existent.

20. In this connection it should be noted that, in his last State of the Union Message, Washington proposed the establishment of a military academy—the future West Point.

21. See below, p. 240, n. 44, for a recent example of how the Viet Cong manipulated and divided American public opinion.

22. See Lyndon Baines Johnson, *Vantage Point* (New York: Popular Library, 1971), p. 475: "Many critics claimed that I was so preoccupied with Southeast Asia that I was . . . passing up opportunities to ease the Cold War tensions with Russia. . . . The Soviet propaganda machine fed this notion, both openly and through informal contacts with individuals."

23. George F. Kennan, *Memoirs 1925-1950* (Boston: Little, Brown & Co., 1967), p. 555. In a letter written in 1923 to an American Negro Communist, Leon Trotsky urged that "The training of black agitators is the most important revolutionary problem of the moment." See "Recognition of Russia", *Hearings Before a Subcommittee of the Committee on Foreign Relations*, U.S. Senate, 68th Cong., 1st sess., Jan. 21-24, 1924 (Washington, D.C.: U.S. Government Printing Office, 1924), Part II, p. 209.

24. *Memoirs 1925-1950*, pp. 558-559. See above, p. 159n.

25. See his *The Use and Abuse of History* (Indianapolis: Bobbs-Merrill Co., 1957). See, also, Henry A. Kissinger, *The Necessity for Choice*, pp. 207-208, 296, 311-312, 321-322, who, as Secretary of State, however, seems to have changed his mind about the corrosive effects of skepticism, judging from the political relativism which underlies his foreign policy.

26. See the present author's *On the Silence of the Declaration of Independence*, Ch. 3.

27. See *ibid.*, and below, p. 225, n. 49.

28. George F. Kennan, *Memoirs 1925-1950*, pp. 563-564.

29. Says Kennan: "Let us not forget Stalin's first reaction when he met Ribbentrop. It was to joke good-naturedly and cynically about the bitter propaganda war which had been waged for so many years between the two countries." (*ibid*). Says Henry A. Kissinger: "Anyone succeeding in Communist leadership struggles must be single-minded, unemotional, dedicated, and, above all, motivated by an enormous desire for power. Nothing in the personal experience of Soviet leaders would lead them to accept protestations of good will at face value." *American Foreign Policy*, p. 37.

30. The failure in question is to be attributed, in part, to a fear of "McCarthyism". In Senator Joseph McCarthy the Soviet Union had its most effective ally; for it was his demagogic and anti-intellectual form of anti-communism that is largely responsible for the ascendancy of anti-anticommunism in the United

States. The form of anti-communism I am advocating is perfectly consistent with reason and civility. It deplores moral fanaticism, but also the moral indifferentism underlying anti-anti-communism.

31. In a letter to the author, a friend recently proposed the following trenchant question: "Is it propaganda *from* the communists which is responsible for th[e present demoralizing] trend, or could one not better say that there already exist, independent of Soviet or other forces, rather deep longings for something like communism among certain segments of the population? Those longings may not be fully articulated, but they are powerful at times and they almost of their own force generate a receptivity to even the slightest hints from the communist powers. In other words, I suggest Marxist rhetoric is significant because it attaches itself to something natural in man and quite widespread; thus, there are a lot of natural communists among men always, or at least in democratic ages. It does not take communist direction to create that sympathy, but [communists] will find it available to some extent everywhere. The real problem seems to be within our society itself; the leaders need to recognize that not all men are naturally in favor of freedom, that some need desperately to be ruled, precisely because of those elements of their souls that make them receptive to Marxism." While I agree with this profound observation, which supplements or qualifies the argument of the text, it should be noted that Communism has also had a peculiar appeal to certain elements of the wealthy. See S. Orwell & I. Angus (eds.), *The Collected Essays, Journalism and Letters of George Orwell* (4 vols.; New York: Harcourt, Brace & World, 1968), I. 344-347, 365 (cited hereafter as Orwell, *Essays*). Orwell's penetrating insights into the political attitudes and motivations of the rich and of intellectuals in England before and during World War II reveal much about their American counterparts today.

CHAPTER 4

1. V. I. Lenin, *Selected Works* (New York: International Publishers, 1971), p. 613 (1-vol. ed.).

2. Headnote in Peter Viereck, *Conservatism Revisited* (New York: The Free Press, 1965), rev. ed., p. 29.

3. See T. Timofeyev, "The Communist Manifesto Versus Antiproletarian Utopias", *Kommunist*, No. 3, 1973, in *Reprints from the Soviet Press*, 17:2 (New York: Compass Publications, July 27, 1973), p. 5.

4. See Robert C. McCloskey (ed.), *The Works of James Wilson* (2 vols.; Cambridge: Harvard University Press, 1967), I, 145-146.

5. This point is elaborated in my *Discourse on Statesmanship*, p. 322, n. 12.

6. *Manifesto of the Communist Party*, in Lewis S. Feuer (ed.), *Marx and Engels: Basic Writings on Politics and Philosophy* (New York: Doubleday Anchor Books, 1959), p. 7, cited hereafter as *Communist Manifesto*, with Marx regarded as the principal author, consistently with Engels' own admission (p. 4).

7. Karl Marx and Frederick Engels, *The German Ideology* (New York: International Publishers Co., 1968), pp. 40-41 (henceforth referred to under the authorship of Marx). A critique of this doctrine will be found in my *Discourse on Statesmanship*, pp. 9-12, 154-155, 270.

8. *Communist Manifesto*, p. 26 (italics added). See, also, *The German Ideology*, p. 39, where it is said: "The ideas of the ruling class are in every epoch the ruling ideas:

i.e. the class, which is the ruling material force of society, is at the same time its ruling intellectual force." For a refutation of this statement, see my *Discourse on Statesmanship*, p. 356.

9. *The German Ideology*, p. 113. For a critique, see my *Discourse on Statesmanship*, p. 8, n. 3.

10. But see the *Communist Manifesto*, p. 17, and *The German Ideology*, pp. 69, 72, where Marx deviates from strict determinism—this, to allow, without evident justification, for his own intellectual independence.

11. *Communist Manifesto*, pp. 9-10.

12. *The German Ideology*, pp. 28-29.

13. See Lloyd D. Easton and Kurth H. Guddat (eds.), *Writings of the Young Marx on Philosophy and Society* (New York: Doubleday Anchor Books, 1967), p. 252 (italics in the orginal), cited hereafter as *Writings of the Young Marx*.

14. *Ibid.*, p. 257. Apropos of Marx's lack of a truth orientation, Mr. William Morrisey has pointed out in correspondence to the author that Marx "uses [the words] 'conflict' and 'contradiction' interchangeably, as if the struggle between oligarchs and democrats were somehow illogical. More precisely, he wants it to *seem* illogical—a clever rhetorical device that treats a political community as if it were a logical formula."

15. *The German Ideology*, pp. 14-15.

16. *Communist Manifesto*, p. 18.

17. Alexander Solzhenitsyn, *The Gulag Archipelago* (New York: Harper & Row, 1973), p. 27. Whereas Lenin reduces certain human beings to the level of insects, Nikita Khrushchev reduces them to the level of weeds. See his speech delivered at the CPSU Central Committee Plenum, 21 June 1963, in *Daily Report Supplement USSR & East Europe*, No. 17, July 1, 1963, p. 6, where he says: "Every peasant knows that the worst enemies of the fields are the sonchus (osot), the couch grass, and other weeds. Therefore he carefully protects his crops against weeds. He protects and cultivates the useful plants but destroys mercilessly the weeds. The same holds true of society. . . ."

18. I am well aware that Lenin, unlike Marx, was simply a philosophical materialist (at least judging from his *Materialism and Empirio-Criticism*). But here I am not concerned with Lenin's epistemology, but with his *political* teachings. Similarly, while it is true that Marx sought to synthesize French materialism and German idealism, the influence of his philosophy on the politics and political thinking of the twentieth century has been overwhelmingly materialistic. What this means is that Marx's writings should be understood not only for their theoretical significance, and as they might be understood by scholars (who are themselves divided in their interpretation of Marxism), but also for their impact on the public in general, and on revolutionary statesmen in particular.

Leaving Marxist revisionists aside (on which, see Oscar Gruenwald, "Marxist Humanism", *ORBIS* 18:3 (Fall 1974), pp. 888-916; Thomas Molnar, "Marxist Revisionism: A Commentary," *Modern Age* 16:3 (Summer 1972 , pp. 301-308), consider Zbigniew Brzezinski, *Between Two Ages: America's Role in the Technetronic Era* (New York: Viking Press, 1971), a work frequently perceptive but lacking philosophical and analytical rigor when dealing with the most serious issues, such as Marxism and the so-called "end of ideology". Apparently influenced by Marxist revisionism, which magnifies out of all proportion the significance of Marx's "early" writings (but which writings, we shall presently see, are fully consistent with those of the "later" Marx), Brzezinski has succumbed to the notion that Marxism is in the rationalist and humanist tradition (pp. 72-73, 83, 123, 126-127, 136-137, 147-148, 154, 162, 241). He thereby slights Marx's most important theory, that of dialectical or historical materialism, a theory which degrades the role of reason on the one hand, and which consequently emphasizes the role of violence (which it encourages) on the other. At the same time, while deploring ideology, Brzezinski does not explicitly analyse or define this historically ambiguous and many-sided concept (pp. 63, 93, 117-119, 136-137, 154, 281-285 *passim*, 293, 307, 308-309). Finally, it is a pity that this perspicacious expert on international relations should also come very close to succumbing to the still fashionable cultural relativism of the present era (pp. 66n, 93, 118, 162, 176, 214n, 272), despite his recognition that skepticism is destructive of society (pp. 196, 241). Indeed, vis-à-vis the Soviet Union, nothing would more undermine the survival of the United States than a foreign policy based on skepticism or cultural relativism.

19. As suggested in the previous footnote, this doctrine derives from Marx's materialistic theory of history. I emphasize the doctrine of revolution, however, because of its more obvious historical significance. Here I should also mention that Marx himself would no doubt have based his claim to greatness on his critique of political economy in *Capital;* but much of the theoretical underpinning of that monumental work seems to have been discredited.

20. Niccolo Machiavelli, *The Prince*, Ch. XV.

21. See Henry A. Kissinger, *The Necessity for Choice*, p. 335, comparing Eisenhower's and Khrushchev's behavior at the United Nations General Assembly in September, 1960.

22. V. I. Lenin, *Selected Works* (New York: International Publishers, 1943), Vol. X, p. 138. See, also, Leonid Brezhnev, *On the Policy of the Soviet Union and the International Situation* (New York: Doubleday & Co., 1973), p. 23 (cited hereafter as *The Policy of the Soviet Union*), where Brezhnev writes: "Lenin warned that the road to socialism 'will never be straight; it will be incredibly involved.' " For examples of Soviet zigzags, see Orwell, *Essays*, IV, 153-160, and note the critique of moral relativism.

23. Consider the forced evacuation of Phnom Penh and other Cambodian cities after their fall to the Communists in 1975. Hundreds of thousands of men, women, and children are reported to have died of the resulting starvation and outbreaks of disease. See *Los Angeles Times*, Aug. 12, 1975, Pt. I, pp. 1,14.

24. *Communist Manifesto*, p. 34.

25. *Ibid.*, p. 35. See, also, *The German Ideology*, pp. 32, 34, 80-81, 112, where Marx repeatedly uses quotation marks around man or mankind.

26. *Communist Manifesto*, p. 14.

27. *Ibid.*, p. 19. The most ominous harbinger is contained in the ninth of the ten measures Marx prescribes for the proletarian dictatorship, namely, "gradual abolition of the distinction between town and country, by a more equable distribution of the population" (p. 28). The word "gradual" notwithstanding, in practice this cannot but lead to forced proletarianization, hence mass terror.

28. But see his estimate of the proletariat in the *Critique of Hegel's Philosophy of Law*, in *Writings of the Young Marx*, pp. 261-263, as well as of "crude communism" in *Economic and Philosophic Manuscripts, ibid.*, p. 302. On the other hand, consider

his high regard for the material accomplishments of the bourgeoisie which he praises for having "rescued a considerable part of the population from the idiocy of rural life", *Communist Manifesto*, pp. 10-12.

29. In the *Manifesto*, Marx writes: "Hitherto, every form of society has been based, as we have already seen, on the antagonism of oppressing and oppressed classes" (p. 19).

30. *Capital* (New York: Modern Library, n.d.), p. 15.

31. See *The German Ideology*, p. 7, and compare Nathan Rotenstreich, *Basic Problems of Marx's Philosophy* (Indianapolis: Bobbs-Merrill Co., 1965), pp. 34-46.

32. *Economic and Philosophic Manuscripts*, p. 304. See *ibid.*, pp. 311-312.

33. *Ibid.*, p. 306.

34. *Ibid.*, p. 294, and compare my own theory of sociological individualism in *A Discourse on Statesmanship*, pp. 270-276.

35. *Communist Manifesto*, p. 22. As suggested above, such a teaching justifies, and has in fact contributed to, the extermination of countless millions. According to Solzhenitsyn, *"In addition* to the toll of two world wars, we have lost, as a result of civil strife and tumult alone—as a result of internal political and economic 'class' extermination alone—66 (sixty-six) million people!!! That is the calculation of a former Leningrad professor of statistics, I. A. Kurganov. . . . " See Solzhenitsyn, *Letter to the Soviet Leaders*, p. 30. Solzhenitsyn attributes this monstrous slaughter to Marxist ideology. See *ibid.*, p. 48, and *The Gulag Archipelago*, p. 174.

36. See V. I. Lenin, *State and Revolution*, in *Selected Works*, 1-vol. ed., p. 277, referring specifically to Engels, but equally applicable to Marx.

37. See *ibid.*, " 'Left-Wing' Communism—An Infantile Disorder", p. 535, where Lenin says: "The dictatorship of the proletariat means a persistent struggle—bloody and bloodless, violent and peaceful, military and economic, educational and administrative—against the forces and traditions of the old society. The force of habit in millions and tens of millions is a most formidable force." For a not so subtle justification of terror, see also *ibid., State and Revolution*, p. 329, and "Where to Begin?" p. 39. On *permanent revolution* see Karl Marx, *the Class Struggles in France, 1848 to 1850*, in Lewis Feuer (ed.), *Marx and Engels: Basic Writings*, p. 317, who writes: "This [revolutionary] socialism is the *declaration of the permanence of the revolution*, the *class dictatorship* of the proletariat as the necessary transit point to the *abolition of class differences generally.* . . ." A similar statement will be found in Marx's *The Eighteenth Brumaire of Louis Bonaparte, ibid.*, p. 324. Stalin draws the doctrine of permanent revolution from Marx's "Address to the Communist League" (1850). See Joseph Stalin, *Foundations of Leninism* (New York: International Publishers, 1939), pp. 42-43. The topics of permanent revolution and terror are discussed in my essay, "The Temptation of Herbert Marcuse", *The Review of Politics*, 31:4 (Oct. 1969), pp. 454-456.

38. *Critique of Hegel's Philosophy of Law*, in *Writings of the Young Marx*, p. 264.

39. Inasmuch as man, according to Marx, is a man-made product, there is no reason why, within the purview of Marxism, he should not experiment upon himself or upon other men, say by altering the genetic code. But consider Marx's *Economic and Philosophic Manuscripts, ibid.,* pp. 293, 295.

40. V. I. Lenin, "A Contribution to the History of the Question of Dictatorship", *Communist International*, No. 14, Nov. 6, 1920, *Collected Works*, XXXI, 326, cited

in Bertram D. Wolfe, *Khrushchev and Stalin's Ghost,* (New York: Praeger Publications, 1957), p. 9. See, also, Alexander Solzhenitsyn, *The Gulag Archipelago Two* (New York: Harper & Row, Publishers, 1975), p. 17, *in re* Lenin's order to "carry out merciless mass terror".

CHAPTER 5

1. Anatole Kuznetsov, the Russian novelist who defected to Britain, whom Amalrik reproaches for having collaborated with the KGB. See below, p. 238, n. 32.

2. Andrei Amalrik, *Will the Soviet Union Survive Until 1984?* (New York: Perennial Library, 1970), p. 103 (cited hereafter as *Amalrik*).

3. But see Jeri Laber, "The Real Solzhenitsyn", *Commentary,* 57:5 (May, 1974), p. 32, where Solzhenitsyn is condemned for being a "reactionary", i.e., for his failure to be an advocate of "liberal values".

4. For my initial explanation of this phenomenon, see above, p. 47.

5. *Amalrik*, p. 96. On internal and external freedom, see also Alexander Solzhenitsyn, *From Under the Rubble* (Boston: Little, Brown & Co., 1975), pp. 21-22, 255.

6. *Ibid.,* pp. 36-37.

7. Various nations have submitted to Peking's pressure to derecognize Taiwan as a condition for establishing diplomatic relations.

8. This is the position taken by John Bassett Moore, *The Collected Papers of John Bassett Moore,* cited and uncritically accepted by Edward M. Bennett, *Recognition of Russia* (Waltham: Blaisdell Publishing Co., 1970), p. 125. It should be noted that Bennett's work is influenced by moral relativism, symptoms of which appear on pp. 6, 49, 51, 60, 69, 124, 137.

For a contemporaneous discussion of the legal meaning and political significance of recognition and non-recognition, see Chesney Hill, "Recent Policies of Non-Recognition", in *International Conciliation, Documents for the Year 1933* (New York: Carnegie Endowment for International Peace), pp. 380, 387-388.

9. Prior to recognition, President Roosevelt and Maxim Litvinov signed a series of agreements covering such issues as non-interference in internal affairs, religious and civil rights of American nationals, economic espionage, etc. By holding the 1935 Comintern meeting in Moscow, Russia violated the fourth article of the agreement, on which see above, p. 104.

10. *Time,* 26:11 (Sept. 9, 1935), p. 21.

11. According to Bennett, *Recognition of Russia,* pp. 122-123, President Roosevelt, in announcing the results on his negotiations with Litvinov on November 17, 1933, deliberately avoided the use of the word "recognition". Professor Bennett comments: "It was his desire that the nation be made to understand that 'recognition' of the Soviet Union was not the subject of the negotiations, but rather it was merely the resumption of 'normal relations' with Russia." Needless to say, this face-saving fiction could only mislead rather than educate the public.

12. Thomas B. Brockway (ed.), *Basic Documents in United States Foreign Policy* (New York: D. Van Nostrand Co., 1957), p. 104. Note, however, the tension

between the disclaimer of the *de jure* element and the position taken by Secretary of State Elihu Root appearing in the first headnote of this chapter.

13. Cited in Donald C. Bishop, *The Roosevelt-Litvinov Agreements* (Syracuse: Syracuse University Press, 1965), p. 16. Bishop notes earlier (p. 15) that Philip Marshall Brown, a former American diplomat, wrote to Hull on October 27:

"Please allow me to express my conviction that no reliance whatever can be placed upon the foreign policy and diplomatic relations of the Soviet Union. These are based on cynical grounds of expediency without the least respect for fundamental principles either of law or of honor. Any assurances they might offer either in treaties or otherwise have but slight value if they believe Marxian principles are endangered."

14. Recall Washington exhorting his countrymen to "observe good faith and justice towards all Nations. Cultivate peace and harmony with all."

15. See *ibid.*, pp. 9-10.

16. See Robert Paul Browder, *The Origins of Soviet-American Diplomacy* (Princeton: Princeton University Press, 1953), pp. 38-82, 171 (hereafter cited as Browder, *Soviet-American Diplomacy*), and Louis Fischer, *Why Recognize Russia?* (New York: Jonathan Cape and Harrison Smith, 1931), pp. 147-166 *passim.*

Shortly after the Soviet repudiation of the 1972 trade agreement, Donald M. Kendall, Chairman of Pepsi Cola Co. (who, together with Soviet Foreign Minister Vladimir S. Alkhimov, is co-chairman of the U.S.-USSR Trade and Economic Council), told reporters that without credit restrictions, $2 billion in U. S. governemnt credits for the Soviet Union would finance $6 billion worth of Soviet business in this country, which in turn could create 240,000 jobs. See *Los Angeles Times*, Feb. 22, 1975, Pt. I, p. 6.

17. See Bishop, *The Roosevelt-Litvinov Agreements*, p. 8, and Browder, *Soviet-American Diplomacy*, pp. 108, 219.

18. See *ibid.*, Appendix A, Table III, pp. 224-225. The American export trade to Russia rose from $16,000,000 in 1921 to $114,000,000 in 1930, declined to $9,000,000 in 1933, and increased to $70,000,000 in 1938.

19. See, *ibid.*, chs. 8-9, *passim.*

20. See Antony C. Sutton, *Western Technology and Soviet Economic Development 1917-1930* (Stanford: Hoover Institution Publications, 1968), p. 295.

21. This was admitted by Litvinov after recognition. See Browder, *Soviet-American Diplomacy*, pp. 178, 191-192.

22. Robert Conquest, *et al.*, *Détente: An Evaluation*, p. 10. Notice how even the South and mid-West in 1975 pressed for U.S. grain shipments to the Soviet Union. If the most passionately anti-communist regions in the U.S. could succumb to the manipulations of "détente". . . . See, also, Mikhail Agursky, "Contemporary Socioeconomic Systems and Their Future Prospects", in Solzhenitsyn, *From Under the Rubble*, who claims that one "incorrigible defect of the existing systems is their growing political instability as a result of the West's increasing dependence on external commodities markets and sources of raw materials, and the Communist countries' drive to expand. The saturation of their own markets leads the Western countries to seek new markets indiscriminately, so as to keep their industry working. This makes them increasingly dependent on raw material supplies from other countries, for the most part those that possess no manufacturing industry of their own [i.e., the Third World]. Therefore, if some state poses a threat to peace and freedom, business circles, fearing the loss of markets or sources of raw material, begin to put pressure on their governments to soften their policies toward that state. This is why Western countries,

despite their own enormous potential, are incapable of resisting dictatorships and totalitarian regimes" (p. 73). In the sequel, Agursky claims that business interests in Britain and France were behind the Munich Agreement of 1938.

23. See Whittaker Chambers, *Cold Friday* (New York: Random House, 1964), p. 223, who writes: "Almost without exception the great businessmen are charmed and impressed by the great Communists whenever history (or trade) has brought them together face to face. They find they speak the same language, i.e., the language of power and action stripped of intellectual baggage. But fate is glimpsed grimly in this fact: though the great Communists fool and baffle the great businessmen, the great businessmen are no puzzle to the great Communists who see straight through and beyond them."

24. *Economic Review of the Soviet Union*, 9:3 (March 1934), p. 59. Mr. Watson went on to express the "hope that Russia will not allow any criticism to be spread in this country against the form of governemnt which we operate." Commenting on this very same statement in his *Soviet-American Diplomacy*, Browder points out, with uncommon perspicuity, that "Apparently, he [Mr. Watson] did not see the distinction between domestic criticism of a foreign regime and foreign agitation within the United States" (p. 171). Dr. Kissinger also fails to make this distinction. See above, p. 188.

25. Robert Conquest, *et al.*, "Détente: An Evaluation", p. 13.

26. See Orwell, *Essays*, I, 333, III, 202-204, IV, 195 (on press "censorship" of anti-Soviet writings); IV-173-174, 178-179 (quoted on p. 180n* above); and III, 222-223 (*in re* moral relativism).

27. Quoted by George Meany in "Détente", *Hearings Before the Committee on Foreign Relations*, U.S. Senate, 93rd Cong., 2nd sess. (Washington, D.C.: U.S. Government Printing Office, 1975), p. 377 (cited hereafter as *Senate Hearings of 1974 on Détente*). See, also, Dean Acheson, *Power and Diplomacy* (Cambridge: Harvard University Press, 1959), p. 96, who writes: "No matter how plainly the Russians talk and act, we simply refuse to believe what they say and to understand the meaning of what they do." But as Marx and Engels wrote in the *Communist Manifesto:* "The communists disdain to conceal their views and aims." For the attitudes of the British intelligentsia toward Communism in the 1930s, see Orwell, *Essays*, I, 512-516.

28. For additional evidence in support of this conclusion, see the statement of Secretary of State Cordell Hull quoted in Bishop, *The Roosevelt-Litvinov Agreements* p. 8 *et seq.*, and Browder, *Soviet-American Diplomacy*, p. 108. Here it should be noted that I have deliberately avoided the relatively minor issue of the Russian debts, on which see *ibid.*, pp. 72, 135-140, and Bishop (just cited), Ch. 5 *passim*.

29. See Browder, *Soviet-American Diplomacy*, pp. 67-71, 107-112, 165-168, 198, and Bennett, *Recognition of Russia*, pp. 137, 161-164, 179-186.

30. See *Laqueur*, p. 53. Whittaker Chambers put the matter more tellingly: "Surely it is not too sweeping to say that there in nothing secret about Communism. For decades, its motives, purposes, and specific strategies have been explicitly stated by Communists themselves, and freely disseminated in the West. Even its guiltiest secrets are known in wearisome detail. Seldom in history can the actions of any cause have been subjected to so minute a picking-over in the very course of their occurence. It makes not the slightest practical difference. On the one hand, the disclosures lead to a hue of moral outrage. On the other hand, the West continues to deal with the Communist center as if this were not true. Thus the West itself engages with respect to Communism in a kind of double-think which it supposes to be one of Communism's distinctive faculties." See his *Cold Friday*, p. 75 *et seq.*

31. Solzhenitsyn, *The Gulag Archipelago*, p. 178. See, also, Orwell, *Essays*, III, 227, condemning British intellectuals as "boot-licking propagandists of the Soviet regime."

32. See below, p. 186.

33. *The Gulag Archipelago*, p. 46.

34. See below, p. 225, n. 50.

35. See p. 241, n. 52. below, *in re* the 1973 Senate confirmation hearings on Dr. Kissinger, and compare my own recommendations for the recognition of Communist China, pp. 153-155 above.

36. Two things, however, must be remembered. First, by July, 1936, the time of Franco's military uprising, Republican Spain was already in an advanced state of disintegration. Political, regional, and anticlerical fanaticism was propelling the regime toward some form of dictatorship. See Franz Borkenau, *The Spanish Cockpit*, (London: Faber & Faber Ltd., 1937), Chs. 1 & 5. Second, some Western governments may have preferred Franco to the Republicans because there were among the latter communists, socialists, and anarchists. According to Orwell (*Essays*, I, 412), "from the middle of 1937 until nearly the end of the war the Spanish Government was directly under the control of Moscow." A communist Spain might have posed a greater threat to the West. Orwell contends, however, that "If the British and French Governments had really wanted to counter the Russian influence, by far the quickest way was to supply the Spanish Government with arms, for . . . any country that supplied arms could control Spanish policy" (*ibid.*). Whatever the case, the withholding of arms may have been a decision based on moral judgement or prudence as opposed to moralism or doctrinairism. See *ibid.*, I. 316-317, 346-247, 269-278; II, 262-263; IV, 493.

37. Japan had invaded Manchuria six years earlier.

38. Of course, one could lead to the other, as a hostile conservative press was soon to point out.

39. As tyrannical ideologies, Communism and National Socialism have much in common. Western statesmen would be well advised to regard and occasionally to refer to Communism as pseudo-philosophical Fascism. See Orwell, *Essays*, II, 25-26, 80.

40. See my *Discourse on Statesmanship*, Chs. 10-12 *passim*, and Archibald MacLeish, *The Irresponsibles* (New York: Duell, Sloan & Pearce, 1940), p. 28. referring, implicitly, to the moral relativism prominent among American scholars. Compare Orwell, *Essays*, III, 99-100.

41. Quoted in Charles E. Bohlen, *Witness to History 1929-1969* (New York: W. W. Norton & Co., 1973), p. 150. Bohlen comments: "It is tragic to think that these noble, eloquent words were to be proved so wrong in so few years. As naïve as they sound now, the words did express his [Roosevelt's] hopes for the future, and even I, with all my doubts, shared them." That Mr. Bohlen should find nobility in these words strikes me as naïve, to say the least. The same naïveté may be seen in W. Averell Harriman & Elie Abel, *Special Envoy to Churchill and Stalin 1941-1946* (New York: Random House, 1975), pp. 277-278. In this connection it should be noted that Roosevelt came to Teheran with knowledge of the Katyn Forest Massacre, where the Russians slaughtered thousands of Poles, mostly from the military and professional elite. See *ibid.*, p. 200; J. K. Zawodny, *Death in the Forest* (Notre Dame: University of Notre Dame Press, 1962), pp. 178-183; E. A. Komorowski, *Night Never Ending* (Chicago: Henry Regnery Press, 1974), Ch. 13.

42. Interestingly enough, Louis Fischer quotes a remark by William Bullitt, our first ambassador to the Soviet Union, soon after his arrival in Moscow. "After all",

said Bullitt, "the President, Jack Reed and I are of the same American strain." John Reed, author of *Ten Days that Shook the World*, was a prominent American Communist who was killed in Moscow during the Bolshevik Revolution. See Louis Fischer, *Men in Politics* (New York: Duell Sloan & Pearce & Co., 1966), p. 299. See, also, Bennett, *Recognition of Russia*, p. 133, according to whom "Roosevelt thought of the Russian diplomats as having a framework of political beliefs very much like those of Americans."

43. If, as legal realists maintain, the just is identical with the legal, then the statesmen of the Declaration were unjust men. Or what is to say the same, if to be just is to be law-abiding, then Amalrik and Solzhenitsyn were justly punished.

44. This suggests that legal realism underlies not only the "spirit of Helsinki". Consider the *de facto* character of the United Nations which, in 1974, recognized or dignified the leader of the PLO terrorists, Yasser Arafat. (In 1975, however, the General Assembly, dominated by despotic regimes, condemned Zionism as racism.)

45. As one economist explains capitalist economics: "We are not concerned with the origin of [men's] wants or with their 'rightness' or 'wrongness' from any absolute point of view. It is a matter of indifference to us whether these wants are due to snobbishness, extravagance, ignorance, or bad habit. We do not wish to distinguish between the want for bread, for holidays on the Riviera, or for opium. We simply note that human beings experience wants." See Erich Roll, *Elements of Economics* (London: Oxford University Press, 1937), p. 42. The same moral relativism will be found even in Frederick Hayek, *The Road to Serfdom* (Chicago: University of Chicago Press, 1944), pp. 58-59.

46. The problem is to synthesize capitalism and morality, or freedom and virtue. On the latter, see my *Discourse on Statesmanship*, pp. 273-275.

47. See Antony C. Sutton, *Western Technology and Soviet Economic Development 1917-1930*, pp. 348, 317-340 *passim*.

48. This anecdote is told by Senator Henry Jackson in *Laqueur*, p. 30.

49. The mere fact that relativists deny the immortality of the soul would psychologically (though illogically) predispose them to regard violent death as the *summum malum*. Consider the abolition of capital punishment in this light.

50. See above, pp. 38-41 and my *Discourse on Statesmenship*, p. 280. True, Wilson refused to recognize not only the Soviet Union, but the Huerta dictatorship of Mexico. It is the case, however, that Wilson was what may be called a first-generation democrat whose moral fervor had yet to succumb to the "pragmatism" of second-generation democrats. It is also true that non-democratic regimes maintained diplomatic relations with the Soviet Union (such as Nazi Germany, although Nazism is a form of relativism). But the point of my argument is not that a regime's democratic or relativistic character is sufficient to determine whether it will accord diplomatic recognition to a communist or fascist dictatorship. No, the point is that such a regime will be the more prone to moral indifferentism or obscurantism, with the consequence that material interests, rather than moral considerations, will be sufficient to determine the question of recognition. And here I do not wish to be construed as a "moralist". The "moralist" tends to make an absolute distinction between material interests and moral considerations. This is an error if only because a nation's physical survival is a moral imperative. On the other hand, no less important than a nation's physical survival is its moral or political survival, that is to say the survival of what it stands for as a nation. Finally, unlike the doctrinaire moralist, I hold that the question of recognition cannot be determined solely by reference to moral precepts.

Moral precepts facilitate but cannot replace moral judgement, on which see *ibid*., pp. 154-157, 171-173, 437-440, and my work, *On the Silence of the Declaration of Independence*, Ch. 4, esp. pp. 64-65.

51. See Browder, *Soviet-American Diplomacy*, p. 158. Browder notes (on p. 159) that Stalin referred to Roosevelt as a "realist" who sees things as they are. Leaving aside the naïve epistemological realism (on which, see my *Discourse on Statesmanship*, pp. 270-276 *passim*), is a realist also to be defined as one who *accepts* things as they are?

52. John Spargo, "The Soviet Union: Question of Recognition", *Current History* (Sept. 1930), p. 1075.

53. Cited in my *Discourse on Statesmanship*, p. 384.

54. The theme of honor is discussed in *ibid*., pp. 258-262 (see Index, under Honor), and is further elaborated in *On the Silence of the Declaration of Independence*, Ch. 2.

55. In *The Papers of Alexander Hamilton* (15 vols., t.d.; New York: Columbia University Press, 1961-1969), Harold C. Syrett, ed., XIV, 309-3 (italics in the original), hereafter cited as *Papers*.

56. *Ibid*., XIV, 372, 374-375.

57. The principle of self-determination is discussed above, pp. 165-166, and in my work *On the Silence of the Delcaration of Independence*, Ch. 5, esp. pp. 94-96.

58. Hamilton, *Papers*, XIV, 386. With Hamilton's humanity and magnanimity compare Lenin: "It was, of course, only on grounds of expediency that we rejected individual terrorism." (*Selected Works*, 1-vol. ed., p. 526), and Stalin: "The freedom of the people can be built only on the bones of the oppressors, the soil for the self-rule of the people with the blood of the oppressors!" (Cited in Nathan Leites, *A Study of Bolshevism* (Glencoe: Free Press, 1953), p. 350.

59. In a letter dated May 18, 1793 (*Papers*, XIV, 475-476), Hamilton had this to say of those who would compare the American and French Revolutions:

The cause of France is compared with that of America during its late revolution. Would to Heaven that the comparison were just. Would to Heaven that we could discern in the Mirror of French affairs, the same humanity, the same decorum, the same gravity, the same order, the same dignity, the same solemnity, which distinguished the course of the American Revolution. Clouds & Darkness would not then rest upon the issue as they now do.

I own, I do not like the comparison. When I contemplate the horrid and systematic massacres . . . of September—When I observe that a Marat and a Robespierre, the notorious prompters of those bloody scenes—sit triumphantly in the Convention . . .—When I see an unfortunate Prince, whose reign was a continued demonstration of the goodness & benevolence of his heart, of his attachment to the people, of whom he was Monarch—who though educated in the lap of despotism, had given repeated proofs, that he was not the enemy of liberty—brought precipitately and ignominiously to the block,—without any substantial proof of guilt, as yet disclosed—without even an authentic exhibition of motives, in decent regard to the opinions of mankind—When I find the doctrines of Atheism openly advanced in the Convention and heard with loud applauses—When I see the sword of fanaticism extended to force a political creed upon citizens who were invited to submit to the arms of France as the harbingers of Liberty—When I behold the hand of Rapacity outstretched to prostrate and ravish monuments of religious worship erected by those citizens and their ancestors—When I perceive passion, tumult and violence usurping those seats, where reason and cool deliberation ought to preside—

I acknowledge, that I am glad to believe, there is no real resemblance between what was the cause of America & what is the cause of France—that the difference is no less great than that between Liberty & Licentiousness. I regret whatever has a tendency to confound them, and I feel anxious, as an American, that the ebullitions of inconsiderate men may not tend to involve our Reputation in the issue.

CHAPTER 6

1. The full text of these agreements is contained in "Establishment of Diplomatic Relations with the Union of Soviet Socialist Republics", Department of State, Eastern European Series, No. 1 (Washington, D.C.: Government Printing Office, 1933).

2. *Communist Manifesto*, p. 41 (italics added).

3. For an elaboration of this topic, see my *Discourse on Statesmanship*, pp. 230-231, and above, p. 138 *et seq*.

4. It may be objected that the United States and the Soviet Union have a common interest in the avoidance of nuclear war which transcends their ideological differences. Such an objection suggests a renunciation of ideology (recalling the "end of ideology" school referred to in Chapter 3). It should be emphasized, however, that neither the Declaration of Independence nor the *Communist Manifesto* regards violent death as the greatest evil. But more on this topic later.

5. *Adventures of Ideas*, p. 367 (italics added).

6. *Khrushchev Remembers* (Boston: Little, Brown & Co., 1970), p. 512.

7. Three of the eight factors of the Soviet strategy of octangular war will now come under discussion. The others portrayed in Chapter 1 will be considered *en passant*.

8. See above, pp. 4-6 (*in re* Lincoln), 138-139, and my *Discourse on Statesmanship*, pp. 437-440.

9. *Ibid.*, pp. 266-269.

10. It has been estimated that some 5 billion dollars worth of American arms have been lost to the Communists. But infinitely more important are the 17 million people of South Vietnam.

11. Cited in Kohler, *Middle East War*, p. 23. Documentary evidence of Soviet encouragement of the Arab oil embargo is provided in *ibid.*, pp. 59-60, 69, 73-75, 80-85. Even Dr. Kissinger admits that "the use of the oil weapon . . . is partly due to the Soviet Union." See *Senate Hearings of 1974 on Détente*, p. 267. It should be noted that Russia replaced the United States in 1974 as the world's leading oil refiner.

12. Quoted in Kohler, *Middle East War*, p. vii. In view of Russia's historic ambitions in the Middle East, it is simply untrue that Soviet influence in that crossroads

of three continents depends largely on the continued existence of Israel. There are enough differences among Arab states for Moscow to exercise its skill in *divide et impera.*Not that the Politburo is committed to Israel's extinction. It simply regards the survival of that democracy as strategically less significant than the elimination of the United States from the Middle East.

12a. Quoted in *ibid.*, p. x.

13. See Martin Schiff, "The United States and United Nations: On a Collision Course", *ORBIS*, 18:2 (Summer 1974), pp. 553-581 *passim.*

14. In view of the declining power of the United States resulting from the various forms of non-nuclear conflict discussed earlier—a decline resulting, in part, from a diminished understanding and consequent soft-pedalling of our ideological differences with the Soviet Union—it is misleading merely to say with former Senator J. William Fulbright that "Détente, in its essence, is an agreement not to let these differences explode into nuclear war." Cited in Theodore Draper, *Commentary* (June 1969), p. 39.

15. Compare the present discussion with Whitehead's discussion of "The Order of Nature" in *Process and Reality* (New York: Harper Torchbooks, 1960), Pt. II, Ch. III *passim.*

16. The success of the rescue obscures the more fundamental failure of the United States in Indochina. Indeed, as Professor Rood has said in a note to the author, that success appears almost as though the Communists had thrown us a sop for our pride.

17. See my essay *On the Silence of the Declaration of Independence,* Ch. 4, for a discussion of the sometimes non-conflicting relationship between force and reason.

18. See Washington's Farewell Address, p. 199 above, for a related teaching.

19. In view of the argument presented in the Introduction (p. 5), Lincoln's contention that "this government cannot endure, permanently half *slave* and half *free*" suggests that peaceful coexistence between the Soviet Union and the United States is, in the long run, impossible—as Khrushchev tacitly admitted in his memoirs.

20. Here it will not do to speak of the possibility of "convergence" between the two regimes, for in that event one or the other (or both) will, in the process, have ceased to retain its teleological existence or defining characteristics. Interestingly enough, in his speech to the CPSU Central Committee Plenum on June 21, 1963 (cited earlier), Khrushchev ridiculed the "convergence theory" saying: "Imperialist ideologists [believe] . . . that the more educated people there are in the Soviet Union, the more vulnerable Soviet society will become to the ideological sphere . . . and that with the growth of material well-being and culture, the Soviet people will come out against party leadership" (p. 17). For a penetrating critique of "convergence theory", see Henry A. Kissinger, *The Necessity for Choice*, pp. 287-308. See, also, Solzhenitsyn' *From Under the Rubble*, p. 17.

21. On Penkovskiy, see below, p. 232, n. 47. Surely it is wise to assume that missiles with 25 megaton warheads are intended to destroy hardened ICBMs, hence retaliatory forces. The Soviet Union is reported to have 313 of such missiles. See Edward Luttwak, *The U.S.-USSR Nuclear Weapons Balance* (Beverly Hills: Sage Publications, 1974), and the recent statement of former Secretary of Defense James R. Schlesinger reported in the *Los Angeles Times*, June 21, 1975, Pt. I, p. 1.

22. Both cited in S. T. Cohen and W. P. Lyons, "A Comparison of U.S.-Allied and Soviet Tactical Nuclear Force Capabilities and Policies", *ORBIS*, 19:1 (Spring

1975), p. 82. See, also, Roger W. Barnett, "Trans-Salt: Soviet Strategic Doctrine", *ORBIS*, 19:2 (Summer 1975), pp. 533-561.

23. "It is well to remember", Professor Kissinger has nonetheless warned, "that Mr. Khrushchev has justified the need for peaceful coexistence primarily by one argument: the disastrous nature of modern war for *both* sides. Should the strategic balance shift so that this condition is no longer met, the reason for even the formal defense of peaceful coexistence will fall away." *The Necessity of Choice*, p. 97.

24. The Brezhnev Doctrine is printed as Appendix 4. Note that it would justify Soviet intervention in Red China.

25. "Peaceful coexistence" is thus related to the communist notion that what is mine is mine, and what is yours is negotiable.

26. Richard M. Nixon, *Six Crises* (Garden City: Doubleday & Co., 1962), pp. 241-242.

27. *Ibid.*, pp. 244, 245, 256, 261, 267. "If", writes Nixon, "we are not constantly to be in the position of negotiating the rate of our retreat, we must counter [Khrushchev's] demands—which are designed to extend slavery—with our own, which have the objective of extending freedom." (273). See p. 228, n. 19 above.

27a. See Kohler, *Middle East War*, pp. 12-20 for statements by Brezhnev, Kosygin, and Marshal Grechko unambiguously affirming the Soviet intention to assist by military and other means revolutionary movements directed against the status quo.

28. Quoted more fully on pp. 147-148 above.

29. I have especially in mind former Senator J. William Fulbright who, during the Senate hearings on Vietnam in 1966, posed the following rhetorical question to General Maxwell Taylor: "How do you describe the war of 1776? Was that a war of national liberation, or wasn't it?" See "Supplemental Foreign Assistance, Fiscal Year 1966—Vietnam", *Hearings Before the Committee on Foreign Relations*, U.S. Senate, 89th Cong., 2nd sess. (Washington, D.C.: U.S. Government Printing Office, 1966), p. 441. This blurring of distinctions is typical of moral relativists.

30. Cited in *Laqueur*, p. 7. See, also, Foy D. Kohler *et al, Soviet Strategy for the Seventies: From Cold War to Peaceful Coexistence* (University of Miami: Center for Advanced International Studies, 1973), p. 135, *et seq.*

31. Quoted more fully on p. 147 above.

32. According to Dr. Kissinger, "the significance of cultural exchange in reducing immediate political tensions is vastly overrated." *The Necessity of Choice*, pp. 181, 190. This is an understatement. Helsinki clearly reveals that Moscow uses cultural exchange as "concessions" for more significant concessions from the West. Furthermore, as an element of its octangular strategy, cultural exchange is used to lull the West and to increase the number of KGB agents in the United States. See Oleg Penkovskiy, *The Penkovskiy Papers* (Garden City: Doubleday & Co., 1965), Chs. 2 and 7, (cited hereafter as *The Penkovskiy Papers*).

33. A cardinal objective of Soviet psychological warfare is to silence anti-Soviet or anti-communist criticism in the West. As noted in the *New York Times* (Feb. 7, 1974), "The Soviet contention clearly is that Moscow is free to tell lies about the West but the West must not tell the truth about the Soviet Union." This recalls Lincoln's Cooper Union Address wherein he asked, What must the North do to satisfy Southern slave holders? "This", he answered, "and this only: cease to call slavery *wrong*, and join them in calling it *right*." *Works*, III, 547.

34. These five tendencies are promoted by the "revisionist theory" of the "cold war", for a critique of which see Raymond Aron, *The Imperial Republic* (Englewood Cliffs, N. J. : Prentice-Hall, Inc., 1974), Ch. 1.

35. Cited by *Labedz*, pp. 53-54.

36. *Ibid.*, p. 54.

37. See "United States/Soviet Military Balance", A Study by the Library of Congress, printed for the use of the Senate Committee on Armed Forces (Washington, D.C.: U.S. Government Printing Office, 1976); "Hearings on Military Posture", *Department of Defense Authorization for Appropriations for FY 1977 Before the Committee on Armed Services*, House of Representatives, 94th Cong., 2nd sess., Part 1 of 5 Parts, *Military Posture*, 1976, pp. 117, 147, 366, 1021-1022, 1540-1541; "Hearings on Military Posture", *Committee on Armed Services*, House of Representatives, 94th Cong., 2nd sess., Part 4 of 5 Parts, *Subcommittee on Sea Power and Strategic and Critical Materials—Navy Shipbuilding and Conversion (SCN) Program for FY 1977, Torpedoes and Other Weapons*, 1976, p. 619; *Report No. 94-967 of the Committee on Armed Services*, House of Representatives, 94th Cong., 2nd sess., "Authorizing Appropriations, FY 1977, for Military Procurement, Research and Development . . .", 1976, pp. 20-23; *Hearings before the Committee on Armed Services*, U.S. Senate, 93rd Cong., 2nd sess., on S. 3000, "Fiscal Year 1975 Authorization for Military Procurement, Research and Development . . .", Part 2, *Authorizations*, 1974, pp. 424, 426-427, 440, 455.

38. See Conquest, *et al.*, "Détente: An Evaluation", p. 7.

39. Cited in *Labedz*, p. 55.

40. Admittedly, the ground for anti-anticommunism was prepared by Senator Joseph McCarthy, a demagogue who surely was the Soviet Union's most effective though unwitting agent in this country.

41. Cited in *Labedz*, p. 113.

42. The *New York Times* (Dec. 11, 1972), reports that, "As the Soviet Union has moved toward improved relations with the West this year, its secret police have mounted a determined campaign of repression against the domestic dissident movement that has left some dissenters feeling weaker, more vulnerable and more on the defensive than at any time since the mid-nineteen-sixties" (p. 1). Furthermore, "Mr. [Andrei] Sakharov, the physicist, had remarked privately that the situation has become worse for dissenters as Soviet relations have improved with Western nations, especially since the visit to Moscow last May of President Nixon. He contends that Soviet authorities now believe Western public opinion is more concerned with improving relations and trade and will thus ignore police actions against Soviet civil-rights activists" (p. 26). Mr. Sakharov's predictions have proven accurate. Only consider President Ford's failure (under Kissinger's advice) to receive Solzhenitsyn at the White House in 1975—on the eve of the . . . ! See the *Senate Hearings of 1974 on Détente*, testimony of George Meany, pp. 378-379, as well as that of Dr. Kissinger who contends (on p. 249) that the Soviet Government has sought " . . . . . . to calm its public opinion by joining in a relaxation of tensions". Dr. Zhores A. Medvedev, who was expelled from the Soviet Union in August, 1973, also claims that there has been a relaxation of repression since the Khrushchev era (*ibid.*, pp. 428-431). Meanwhile, Solzhenitsyn gives evidence of an increase in repression under Brezhnev. See his *From Under the Rubble*, p. 252. Recently, Moscow poet Vladimir Bukovsky

and Ukrainian Historian Valenty Moroz have both been incarcerated for their advocacy of civil liberties. And in Yugoslavia, Mihaljo Mihaljov was sentenced to seven years of hard labor for contributing five articles to American media and Russian emigré journals in Western Europe. See the statement by Senator Henry Jackson, *Congressional Record*, 121:5 (March 26, 1975), and *The Christian Science Monitor*, Jan. 27, 1975, p. 3. These contradictory impressions may be resolved as follows: First, it is true that the Soviet Union under Brezhnev is less repressive than it was under Stalin, given the absence of unadulterated terror. But the absence of such terror may only be indicative of its lasting success, rather than of "liberalization". Second, it is not uncommon for tyrants to tolerate, occasionally, the public expression of criticism in order to identify and place under closer scrutiny potential rallying points of opposition. (Consider, in this connection, Mao's policy of "Let a Hundred Flowers Blossom, Let a Hundred Schools of Thought Contend", a policy which flushed out critics of the regime and which resulted in their brutal repression.) Finally, by allowing a handful of dissidents to speak out, while suppressing one or another outstanding figure (like Amalrik), the rulers of the Soviet Union can cow the timid and still convey to the unwary the impression of "liberalization".

43. Statements of Italian and French communist party leaders issued during the twenty-fifth Congress of the CPSU in 1976 to the effect that they would pursue an independent foreign policy and work within the democratic process should be treated with skepticism, to say the least. Such statements are intended to disarm the West on the one hand, and to win votes away from democratic socialists on the other.

44. Needless to say, these are hardly the conclusions of Secretary of State Henry Kissinger. See his testimony before the Senate Foreign Relations Committee, presented on September 19, 1974, in the *Senate Hearings of 1974 on Détente*, pp. 247-260, which is emphatically silent about the role of the Soviet Union in the Middle East War of October 1973.

45. Inasmuch as détente is publicly understood to mean the end of the "cold war" and the beginning of amiable relations with the Soviet Union, its mendacity should be evident by the mere absence of détente *within the United States itself.* Considering the extent of hostility between American citizens or the tensions and conflicts between various groups in American society, not to mention the domestic crime and violence, the political and economic fraud and deception, the extortion and economic blackmail—all displayed in one country whose people ostensibly share the same traditions, or who are supposedly governed by the same laws and institutions—in view of all this internal hostility, it is simply foolish or self-demeaning nonsense to think that genuine détente is possible between two nations so fundamentally opposed in their principles and purposes as Soviet Russia and the United States. But is it any wonder that our civil authorities, during the period of Soviet-American "détente", have become increasingly willing to negotiate with and thereby dignify domestic criminals and militant groups engaged in violence and blackmail? Finally, given the precedent of "détente", is it any wonder that the United Nations should recognize and thereby dignify the gun-slinging Yasser Arafat?

46. According to KGB defector Anatol Golytsyn, Khrushchev planned to have Richard Nixon assassinated if the latter had won the 1960 election. See *Los Angeles Times*, March 18, 1975, Pt. I, p. 5.

Beyond Détente

47. See *The Penkovskiy Papers*, pp. 52, 73, 84-85, 184, 249-259, 334, 368. Penkovskiy was a colonel in the GRU. Disillusioned with the Soviet regime, and fearful of its aggressive intentions toward the West, he photographed and passed to British and American intelligence thousands of top-secret documents, including the Soviet war plans—all this during the period of 1961-62. (See esp. pp. 249-259.) Although Penkovskiy knew he was under the surveillance of the KGB, rather than defect to the West (as he was urged to do once his British and American contacts became aware of his imminent danger), he preferred to remain in Russia to continue working for the ultimate freedom of his country. Arrested in 1962, he was subsequently tried and executed.

48. *Senate Hearings of 1974 on Détente*, pp. 247, 248.

49. *Ibid.*, p. 260. Of the various factors which may explain the differences between *Professor* and *Secretary of State* Kissinger, consider Orwell's observation that political responsibility makes men timid and foreshortens their perspectives. *Essays*, II, 430. See, also, below, p. 234, n. 68.

50. *Senate Hearings of 1974 on Détente*, p. 247.

51. See his statement in *ibid.*, p. 259.

52. In his press conference of October 25, 1973, Secretary Kissinger indicated that détente means little more than that "confrontations are kept within bounds that do not threaten civilized life." Cited in Theodore Draper, "Détente", *Commentary* (June 1974), p. 39.

53. For an account of legislative restrictions on East-West trade, see John P. Hardt and George D. Holliday, "U.S.-Soviet Commercial Relations: The Interplay of Economics, Technology Transfer, and Diplomacy" prepared for the *Subcommittee on National Security Policy and Scientific Developments of the Committee on Foreign Affairs*, House of Representatives, (Washington, D.C.: U.S. Government Printing Office, 1973), pp. 48-50 (cited hereafter as Hardt, *U.S.-Soviet Commercial Relations*).

54. Hardt, (*ibid.*, p. 7) claims that "the U.S. domestic economic recession of 1969-70 and the recurring balance-of-payments deficits gave rise to a far-reaching review by the Nixon Administration of foreign economic policy." This may be the case. But to suggest that domestic economic factors were decisive in relaxing our trade policy with the Soviet Union is merely to acknowledge the ideological shift from determined containment to "détente".

55. See *ibid.*, p. 31, and, more recently, the *Los Angeles Times*, April 3, 1975, Pt. I, pp. 1, 16, which reports that the Ford Administration has approved the sale of one of IBM's more advanced computers to the Soviet Union.

56. Compare the testimony of George Meany in the *Senate Hearings of 1974 on Détente*, p. 383, and *GIST*, Bureau of Public Affairs, Department of State, June 1975. See, also, Dr. Kissinger's statement on the subject in the *Senate Hearings of 1974 on Détente*, pp. 252-253.

57. According to Dr. Medvedev's testimony in *ibid.*, p. 417, not only is "Trade not . . . a serious economic issue for the Russian Government" but it does not affect their military policy. "[I]f these purchases [of 'grain, the tens of thousands of tons of European butter and . . . some 100,000 tons of meats from the Common Market'] had not been possible, then the Soviet government would not have fallen, and the main difficulties would have been felt by the lowest layers of the state system. . . . But neither

military industry nor the production of rockets and submarines would have been slowed down. It is enough to remember that in considerably more difficult times, for example during collectivisation and the beginning of industrialization(1928-32), when there was a real famine in the southern areas of the USSR with at least 3 million deaths, the USSR *exported* and sold grain and flour primarily in Europe" (p. 427). This suggests that Western exports to the Soviet Union can only subsidize her military establishment.

58. As *Labedz* notes, quoting Bismark: "No-one will ever be rich enough to buy his enemies with concessions" (p. 107).

59. Hardt, *U.S.-Soviet Commercial Relations*, pp. 13-14.

60. See Kohler, *Middle East War*, p. 59. For data on Soviet arms shipments to Egypt and Syria prior to and during the Yom Kippur War, see *ibid.*, pp. 35-43, 49, 63-65. See, also, George Meany's testimony in *Senate Hearing of 1974 on Détente*, p. 376; *Aviation Week & Space Technology* (Nov. 19, 1973), pp. 13-15: "Soviet Buildup for Mideast Worries West", referring to the "Transfer of an airborne division from Tula, in central European Russia, to a base near Belgrade. . . . Staff of the division is in Damascus. . . ."; and Zeev Schiff, *October Earthquake: Yom Kippur 1973* (Tel Aviv: University Publishing Projects, Ltd., 1974). pp. 13, 150-151, 167-168. 186, 192-194, 196-197, 201, 248, 288-290 (*in re* Scud missiles), 313. A mechanized division of 200 Iraqi tanks, a Jordanian armored brigade of 80 Patton tanks, and Saudi armored vehicles fought on the Syrian front. Egypt had the assistance of a small armored brigade from Kuwait and Mirage aircraft from Libya.

61. Quoted in Theodore Draper, "From 1967-1973: The Arab-Israeli Wars", *Commentary* (Dec. 1973), p. 38. See also *Senate Hearings of 1974 on Détente*, p. 249, where Dr. Kissinger contends that "The prospect of achieving a military position of near parity with the U. S. in strategic forces could have tempted Moscow to use its expanding military capability to strive more determinedly for expansion; in fact it tempered the militancy of *some* of its actions and sought to stabilize *at least some* aspects of its military competition through negotiations." (Do the words I have italicized indicate that Dr. Kissinger was not wholly forgetful of the nuclear alert he or President Nixon instituted during the war in question?) No doubt Dr. Kissinger knows whereof he speaks. Unfortunately, the public does not. See Bernard Lewis' testimony of March 17, 1971, before the Senate Subcommittee on National Security (Washington, D.C.: U.S. Government Printing Office, 1971), p. 98, who predicted that "the Soviets have a great need to gain some sort of victory over Isreal . . . to convince the Arabs of value of their protection. For this they must persuade the United States to provide them with one—a task that is not as difficult as it ought to be." The following month, on April 30, 1971, Robert Conquest, testifying before the same subcommittee, clarified Professor Lewis' prediction by saying that the Soviets are "naturally seeking the *political* defeat of Isreal and the opening of the [Suez] Canal as their two main objectives, for both political and strategic reasons" (p. 168). For a penetrating study of the Soviet role in the Middle East War of October 1973, see Kohler, *Middle East War* (cited earlier). See, also, "Middle-East: Some Reflections on the Soviet Decision-Making Process", ORBIS, 17:3 (Fall, 1973), pp. 946-977, and Theodore Draper, "Road to Geneva", *Commentary* (Feb. 1974), pp. 23-39.

62. *Senate Hearings of 1974 on Détente*, p. 247 (italics added).

63. See below, p. 234, n. 70.

64. Henry A. Kissinger, *The Necessity for Choice*, p. 207.

65. The difference arises from the fact that whereas Hitler resorted to direct invasion of other countries, the Soviets often employ "proxies" or "clients" to achieve their objectives.

66. *Ibid.*, pp. 207-208.

67. The fact that Brezhnev had clients in the Middle East does not affect the essential sameness of his and Hitler's insincerity or lack of honor which, like Henderson, Secretary Kissinger has chosen to ignore, at least in public.

68. For a perceptive study of Kissinger's increasingly mellow attitude toward the Soviet Union, see James E. Dornan, Jr., "Kissinger's Foreign Policy: Grand Design or Grand Illusion?" *Washington Report* (Washington, D.C.: American Security Council, Dec., 1975), Special Issue.

69. *The Necessity for Choice*, p. 208. This surely applies to Senator J. William Fulbright who, while in office, was the champion of Secretary of State Kissinger. The "convergence" of Fulbright and Kissinger is another paradox of "détente". But see my *On the Silence of the Declaration of Independence*, pp. 36-42.

70. Dr. Kissinger is not consistent on this point. Thus, in *The Necessity for Choice* he writes: "Most Americans are convinced that no one is ever entirely 'right', or, as the saying goes, that if there is a disagreement each party is probably a little in error. The fear of dogmatism [which Kissinger rightly refuses to identify with morality (p. 352)] pervades the American scene. But the corollary of the tentativeness of most views is an incurable inner insecurity" (p. 343). I wonder whether this fear, tentativeness, and insecurity are as widespread among ordinary men as among relativistically inclined intellectuals?

71. *Ibid.*, p. 296.

72. *Ibid.*, p. 86 and see *ibid.*, pp. 97, 184.

73. *Senate Hearings of 1974 on Détente*, p. 248.

74. Of course, the great statesman will possess intellectual detachment in the sense of possessing a more comprehensive view than his countrymen. But detachment as such will not be a conspicuous element of his public rhetoric.

75. *The Necessity for Choice*, p. 202 (italics in the original). See, also, *American Foreign Policy* (New York: W. W. Norton, 1974), exp. ed., pp. 85-89, where Dr. Kissinger discusses and again minimizes the importance of Soviet intentions.

76. *Senate Hearings of 1974 on Détente*, p. 248.

77. As Professor Kissinger has written in *The Necessity for Choice:*

> For over a generation now the Communist leaders have proclaimed their devotion to the overthrow of the capitalist world. They have insisted that the economic system of their opponents was based on exploitation and war. They have never wavered from asserting the inevitability or the crucial importance of their triumph. To be sure, periods of peaceful coexistence have alternated with belligerence, particularly since the advent of Mr. Khrushchev. But one of the principal Communist justifications for a *détente* can hardly prove very reassuring to the free world: peace is advocated not for its own sake but because the West is said to have grown so weak that it will go to perdition without a last convulsive upheaval (172).

78. Winston Churchill, *The Gathering Storm* (Boston: Houghton Mifflin Co., 1948), pp. 17-19, and see *ibid.*, p. 89.

CHAPTER 7

1. Alfred North Whitehead, *Science and the Modern World* (New York: Free Press, 1967), pp. 5, 18.

2. Alfred North Whitehead, *The Function of Reason* (Boston: Beacon Press, 1966), p. 20.

3. Marx himself admitted that "crude communism" engenders "universal envy". This is precisely what is implied in Amalrik's assessment of the psychology which now dominates the Russian people. He writes:

In practice, "justice" involves the desire that "nobody should live better than I do". . . . This idea of justice is motivated by a hatred of everything that is outstanding. . . . See *Amalrik*, p. 35, and below, p. 237, n. 27.

CHAPTER 8

1. See below, p. 236, n. 17, and Fred C. Iklé, "American Shortcomings in Negotiating with Communist Powers", *Memorandum Prepared at the Request of the Subcommittee on National Security and International Operations of the Committee on Government Operations*, U. S. Senate (Washington, D.C.: U.S. Government Printing Office, 1970), p. 5 (hereafter cited as *American Shortcomings in Negotiating;* also, this subcommittee will henceforth be referred to as the *Subcommittee on National Security*). See, also, Philip E. Mosely, "Some Soviet Techniques of Negotiation," in "The Soviet Approach to Negotiation: Selected Writings, compiled by the *Subcommittee on National Security* (Washington, D.C.: U.S. Government Printing Office, 1969), p. 22 (cited hereafter as *Soviet Approach to Negotiation*).

2. See *Soviet Approach to Negotiation*, pp. 21-22. Two years after the Yalta Agreement, which were systematically violated by the Soviet Union, the United States forcibly repatriated Russian prisoners of war, returning them as required by Yalta, but to their certain death or imprisonment. See Nicholas Bethell, *The Last Secret* (New York: Basic Books, 1974), pp. 193, 203. See, also, Orwell, *Essays*, IV, 62 *et seq.*

3. See Fred C. Iklé, *American Shortcomings in Negotiation*, p. 5, as well as the previous note.

4. See above, p. 147, *in re* J. William Fulbright. See, also, the testimony of William R. Van Cleave, *Hearings Before the Subcommittee on National Security*, July 25, 1972 (Washington, D.C.: U.S. Government Printing Office, 1973) *passim.* Dr. Van Cleave's testimony confirms the advice once tendered by George F. Kennan concerning the Soviet Union: "*Don't assume a community of aims with them which does not really exist.*" *Memoirs 1925-1950*, p. 561. See J. William Fulbright, *The Arrogance of power*, pp. 197-198, and his *Russia and the West* (Cambridge: Harvard University Press, 1963), pp. 11-14. Finally, consider Franklin Roosevelt's "mirror-imaging" during the Teheran Conference, in Charles E. Bohlen, *Witness to History 1929-1969*, Ch. 9 *passim.*

5. J. William Fulbright, *The Arrogance of Power*, pp. 256-257 and 79-80. See, also, his *Old Myths and New Realities,* pp. 9-10. It should be noted that Fulbright is a cultural relativist (see below, p.000, n. 12). His relativism is discussed in my essay, "Intellectual and Moral Anarchy in American Society", *The Review of Politics*, 32:1 (Jan. 1970), pp. 41-43, and more extensively in my *On the Silence of the Declaration of Independence*, pp. 36-42.

6. Cited in Nathan Leites, *The Operational Code of the Politburo* (New York: McGraw-Hill Book Co., 1951),p.7.

7. Vladimir Ilyich Ulyanov (1870-1924) Soviet premier 1918-24.

8. "Fifty Years of Great Achievements of Socialism", Report by L. I. Brezhnev to the Central Committee of the CPSU (Moscow: Novosti Press, 1967), p. 75.

9. Cited in *Laqueur*, p. 7.

10. Cited in *Soviet Approach to Negotiation*, p. 31.

11. See Fred C. Iklé, *American Shortcomings in Negotiating*, pp. 2, 16.

12. See J. William Fulbright, *The Arrogance of Power*, pp. 168-170, 177, 204, and compare the somewhat conflicting position taken in his *Russia and the West*, p. 14. Fulbright's relativism is modulated by positivism. Thus, notwithstanding the conventional morality (which he calls "democratic humanism") evident from time to time in his writings, he generally tends to explain moral values, hence ideological conflicts, in psychological or nonrational terms, as when he claims that "the sources of ideological belief are largely accidental and irrational". *Arrogance of Power*, p. 163.

13. *Ibid.*, pp. 197-198.

14. V. I. Lenin, " 'Left-Wing' Communism—An Infantile Disorder", *Selected Works* (1-vol. ed.), p. 535.

15. Leonid Brezhnev, *The Policy of the Soviet Union and the International Situation*, pp. 55-56, 58.

16. *The Penkovskiy Papers,* p. 73.

17. Cited in M. Stanton Evans, *The Politics of Surrender* (New York: Devin-Adair Co., 1966), p. 44. Notice how Kennan shifts from "Soviet *leaders*" to "the *people* on the other side", suggesting an identity between the two. (But see above, p. 81, and below, p. 237, n. 27, for Andrei Amalrik's assessment of the character of the Russian people.) As for Kennan, see his *Memoirs 1925-1950*, p. 474, where he says of the United States: "[W]e remain prepared to go very far, to show considerable confidence in others, and to accept a certain risk for ourselves, in order to achieve international agreement on the removal [of nuclear weapons] from international arsenals. . . . " Yet, as noted earlier, it was Kennan who, in speaking about the leaders of the Soviet Union, had once urged: "*Don't assume a community of aims which does not really exist*" (p.561), to which he added, "*Don't make fatuous gestures of good will."* Admittedly, this advice was tendered in 1946, and may therefore be said to apply only to Stalin. Nevertheless, the advice is included without qualification in Kennan's *Memoirs* published in 1967. For statements similar to Kennan's more recent views on the Soviet Union and on Marxism, see, respectively, John F. Kennedy's American University Address of 1963 in Peter G. Filene (ed.), *American Views of Soviet Russia* (Homewood, Ill.: Dorsey Press, 1968), p. 387, and J. William Fulbright, *The Arrogance of Power*, pp. 79-80.

18. Cited above, p. 220, n. 35.

19. See Fred C. Iklé, *American Shortcomings in Negotiating*, p. 5, and Charles E. Bohlen, *Witness to History 1929-1969*, p. 151, *in re* President Roosevelt's frankness with Stalin at Teheran.

20. Speech delivered at the CPSU Central Committee Plenum, July 21, 1963 (cited earlier), pp. 10-11.

21. G. Arbatov, "The New Stage in Soviet-American Relations", *Pravda*, July 27, 1973, *Reprints from the Soviet Press*, 17:5 (Sept. 7, 1973), pp. 31, 34-35. It should be noted that Arbatov (who is Director of the Institute of U. S. Studies in the Soviet Academy of Sciences) does not attribute the change in Soviet-American relations, or détente, to any changes in the attitudes of the Soviet Union. Instead, he ascribes the causes of détente to the military, political, and economic decline of the United States and to the consequent deterioration of American will. Nevertheless, he concludes that the struggle between the United States and the Soviet Union will become more intense and complicated (p. 37).

22. *Amalrik*, p. 40.

23. Karl Marx, *Capital*, p. 15.

24. Cited in *Soviet Approach to Negotiation*, p. 85.

25. Oleg Penkovskiy, *The Penkovskiy Papers*, pp. 56, 216.

26. Cited in Nathan Leites, *A Study of Bolshevism*, p. 332.

27. V.I. Lenin, *Selected Works* (1-vol. ed.), p. 63. According to *Amalrik* (p. 34):

> To the majority of the [Russian] people, the very word "freedom" is synonomous with "disorder". . . . As for respecting the rights of an individual as such, the idea simply arouses bewilderment. One can respect strength, authority, even intellect or education, but it is preposterous to the popular mind that the human personality should represent any kind of value.

This contempt for the rights of the individual is consistent with the egalitarian notion of justice: that "nobody should live better than I do", and helps to explain why, in Amalrik's words, so many Russians are "motivated by hatred of everything outstanding" (p. 35). From such egalitarian envy follows the official persecution and/or execution of outstanding individuals. I attribute this aristocide primarily to the teachings of Marx and Lenin (rather than to the influence of tsarism), in defense of which one may call forth even the evidence of Marx himself. Thus, it was Marx who foresaw "Universal *envy* establishing itself as a power" with the establishment of what he called "crude communism". See his *Economic and Philosophic Manuscripts*, in *Writings of the Young Marx*, p. 302.

28. Solzhenitsyn, *The Gulag Archipelago*, pp. 46, 161, and above, pp. 91-92.

29. *Amalrik*, pp. 36-37.

30. Alfred North Whitehead, *Modes of Thought* (New York: Free Press, 1968), p. 131. See *ibid.*, pp. 148-168 for Whitehead's critique of positivism. Some fifty years ago Whitehead warned in *Science and the Modern World* that

> The dangers arising from this aspect of professionalism are great, particularly in our democratic societies. The directive force of reason is weakened. The leading intellects lack balance. They see this set of circumstances, or that set; but not both sets together. The task of coordination is left to those who lack either the force or the character to succeed in some definite career. In short, the specialized functions of the community are performed better and more progressively, but the generalized direction lacks vision (p. 197).

Whitehead attributes this lack of vision and coördination to the impact of positivism on the social sciences and the humanities which, he says, "exclude from rationalistic thought more of the final values of existence. The intimate timidity of professionalized [i.e., of specialized and empirically oriented] scholarship circumscribes reason by reducing its topics to triviality, for example, to bare sensa and to tautologies." *Adventures of Ideas,* p. 151. Trivialization is inevitable so long as universities exclude from the province of objective truth the most important questions of human life, which is precisely what follows from the behavioral denial that reason is capable of apprehending universally valid standards of how men should live or of how society should be governed. Lacking such standards, intellectual coördination is impossible. Nor is this all. For if reason is incapable of apprehending universally valid standards of what is good or bad, right or wrong, honorable or dishonorable, then our universities possess no more wisdom on the ultimate questions of human life than is to be found among ordinary men. (Perhaps this helps to explain why enormous sums and energies are devoted to prove the obvious.)

31. In contrast, the Ho Chi Minh Declaration of Independence of 1945 asserts the right of all peoples to *"be* happy".

32. Let us avoid sentimental egalitarianism by refusing to admit that the character of one people may, on the whole, be superior to that of another. Here, a passage from Amalrik's "Open Letter to Kuznetsov" is instructive:

> If an individual person or the whole country actively wanted to be free they must achieve freedom somehow even if it be by means of non-cooperation with their oppressors. But sometimes to obtain this one must risk even the freedom one has—which, as I understand it, you were afraid to do.
>
> The question . . . often put to you in the West, namely, why do the people in the USSR not change the government if it be so bad, seemed to you naïve. This question seems completely reasonable to me. I would reply to it in this way: it is not that the people do not change the government because the government is good but because we ourselves are bad. We are passive, ignorant and fearful . . . (p. 100).

Consider, too, these words of the Declaration: "all experience hath shown, that mankind are more disposed to suffer, while evils are sufferable, than to right themselves by abolishing the forms [of government] to which they are accustomed." Or as Aristotle has written: "The masses covet profits more than they covet honours; witness the patience with which they bore the old-time tyrannies, and still continue to tolerate oligarchies if only they are allowed to get on with their work and are not robbed of their earnings." See *The Politics of Aristotle* (London: Oxford University Press, 1952), Ernest Barker, trans., p. 263.

33. Here I am not about to recommend the so-called "pentagonal" system of checks and balances associated with the "Nixon Doctrine". In an interview with *Time* magazine (Jan. 3, 1972) President Nixon said: "We must remember the only time in the history of the world that we have had any extended periods of peace is when there has been balance of power. It is when one nation becomes infinitely more powerful in relation to its potential competitor that the danger of war arises [N.B.]. So I believe in a world in which the United States is powerful. I think it will be a safer world and a better world if we have a strong, healthy United States, Europe, Soviet Union, China, Japan, each balancing the other, not playing one against the other, an even balance." The absurdity of this public teaching surpasses belief. To begin with, if the United States were *infinitely* stronger than the Soviet Union, and the latter knew this, then so long as this country remained true to its principles and did not abuse its power—and recall how we were willing to turn over to the United Nations control of the atomic bomb when we had a monopoly of this weapon—that being the case, Russia (and China) would cease to endanger world peace. On the other hand, would it be "a safer world and a *better* world if we have a strong . . . Soviet Union [or] China. . . . "?

238

Notice that the former President abstracts from ideology, that is, from the fundamental political and moral differences between the United States, a liberal democracy, and the Soviet Union, a communist tyranny. (This politcally neutral posture—I do not say conviction—may be seen in Mr. Nixon's report to a joint session of Congress after the conclusion of the SALT-ABM agreements of 1972: "Recognizing that the quest for useful knowledge transcends the differences between ideologies and social systems, we have agreed to expand United States and Soviet co-operation in many areas of science and technology.")

Raymond Aron criticizes the same *Time* magazine interview as follows:

> Even if Europe between 1815 and 1914 comprised five major protagonists (Great Britain, France, Germany, Austria-Hungary, and Russia), there was no magic virtue in the number five. The European order of the Congress of Vienna was proof against the limited conflicts of the nineteenth century for a great many reasons which have nothing to do with the number of principals. Moreover, the five actors listed by the President exist only in his imagination, or at least differ from each other in ways totally unlike those evident among the actors in the European system. They comprise two global powers; a great unarmed economic power (Japan); a continental power, poor but equipped with an embryonic nuclear force (China); and an ensemble of industrialized nations without a common government and without the ability or determination to assert itself abroad (Europe). . . .
>
> The notion of a pentagonal balance must make the Japanese even uneasier than the Europeans; for it implies a failure to make an explicit distinction between allies and adversaries. The refusal to make such a distinction would indeed mark a drastic break with American postwar diplomacy.

See Raymond Aron, *The Imperial Republic*, pp. 141-142.

Finally, for an implicit critique of Nixon's formula for a safer and better world, see Henry A. Kissinger, *The Necessity for Choice*, p. 37; *American Foreign Policy*, pp. 56-57. and the computer study cited above, p. 215, n. 14, which offers the following conclusion:

> . . . the managers of détente have approached power in the wrong way. It is not power parity that enhances peace. It is not equality in power that reduces hostility and conflict. Rather, it is power dominance or submission. Peace is purchased by making yourself much stronger than your adversary. Or, by abdicating power.

Recently, however, Secretary of State Kissinger has asked: "What in the name of God is [nuclear] superiority? How do you use it?"—a position perhaps foreshadowed in his *American Foriegn Policy*, p. 60 (1969) and reiterated in the expanded edition, on p. 266 (1973). (The answer to Dr. Kissinger's question is that Russia is using it quite effectively in the form of nuclear blackmail, even as the Professor once predicted.)

34. With one strategically important qualification, these four consequences would also follow the loss of America's military and political credibility, which appears to have happened as a result of the defeat of the United States in Indochina. The qualification is this. In view of Moscow's predominant influence in Hanoi—it was primarily Russian arms that conquered South Vietnam—the rapidly expanding Soviet fleet will be able to use the excellent American-built facilities of Camranh Bay, the consequence of which would be to restrain Chinese ambitions throughtout Southeast Asia. Russia would have then taken the place vacated by the United States, thereby creating strains on our various alliances with Japan, the Philippines, Australia and New Zealand.

35. But here a caveat is in order. For as Penkovskiy points out: "I wish only to warn the Western states that despite the serious differences that exist between the USSR and China at the present time [1962], these differences could disappear if a serious situation develops in the world. The argument and the differences between Khrushchev and Mao Tse-tung are basically concerned with the problem: which is the best and quickest method of burying capitalism. This must not be forgotten". (p. 367).

36. See Harold W. Rood, "Distant Rampart", *United States Naval Institute Proceedings*, March 1967, p. 31.

37. By Western Europe is meant the 15 nations comprising the North Atlantic Treaty Organization (NATO) which includes, however, Canada and Iceland.

38. *Ibid.*

39. As Hamilton points out in *Federalist* 7: ". . . America, if not connected at all, or only by the feeble tie of a simple league, offensive and defensive, would, by the operation of such jarring alliances, be gradually entangled in all the pernicious labyrinths of European politics and wars; and by the destructive contentions of the parts into which she was divided, would be likely to become a prey to the artifices and machinations of powers equally the enemies of them all. *Divide et impera* must be the motto of every nation that either hates or fears us."

40. Rood, "Distant Rampart," p. 37.

41. *Ibid.*, p. 34.

42. ". . . the U.S. imports, in full or in part, 69 of the 72 materials designated by the Department of Commerce as critical to its industrial base—and over 99 percent by weight of those materials is carried by shipping over the adjoining seas." *Hearings Before the Committee on Armed Services*, U.S. Senate, 93rd Cong., 2nd session, "Fiscal Year 1975 authorization for Military Procurement, Research and Development" (U.S. Government Printing Office: 1974), Part 2, pp. 424, 426-7, 440, 445.

43. Without denying the delicate nature of the nuclear age, excessive secrecy cannot but engender public cynicism, irresponsible "leaks", and a declining confidence in government. It should be understood, however, that what is most wanting is not candor, but wisdom and courage.

44. During Hollywood's Academy Award festivities of April 1975, while South Vietnam was being overrun by communist forces, the producer of "Hearts and Minds", an Oscar-winning antiwar film, read a telegram from a Viet Cong diplomat in Paris thanking the American people for "the *liberation* of South Vietnam". One cannot but admire the quick and cunning intelligence facilities of our enemies, so skilled in the art of *divide et impera*. See the *Los Angeles Times*, April 9, 1975, Pt. I, p. 1.

45. In this connection, see *Federalist* 49, where *Publius* says: "We are to recollect that all the existing constitutions were formed in the midst of a danger which repressed the passions most unfriendly to order and concord; of an enthusiastic confidence of the people in their patriotic leaders, which stifled the ordinary diversity of opinions on great national questions. . . ."

46. Quoted at length above, p. 226, n. 59. Compare Lincoln's "Address to the Young Men's Lyceum of Springfield, Illinois," *Works*, I, 114.

47. See above, p. 215, n. 14, regarding the twelve-year computer study which concludes that cultural exchange and trade on the one hand, and international conflict on the other, are statistically independent.

48. The increasing cynicism among American youth also calls for a political rhetoric that avoids sentimentality but which fosters magnanimity.

49. *The Penkovskiy Papers*, p. 67. The Soviet Union has the most extensive espionage network in the world. See *ibid.*, p. 73.

50. The Convention specifies that ". . . Parties undertake to . . . guarantee the right of everyone, without distinction as to race, colour, or national or ethnic origin . . . to leave any country, including his own, and *to return to his country.*" (This Convention implements Article XIII of the Universal Declaration of Human Rights.) I have italicized the right of return because, as Dr. Medvedev points out, "emigration from the Soviet Union is in fact a relaxed form of deportation", as well as a method of ridding Russia of the very people who might exert a liberalizing influence on the regime. See *Senate Hearings of 1974 on Détente*, p. 415.

51. For an incisive critique of the UN, see Martin Schiff, "The United States and the United Nations: On a Collision Course (cited above, p. 228, n. 13).

52. In testimony before the Senate Foreign Relations Committee on his nomination as Secretary of State, Dr. Kissinger declared:

> . . . in the Soviet case our first objective should be to reduce the danger of international war, but at the same time we have an obligation never to leave any doubt about where we stand with respect to the principle of human liberty. We can never imply that we are acquiescing in the suppression of human liberty. . . .
> With respect to other countries, if their domestic policies are morally offensive to us, we should avoid gratuitous associations which cannot be seen as affecting international peace or serving some other overriding international interest. . . .
> The dividing line is very hard to draw. If a country does something that is so repugnant to human morality—if extermination camps are constructed—then this certainly will affect *the degree of coöperation* in which we can engage with such a country. . . .

See Henry A. Kissinger, *American Foreign Policy*, pp. 206-207. From the words I have italicized it appears that Dr. Kissinger would have recognized Stalinist Russia in 1933, maintained diplomatic relations with Nazi Germany up until 1941, which surely would then have "[implied] that we [we]re acquiescing in the suppression of human liberty." But to carry on the charade of "détente" with Russia while it was supplying North Vietnam the very weapons used to kill American servicemen—surely this is shameful self-abasement, the bitter fruits of which have yet to make this country wiser or more honorable. (And I might note in passing that Vietnam is a tragic illustration of how honor is a precondition of wisdom.)

53. See *The Penkovskiy Papers*, pp. 57, 251-258, 332. There is no point in objecting that I am calling for a nuclear arms race. Like it or not, we are in such a race, and we may very well be close to having lost it. On this subject, see the testimony of William Van Cleave before the *Subcommittee on National Security and International Operations of the Committee on Government Operations*, U.S. Senate, 92nd Cong., 2nd sess., (Washington, D.C.: U.S. Government Printing Office, 1973), Pt. 7, pp. 200-246 *passim*.

54. *The Penkovskiy Papers*, p. 213.

55. The following rules also apply to Communist China.

56. *The Penkovskiy Papers*, p. 57. In his *Witness to History 1929-1969*, Charles Bohlen remarks: "I did not share Dulles's view that the spectacle of Eisenhower shaking hands with Khrushchev [at Geneva in 1955] would destroy the moral image of the United States, have a bad effect domestically, and tend to weaken the Allies' will to stand up to Communism. I felt the shoe was on the other foot. The Communist system, being a closed society, was much less able to withstand the impact

of a spirit of détente in regular diplomatic contact between countries." It appears, however, that events have confirmed Dulles's judgment on this matter (see above, p. 230, n. 42). But surely it was unseemly, to say the very least, for the President of the United States to shake hands with the butcher of the Ukraine. Having thus dignified Khrushchev in 1955, was it any easier for the United States to condemn his role in the brutal repression of Hungary in 1956? Indeed, Bohlen himself admits, in connection with the Soviet invasion of Czechoslovakia in 1968, that "the [American] public had grown somewhat callous in regard to Soviet behavior" (*ibid.*, p. 535), thereby refuting his earlier criticism of Dulles, but therefore his own understanding of the effect of "détente" in "open" as opposed to "closed" societies.

56a. See Lawrence W. Beilenson, *The Treaty Trap* (Washington, D.C.: Public Affairs Press, 1969), pp. 198-200, 208-221 *passim*. Despite pledges to Israel neither to recognize nor negotiate with the PLO, the U.S. agreed to a Security Council decision to debate the Middle East problem with PLO participation.

57. *American Foreign Policy*, p. 37.

58. *Ibid.*, p. 35, and *The Necessity for Choice*, pp. 5, 181, 183.

59. In his testimony before the Senate Subcommittee on National Security (cited earlier), Dr. Van Cleave was asked by then-Senator Saxbe: "Now, talking about the political aspects which have to be considered in anything that we are talking about here, do you think it is possible in an election year to have any reasonable approach from our side to a SALT agreement? In other words, can we really be objective?" To this Dr. Van Cleave replied: "It would be very difficult and probably not politically fruitful in this election year, but in general that depends on the leadership" (pp. 215-216). Inasmuch as Senator Saxbe went on to say "I don't think there are a great many in the Senate that are happy with it [the SALT agreement]" (p. 216), the 90 to 2 vote of that august body in favor of SALT I places in question either the accuracy of Senator Saxbe's political judgment or the political courage and patriotism of many of his colleagues.

60. President Johnson admitted his failure to prepare the American public for the Tet offensive early in 1968. See his *Vantage Point*, p. 380, and W. W. Rostow, *The Diffusion of Power* (New York: Macmillan Co., 1972), pp. 481-483, 172, 516, 552. It can be argued that with Tet the United States virtually won the war in Vietnam and lost it in Washington. See *ibid.*, pp. 460-467, and above, p. 180n[†].

61. See Alexis de Tocqueville, *Democracy in America* (2 vols.; New York: Vintage Books, 195), II, 256.

62. Now virtually disarmed, Japan is defenseless against her two principal enemies. It is estimated that, in a conventional war, Russia could conquer Japan in three or four days, assuming the Japanese were to resist. Presumably it would take longer for China.

63. For specific proposals, see Steven L. Canby, "Damping Nuclear Counterforce Incentives: Correcting NATO's Inferiority in Conventional Military Strength", ORBIS, 19:1 (Spring 1975), pp. 47-71, and Marc E. Geneste, "The City Walls: A Credible Defense Doctrine for the West", ORBIS, 19:2 (Summer 1975), pp. 447-496.

64. See William Schneider, *Food, Foreign Policy, and Raw Materials Cartels*, (New York: Crane, Russak & Co., 1976), pp. 51-61.

65. See W. Eugene Hollon, *The Great Western Desert* (New York: Oxford University Press, 1966), which discusses the Alaskan River Diversion Project once under study by a special Senate subcommittee on Western water development. The project was formulated by the Ralph M. Parsons Company of Los Angeles. Through a

system of dams, reservoirs, and canals, the diversion of the rivers in question would supply 4.3 billion acre-feet of storage or twice the available water resources of the seventeen Western states. Enough water would be left for Mexico to develop eight times as much irrigable land as the Aswan Dam. The project—and I have only mentioned a few of its features—would take some thirty years to complete at the then estimated cost of 80 billion dollars. Considering the number of jobs it would create and the number of small cities that could spring up from so magnificent an undertaking, 80 billion dollars over a thirty-year period appears small in comparison with that which would otherwise be spent on welfare and on overcoming the inequities, violence, and decay of contemporary society.

66. See my *Discourse on Statesmanship*, pp. 321-322, 365.

SELECTED BIBLIOGRAPHY

Acheson, Dean. *Power and Diplomacy*. Cambridge: Harvard University Press, 1959.

Amalrik, Andrei. *Will the Soviet Union Survive Until 1984?* New York: Perennial Library, 1970.

Aristotle, *Politics*.

Aron, Raymond. *The Imperial Republic*. Englewood Cliffs, N.J.: Prentice-Hall, Inc., 1974.

Beilenson, Lawrence W. *The Treaty Trap*. Washington, D.C.: Public Affairs Press, 1969.

Bennett, Edward M. *Recognition of Russia*. Waltham: Blaisdell Publishing Co., 1970.

Bethel, Nicholas. *The Last Secret*. New York: Basic Books, 1974.

Bishop, Donald C. *The Roosevelt-Litvinov Agreements*. Syracuse: Syracuse University Press, 1965.

Bohlen, Charles E. *Witness to History 1929-1969*. New York: W.W. Norton & Co., 1973.

Borkenau, Franz. *The Spanish Cockpit*. London: Faber & Faber Ltd., 1937.

Brezhnev, Leonid. *On the Policy of the Soviet Union and the International Situation*. New York: Doubleday & Co., 1973.

Brockway, Thomas B., ed. *Basic Documents in United States Foreign Policy*. New York: D. Van Nostrand Co., 1957.

Browder, Robert Paul. *Soviet-American Diplomacy*. Princeton: Princeton University Press, 1953.

Brzezinski, Zbigniew. *Between Two Ages: America's Role in the Technetronic Era*. New York: Viking Press, 1971.

Burnham, James. *Suicide of the West*. New Rochelle, N.Y.: Arlington House, 1975.

Casey, Francis M. *The Vietnam Policy of President Lyndon Baines Johnson in Response to the Theory of the Protracted Conflict.* Doctoral dissertation, Claremont Graduate School, 1976.

Chambers, Whittaker. *Cold Friday.* New York: Random House, 1964.

Churchill, Winston. *The Gathering Storm.* Boston: Houghton Mifflin Co., 1948.

Clemenceau, Georges. *Grandeur and Misery of Victory.* New York: Harcourt, Brace & Co., 1930.

Confino, Michael & Shimon Shamir, eds. *The USSR and the Middle East* New York: John Wiley & Sons, 1973.

Eidelberg, Paul. *A Discourse on Statesmanship: The Design and Transformation of the American Polity.* Urbana, Ill.: The University of Illinois Press, 1974.

————. *The Philosophy of the American Constitution: A Reinterpretation of the Intentions of the Founding Fathers.* New York: The Free Press, 1968.

————. *On the Silence of the Declaration of Independence.* Amherst: The University of Massachusetts Press, 1976.

Fischer, Louis. *Men in Politics.* New York: Duell, Sloan & Pearce & Co., 1966.

————. *Why Recognize Russia.* New York: Jonathan Cape & Harrison Smith, 1931.

Fulbright, J. William. *The Arrogance of Power.* New York: Vintage Books, 1966.

————. *Old Myths and New Realities.* New York: Vintage Books, 1964.

————. *Russia and the West.* Cambridge: Harvard University Press, 1963.

Gouré, Leon & Morris Rothenberg. *Soviet Penetration of Latin America.* Miami: Center for Advanced International Studies, University of Miami, 1975.

Hamilton, Alexander. *The Papers of Alexander Hamilton.* 15 vols., t.d. New York: Columbia University Press, 1961-69. Harold C. Syrett, ed.

————. *The Works of Alexander Hamilton.* 12 vols. New York: G.P. Putnam's Sons, 1904. Henry Cabot Lodge, ed.

————, John Jay & James Madison. *The Federalist.* New York: Modern Library, 1938. Edward Meade Earle, ed.

Harriman, Averell & Elie Abel. *Special Envoy to Churchill and Stalin 1941-1946.* New York: Random House, 1975.

Bibliography

Jaffa, Harry V. *Crisis of the House Divided*. New York: Doubleday & Co., 1959.

Jefferson, Thomas. *The Political Writings of Thomas Jefferson*. New York: Liberal Arts Press, 1955. Edward Dumbauld, ed.

Johnson, Lyndon Baines. *Vantage Point*. New York: Popular Library, 1971.

Kennan, George F. *Memoirs 1925-1950*. Boston: Little, Brown & Co., 1967.

————. *Memoirs 1950-1963*. Boston: Little, Brown & Co., 1972.

Khrushchev, Nikita. *Khrushchev Remembers*. Boston: Little, Brown & Co., 1970.

Kissinger, Henry A. *American Foreign Policy*. New York: W.W. Norton, Inc., 1974. exp. ed.

————. *The Necessity for Choice*. New York: Harper & Row, 1961.

————. ed. *Problems of National Security*. New York: Praeger Publications, 1965.

————. *A World Restored: Metternich, Castlereagh and the Problems of Peace 1812-1822*. Boston: Houghton Mifflin Co., 1973.

Kohler, Foy D. *et al. Soviet Strategy for the Seventies: From Cold War to Peaceful Coexistence*. Miami: Center for Advanced International Studies, University of Miami, 1973.

————. *The Soviet Union and the October 1973 Middle East War: Implications for Détente*. Miami: Center for Advanced International Studies, University of Miami, 1974.

Komorowski, Eugenjusz A. *Night Never Ending*. Chicago: Henry Regnery Co., 1974.

Leites, Nathan. *The Operational Code of the Politburo*. New York: McGraw-Hill Book Co., 1951.

————. *A Study of Bolshevism*. Glencoe, Ill.: Glencoe Free Press, 1953.

Lenin, V.I. *Selected Works*. New York: International Publishers, 1971. 1-vol. ed.

Lincoln, Abraham. *The Collected Works of Abraham Lincoln*. 9 vols. New Brunswick: Rutgers University Press, 1953-55.

Luttwak, Edward. *The U.S.-USSR Nuclear Weapons Balance*. Beverly Hills: Sage Publications, 1974.

Machiavelli, Niccolo. *The Prince*.

MacLeish, Archibald. *The Irresponsibles*. New York: Duell, Sloan & Pearce & Co., 1940.

247

Madison, James. *The Writings of James Madison.* 9 vols. New York: G.P. Putnam's Sons, 1900-10. Gaillard Hunt, ed.

Marx, Karl. *Capital.* New York: Modern Library, n.d.

_____. *Writings of the Young Marx on Philosophy and Society.* New York: Doubleday Anchor Books, 1967. Lloyd D. Easton & Kurth H. Guddat, eds.

_____. and Frederick Engels. *The German Ideology.* New York International Publishers, 1968.

_____. *Basic Writings on Politics & Philosophy.* New York: Doubleday Anchor Books, 1959. Lewis S. Feuer, ed.

Mill, John Stuart. *Utilitarianism, Liberty, and Representative Government.* New York: E.P. Dutton & Co., 1951.

Nixon, Richard M. *Six Crises.* Garden City: Doubleday & Co., 1962.

Orwell, George. *The Collected Essays, Journalism and Letters of George Orwell.* 4 vols. New York: Harcourt, Brace & World, Inc., 1968. Sonia Orwell and Ian Angus, eds.

Penkovskiy, Oleg. *The Penkovskiy Papers.* Garden City: Doubleday & Co., 1965.

Polmar, Norman. *Strategic Weapons: An Introduction.* New York: Crane, Russak & Co., Inc., 1976.

Roberts, Paul Craig & Matthew A. Stephenson. *Marx's Theory of Exchange, Alienation and Crisis.* Stanford: Hoover Institution Press, 1973.

Rood, Harold W. "Distant Rampart." *United States Naval Institute Proceedings,* March, 1967.

Rostow, W.W. *The Diffusion of Power.* New York: Macmillan Co., 1972.

Schiff, Zeer. *October Earthquake: Yom Kippur 1973.* Tel Aviv: University Publishing Projects Ltd., 1974.

Schneider, William. *Food, Foreign Policy, and Raw Materials Cartels.* New York: Crane, Russak & Co., Inc. 1976.

Scott, William F. *Soviet Sources of Military Doctrine and Strategy.* New York: Crane, Russak, & Co., Inc., 1975.

Solzhenitsyn, Alexander. *From Under the Rubble.* Boston: Little, Brown & Co., 1975.

_____. *The Gulag Archipelago.* New York: Harper & Row, 1973.

_____. *The Gulag Archipelago Two.* New York: Harper & Row, 1975.

_____. *Letter to the Soviet Leaders.* New York: Harper & Row, 1974.

Stalin, Joseph. *Foundations of Leninism*. New York: International Publishers, 1939.

Sutton, Antony C. *Western Technology and Soviet Economic Development 1917-1930*. Stanford: Hoover Institution Publications, 1968.

Washington, George. *The Writings of George Washington*. 39 vols. Washington, D.C.: U.S. Government Printing Office, 1931-44.

Whitehead, Alfred North. *Adventures of Ideas*. New York: Macmillan Co., 1933.

————. *The Function of Reason*. Boston: Beacon Press, 1960.

————. *Modes of Thought*. New York: The Free Press, 1968.

————. *Science and the Modern World*. New York: The Free Press, 1967.

Wilson, James. *The Works of James Wilson*. 2 vols. Cambridge: Harvard University Press, 1967. Robert C. McCloskey, ed.

Wolfe, Bertram D. *Khrushchev and Stalin's Ghost*. New York: Praeger Publications, 1957.

Zawodny, J.K. *Death in the Forest*. Notre Dame: University of Notre Dame Press, 1962.

U.S. Government Printing Office Publications

"Abuse of Psychiatry for Political Repression in the Soviet Union." *Hearings Before the Subcommittee to Investigate the Administration of the Internal Security Laws of the Committee on the Judiciary*. U.S. Senate, 92nd Cong., 2nd sess., Sept. 26, 1972.

"Détente." *Hearings Before the Committee on Foreign Relations*, U.S. Senate, 93rd Cong. 2nd sess., 1975.

Conquest, Robert *et al*. "Détente: An Evaluation". *Subcommittee on Arms Control of the Committee on Armed Services*, U.S. Senate, 1974.

"Establishment of Diplomatic Relations with the Union of Soviet Socialist Republics." Department of State, Eastern European Series, No. 1, 1933.

"American Shortcomings in Negotiating with Communist Powers." *Memorandum Prepared at the Request of the Subcommittee on National Security and International Operations of the Committee on Government Operations*, U.S. Senate, 1970.

"The Soviet Approach to Negotiation: Selected Writings." *Subcommittee on National Security and International Operations of the Committee on Government Operations*, U.S. Senate, 1969.

"Negotiation and Statecraft: A Selection of Readings." *Subcommittee on National Security and International Operations of the Committee on Government Operations*, U.S. Senate, 1970.

"Negotiation and Statecraft." *Hearings Before the Permanent Subcommittee on Investigations of the Committee on Government Operations*, U.S. Senate, 93rd Cong., 1st sess. Part I with Walter Laqueur, April 17, 1973; Part II with Leopold Labedz, July 12, 1973.

"International Negotiation." *Hearings Before the Subcommittee on National Security and International Operations of the Committee on Government Operations*, U.S. Senate, 91st Cong., 2nd sess., Part 2 with Leonard Schapiro, April 16, 1970; Part 4 with Bernard Lewis, March 17, 1971; Part 6 with Robert Conquest, April 30, 1971; Part 7 with William R. Van Cleave, July 25, 1972.

Uri Ra'anan. "The Changing American-Soviet Strategic Balance: Some Political Implications." *Memorandum Prepared at the Request of the Subcommittee on National Security and International Operations of the Committee on Government Operations*, U.S. Senate, 1972.

"Supplemental Foreign Assistance, Fiscal Year 1966—Vietnam." *Hearings Before the Committee on Foreign Relations*, U.S. Senate, 89th Cong., 2nd sess., 1966.

Hardt, John P. and George D. Holliday. "U.S.-Soviet Commercial Relations: The Interplay of Economics, Technology Transfer, and Diplomacy." *Prepared for the Subcommittee on National Security Policy and Scientific Developments of the Committee on Foreign Affairs*, U.S. House of Representatives, June 10, 1973.

"Recognition of Russia." *Hearings Before a Subcommittee of the Committee on Foreign Relations*, U.S. Senate, 68th Cong., 1st sess., 1924.

"United States/Soviet Military Balance," A study by the Library of Congress, *Congressional Research Service*, for the use of the Senate Committee on Armed Services, Jan. 1976.

"Hearings on Military Posture," *Department of Defense Authorization for Appropriations for FY 1977 Before the Committee on Armed Services*, House of Representatives, 94th Cong., 2nd sess., Part 1 of 5 Parts, *Military Posture*, 1976.

"Hearings on Military Posture," *Committee on Armed Services*, House of Representatives, 94th Cong., 2nd sess., Part 4 of 5 parts, *Subcommittee on Sea Power and Strategic and Critical Materials—Navy Shipbuilding and Conversion (SCN) Program for FY 1977, Torpedoes and Other Weapons*, 1976

Report No. 94-967 of the Committee on Armed Services, House of Representatives, 94th Cong., 2nd sess., "Authorizing Appropriations, FY 1977, for Military Procurement, Research and Development. . .", 1976.

Hearings before the Committee on Armed Services, U.S. Senate, 93rd Cong., 2nd sess., on S. 3000, "Fiscal Year 1975 Authorization for Military Procurement, Research and Development . . .", Part 2, *Authorizations, 1974.*

INDEX

Acheson, Dean, 147, 223n27
Adams, John, 37
Adee, Alvey A., 84, 85
Africa, 7, 166, 175. *See* Organization of African Unity; Third World
Afro-Asian bloc, 110, 167
Albania, 155
alliances, 53-58 *passim*, 175
altruism, 45
Amalrik, Andrei, 79-81, 148, 149, 188n, 237n27, 238n32
American Constitution. *See* Constitution
American foreign policy:
central strategic objective of, 155; ends of, 41, 44. *See* democratic foreign policy fragmentation of, 12-13, 14; rationale of, 157. *See also* "selective containment", "selective détente", and "selective liberalism"
American people, 59, 149-150, 161-162
American republic, uniqueness of, 17
American Revolution, 17-18
American-Russian Chamber of Commerce, 87
Amtorg, 87
Angola, 115, 135, 176
anti-anticommunism, 58, 164, 216n30
anti-communism, 163, 181, 182, 212n6, 216n30
appeasement, 127, 130
Arab-Israeli conflict, 12n, 109, 110
Arbatov, G., 148
aristocracy, 38-41
Aristotle, 238n32
Aron, Raymond, 239n33
average man, 34, 132-136 *passim*, 162-164

"Basic Principles of Relations between U.S. and USSR", 129. *See* Appendix 5
benevolence, 48, 79
Bennett, Edward M., 221n8, 11
Bohlen, Charles E., 224n41, 241n56
Brezhnev Doctrine, 114. *See* Appendix 4
Brezhnev, Leonid, 118-119, 129, 131, 146, 147, 188, 219n22
Britain, 94, 107
Brzezinski, Zbigniew, 218n18
Burr, Aaron, 100

Cambodia, 112, 219n23
Camranh Bay, 109, 158, 239n34
Canada, 177
candor, 14, 64, 125, 131n, 155, 159, 162. *See also* truth

Capitalism, 97, 141-142, 222n22, 223n23, 225n45, 46
Central Intelligence Agency (CIA), 124n
Chambers, Whittaker, 223n23, 30
Chile, 81
China (Communist), 153-155, 158
Chou En-lai, 47n, 97n
Churchill, Winston, epigr. 95, 136, 151, 179
civil defense, 174
civil disobedience, 29-30
civility, 22, 65, 139
Clemenceau, Georges, 1-2
"clients" or "proxies". *See under* Soviet Union
Colby, Bainbridge, 77
"cold war", 108, 122-128 *passim*
Communism, 139, 141-142, 165n †, 224n39. *See also* Marx; Marxism
Conquest, Robert, 233n61
consent, 13, 14. *See also* wisdom
conservatives, 47, 95, 106, 128n. *See also* liberals
Constitution, 18, 26-34 *passim*, 41-43, 138, 139, 156
containment, 127. *See also* "selective containment"
convergence, 228n20
correlation of forces, 12
cultural exchange, 118, 229n32, 240n47
Cuba, 135, 182, 216n19

death, 81, 92, 98, 133, 225n49, 227n4
Declaration of Independence, 8-9, 21, 37, 38-39, 43, 48, 51; compared with *Communist Manifesto*, 62-67; 138, 144-145, 150-151, 162, 215n18, 238n32
democracy, 13, 93, 98-99, 151-152, 217n31. *See also* republic
democratic foreign policy, 47-48. *See also* American foreign policy, ends of
"détente", 116-119, 123-125, 127-128, 231n45. *See also* "peaceful coexistence"
dictatorship, 81, 182
diplomacy, 170-173
disengagement, 52-53
Dostoevski, 103, 137
doublethink, examples of, 116, 128-130, 188-189, 223n30
Douglas, Stephen, 6, 166n, 213n11
Dulles, John Foster, 114, 115, 241n56

Eastern Europe, 1, 5, 8, 118, 122, 177
economic interests and morality, 13-14
economic warfare, 14, 109, 156, 175-176, 227n11

252